D0278955

STREETFINDER
EDINBURGH

Contents

Key to street map pages	2-3
Key to street map symbols	4
Key to route planning map symbols	5
City centre map	6-7
Street maps	8-71
Route planning maps	72-75
Index	76-112

Published by Collins
An imprint of HarperCollins Publishers
77-85 Fulham Palace Road, Hammersmith,
London W6 8JB

www.collins.co.uk

Copyright © HarperCollins Publishers Ltd 2005

Collins® is a registered trademark of
HarperCollins Publishers Limited

Mapping generated from Collins Bartholomew
digital databases

Pages 6-71 use map data licensed from
Ordnance Survey ® with the permission of the
Controller of Her Majesty's Stationery Office.
© Crown copyright. Licence number 399302

The grid on this map is the National Grid taken
from the Ordnance Survey map with the
permission of the Controller of Her Majesty's
Stationery Office.

The contents of this publication are believed
correct at the time of printing. Nevertheless,
the publisher can accept no responsibility for
errors or omissions, changes in the detail given,
or for any expense or loss thereby caused.

The representation of a road, track or footpath
is no evidence of a right of way.

Printed in Hong Kong

ISBN-13   978 0 00 720822 7
ISBN-10   0 00 720822 7   Imp 001
SI12097   ADE

e-mail: roadcheck@harpercollins.co.uk

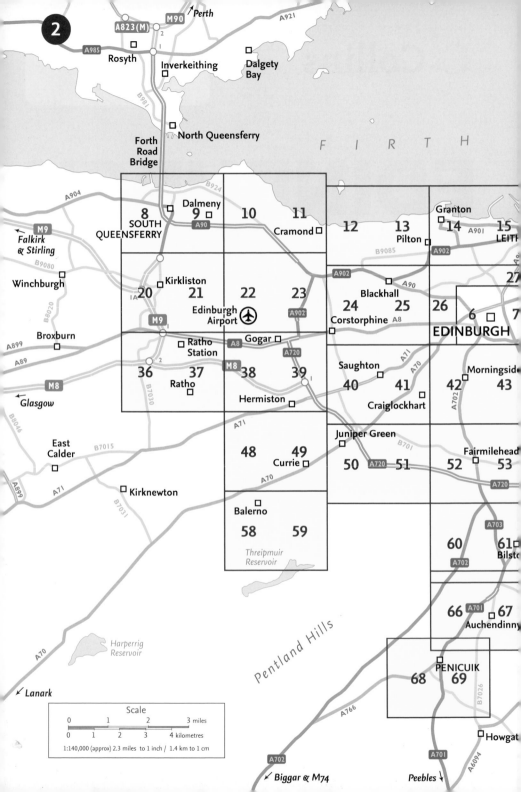

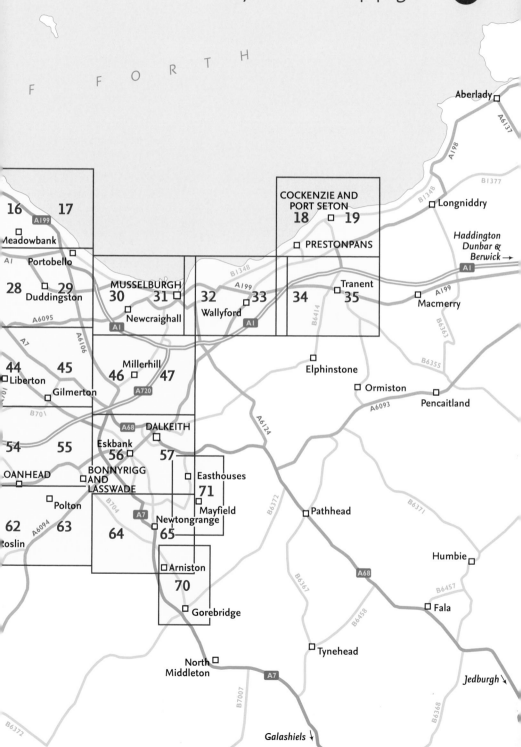

F FORTH

Aberlady

A6137

A198

B1377

16 17

A199

Meadowbank

A1 Portobello

28 29
Duddingston

A6095

A7

A6106

44 45
Liberton

Gilmerton

B701

54 55

OANHEAD

62 63
Roslin

A6094

B704

COCKENZIE AND
PORT SETON
18 19

PRESTONPANS

B1348

MUSSELBURGH
30 31

A199

Newcraighall

A1

32 33
Wallyford

A1

34 35
Tranent

Elphinstone

A720

46 47

Millerhill

A68

DALKEITH

Eskbank
56

57

BONNYRIGG
AND
LASSWADE

Polton

A7

64

Easthouses

71

Mayfield

Newtongrange

65

Arniston

70

Gorebridge

Longniddry

B1348

*Haddington
Dunbar &
Berwick* →

A1

A199 Macmerry

B6363

B6355

Ormiston

A6093 Pencaitland

A6124

B6372

Pathhead

B6371

B6371

Humbie

A68

B6367

B6457

Fala

B6458

Tynehead

North
Middleton A7

B7007

Jedburgh ↓

B6368

Galashiels ↓

B6372

B6414

Key to street map symbols
(see pages 6-71)

M8	Motorway
A720	Primary road dual /single
A70	'A' Road dual / single
B701	'B' Road dual / single
	Other road dual / single
	Motorway / road under construction
4	Key number for street name (See note on page 77 for further details)
Toll	One-way street / Toll
	Restricted access / Pedestrian street
	Minor road / Track
FB	Footpath / Cycle path / Footbridge
EDINBURGH	Unitary authority boundary
EH1	Postcode boundary and number
	Railway station
	Railway tunnel
	Level crossing
	Bus / Coach station
	Health centre
P + 🚌	Park & Ride
P	Car Park
Pol	Police station
PO	Post Office

Lib	Library
	Cinema
	Theatre
⊠ Hilton	Major Hotel
i i	Tourist information centre (all year / seasonal)
+ ☾ ☆	Church / Mosque / Synagogue
▬	Fire station / Ambulance station / Community centre
	Leisure / Tourism
	Shopping / Retail
	Administration / Law
	Education
	Hospital
	Industry / Commerce
	Other notable building
✚	Major religious building
	Wood / Forest
	Park / Garden / Recreation ground
	Public open space
⚑	Golf course
	Cemetery
	Built up area
³15	National Grid reference
15	Page continuation number

Scale

0	1/4	1/2	3/4	1 mile

0	0.25	0.5	0.75	1	1.25	1.5 kilometres

1 : 15,840   4 inches (10.2 cm) to 1 mile / 6.3 cm to 1 km

Key to route planning map symbols
(see pages 72-75)

5

M8	Motorway
8 — 9	Motorway junction with full / limited access
Stirling / Harthill / Hamilton	Motorway service area with off road / full / limited access
A725	Primary route dual / single carriageway
A73	'A' Road dual / single carriageway
B759	'B' Road dual / single carriageway
	Minor road
	Restricted access
	Road proposed or under construction
	Multi-level junction
	Roundabout
6	Road distance in miles
	Road tunnel
	Steep hill (arrows point downhill)
Toll	Level crossing / Toll
	Railway line / station / tunnel
	Car ferry
	Built up area
☐ ☐ ☐	Town / Village / Other settlement
	Forest Park boundary
	National / Regional Park
	Woodland
	Lake / Dam / River / Waterfall
	Canal / Dry canal / Canal tunnel
✈	Airport with scheduled services
Ⓟ	Park and Ride site (operates at least five days a week)
	Lighthouse
•468 ▲941	Spot / Summit height (in metres)
ℹ ⓘ	Tourist information office (all year / seasonal)

�m	Ancient monument
	Aquarium
⤬1738	Battlefield
▲ ⚏	Campsite / Caravan site
	Castle
	Country park
✠	Ecclesiastical building
❀	Garden
⚑	Golf course
曲	Historic house (with or without garden)
⚽	Major football club
£	Major shopping centre / Outlet village
	Major sports venue
	Motor racing circuit
🏛	Museum / Art gallery
	Nature reserve
	Preserved railway
	Racecourse
	Theme park
	University
	Wildlife park / Zoo
★	Other interesting feature
(NTS)	National Trust for Scotland

Land height reference bar

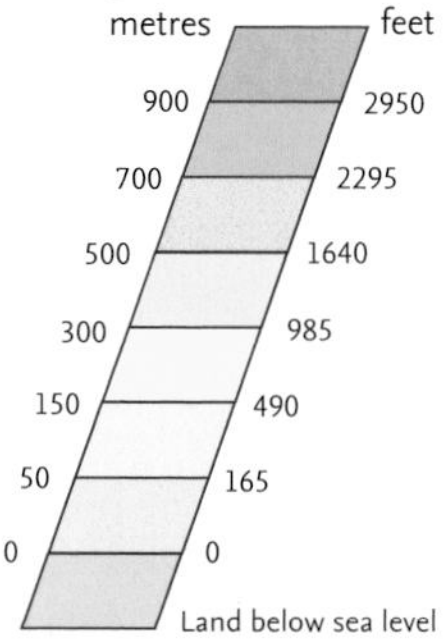

metres	feet
900	2950
700	2295
500	1640
300	985
150	490
50	165
0	0

Land below sea level

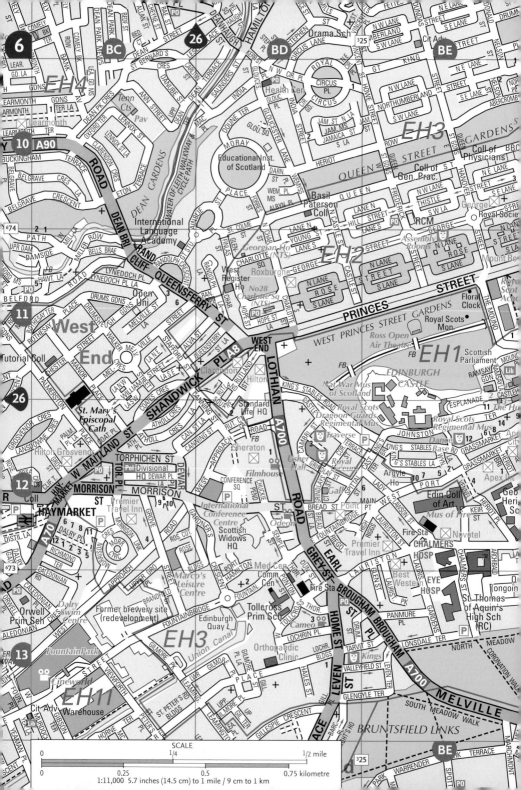

SCALE

| 0 | 1/4 | 1/2 mile |

| 0.25 | 0.5 | 0.75 kilometre |

1:11,000 5.7 inches (14.5 cm) to 1 mile / 9 cm to 1 km

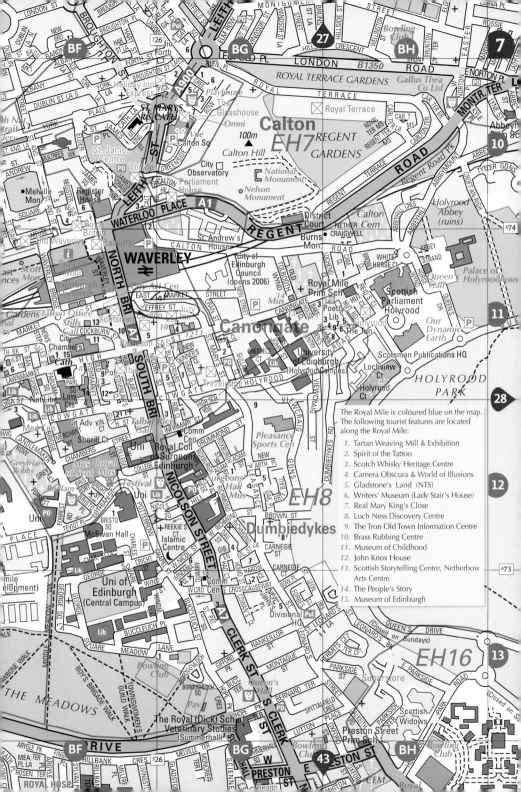

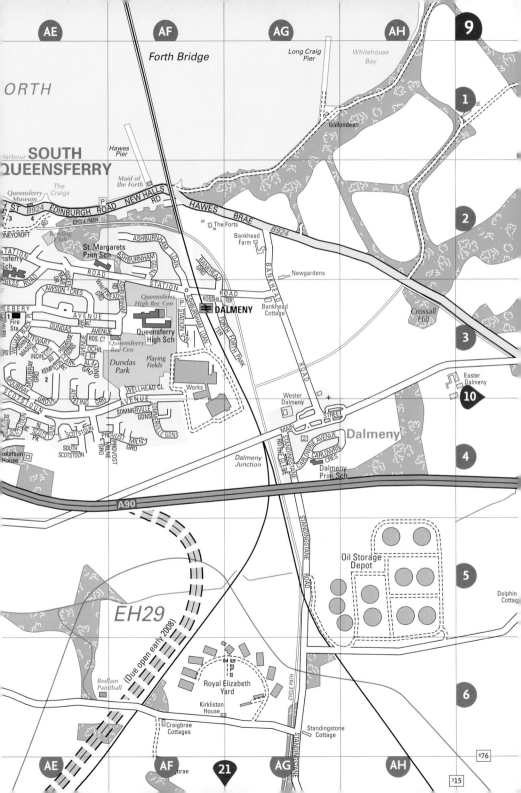

10 **AJ** **AK** **AL** **AM**

1 Leuchold

LEUCHOLD
WOOD

Barnbougl
Castle

2

NEW
ENGLAND

Dalmeny
House

Dalmeny
Stables

Crossall
Hill

3 Dunter
Hill

Chapel Coppice

MOUSE
WOOD

DALMENY PARK

Easter
Dalmeny

9

MANSION HILL
WOOD

4

Home Farm

Dolphington Burn

A90

Cock

CYCLE PATH

B924

Dolphington
House

BURNSHOT
WOOD

Dolphington

5

CRAIGIE
HILL

EH30

Dolphington
Cottages

West
Craigie
Farm

6

Lowoo

Hillsl

HILLS Road TER

⁶76

³15

AJ **AK** **22** **AL** **AM** HILLS

1

FIRTH

OF

2

FORTH

DRUM SANDS

3

Tidal C

Snab Point

12

Long
Green

Eagle
Rock

4 eakwater

LONG GREEN
WOOD

ESPLANA

almeny
ome Farm

P

Cobble
Cottage
Passenger Ferry

Cramond
Tower

Home Farm
Cottages

Cramond
House

Wilderness
Wood

CRAMOND

Hall

Roman Fort
(remains)

Linkie Burn

+

5

MOND
GDNS

BROADHOLM
PARK GN

BRIGHO
PARK CT

THE
GLEBE

RAMON

CRAMOND

GLEBE

CRAMOND GR

CRAMOND PL

EH4

SCHOOL BRAE

CADDELL'S
ROW

FAIR-A-FAR
COTTAGES

Weir

CRAMOND
ROAD

AVENUE

River Almond

New
Burnshot

CYCLE PATH

CRAMOND VALE

CRAMOND TERRACE

CRAMOND PARK

CRAMOND GDN

6

ROAD

East
Craigie

FAIR-A-FAR

WHITEHOUSE
ROAD

INVERLMOND GR

CRAMOND
BK

INVERLMOND DR

CRAMOND
GLN

Cramond
Prim Sch

GAMEKEEPER'S

GAMEKEEPER'S

Cargilfield
Sch

BR

MILL ROAD

COTTAGE

CRAMOND

INVERLMOND

AVO

676

319

12

AS AT AU AV

2

Cramond
Island

The
Knoll

3

F I R T H O

Tidal Causeway

4 Breakwater

Cobble
Cottage
anger Ferry

ESPLANADE SILVERKNOWES ESPLANADE

11 P SILVERKNOWES ESPLANADE

Cramond
Tower MARINE DRIVE

Cramond
House P

5 Hall Roman Fort
(remains) KIRK +

RIVER ALMOND WALKWAY

SCHOOL BRAE THE GLEBE BRIGHOUSE PARK RIGG SILVERKNOWES

CRAMOND GLEBE ROAD BRIGHOUSE PARK GDNS SILVERKNOWES

BRIGHOUSE PARK CRES GOLF COURSE

1 CRAMOND BRIGHOUSE PARK CT

CRAMOND ROAD CRAMOND Clubhouse SILVERKNOWES

CRAMOND TERRACE NORTH SILVERKNOWES PARK

6 AVENUE CRAMOND ROAD EH4 SILVERKNOW
PARK

CRAMOND CRAMOND GAME RD SILVERKNOWES PARKWAY

CRAMOND BK Lauriston SILVERKNOWES SILVERKNOW
Farm SILVERKNOWES

KEEPER S Lauriston
Castle CRAMOND SILVERKNOWES HILL CRESCENT

Cargil BRUNTSFIELD LINKS ROAD LAURISTON SILVERKNOWES SILVERKNO
676 St FARM SILVERKNOWES LOAN DRIVE

GOLF COURSE Clubhouse NORTHLAWN 6 BARNTON SILVERKNOWES
EASTER 3 PARK SILVERKNOWES TER

7 WEST CYCLE PATH RD 5 DRIVE 7 ROAD

4 2 BARNTON GARDENS SILVERKNOWES

AVENUE Superstore
THE GREEN

ROYAL BURGESS BARNTON BARNTON PK BARNTON AVENUE

319 GOLF COURSE BARNTON BARNTON AV B9085 PL QUALITY
LOAN EAST S BARN ST LA CORBIE
GDNS PO CORB

AS AT 24 AU AV

BA   BB   BC   BD

2

3

FIRTH OF

WESTERN BREAKWATER

EASTERN BREAKWATER

GRANTON
HARBOUR

ROAD
WEST PIER
SEALCARR STREET
FINTISH
OXCRAIGS
MIDDLE PIER
FORTH
IND EST

4   GRANTON

WEST HARBOUR
NEW BROO
GRANTON PK AV
CUSTOM HOUSE
GRANTON PK
WATERFRONT AVENUE
ROAD
GRAN SQ
LOCHINVAR DR
GRAN LOWER GRANTON
A903
GRANTON
MCKELVIE PARADE
ROAD
A901
TRINIT CRES

13

Gas
Superstore
GRANTON MDW
GRANTON CRESCENT
GRANTON CRES
Granton Crescent Park
GRANTON TER
GRANTON PLACE
GRANTON VIEW
GRANTON SQ
LUFRA BANK
WARDIE
St. Columba's Hospice
WARDIE STEPS
HOTA RD
BOSWALL RD
BOSWALL ROAD
PRIMROSE BANK RD
LOWER GRAN RD
TRINITY ROW

West
CAROLINE
WEST GRANTON CRESCENT
Bowling Club
ROYSTON MAINS AV
WARDIEBURN PL PS
WARDIEBURN
WARDIE AV
Comm Cen
GRANTON PS
WARDIEBURN DR
WARDIE DELL
BOS GDNS
WARDIE CRESCENT
GRI SQ
GRIERSON AV
LENNOX
Lomond Park
Bowling Club
STIRLING
ZETLAND
EAST TRINITY

5

CREWE
ROYSTON MAINS ST
ROYSTON MAINS
Royston Prim Sch
MAINS
Granton Prim Sch
BOSWALL
DRIVE
GRANTON
TER
PARKWAY
Granton Prim Sch
GRIERSON CRES
PO
GRIERSON GDNS
EH5
Recreation Grounds
Wardie
Pavs
Wardie Prim Sch
SPENCER PL
TRINITY GRO
Trinity

CREWE PATH
BOSWALL CREWE
Pilton
CREWE PL
CREWE LOAN
PILTON CRES
PILTON LOAN
PILTON
PILTON TERRACE
East Pilton
PILTON Pav
PILTON PARK
AVENUE
BOS GDNS
BOS GDNS
BOSWALL CRES
BOSWALL GRN
FRASER CRES
FRASER GDNS
CARGIL CT
CARGIL CT
DARNELL RD
ROSEBANK RD
DENHAM GRN
DENHAM GRN AV
CLARK PL
BANGHOLM
BANGHOLM

6

PILTON
WEST PILTON
BOSWALL QUAD
FRASER AVENUE
FRASER GRO
AFTON TER
AFTON PL
TRINITY CT
ROSE BANK
ROSE CT
BANGS
BANGHOLM
AV

Ainslie Park Leisure Cen
Rec Grds
CYCLE PATH
EAST PILTON FARM RIGG
BOSWALL PL
W FERRYFIELD
BOSWALL AVENUE
CYCLE PATH
WARDIE PK
WARDIE AV
ROAD
TRINITY
INVERLEITH GDNS
ARBORETUM
BOWHILL TER
WARRISTON

76
Works
Superstore
Rec Grd
P
FERRY
ROAD
A902
FERRY
Sports Centre
Edinburgh Academy Junior Sch
SPENCER PL
Golder
George
Sports

7   A902

Works
B9085
Fire Sta
TELFORD RD
A902
Playing Fields
FERRY
ROAD
Clubhouse
Stewarts Melville Sports Ground
Football Grd
Pav
Playing Field
EAST
FETTES
ROCHEID PK
ROCHEID PK
ROAD
FERRY
Sports Ground
Edinburgh College of Art (Inverleith)
EH3
INVERLEITH
RUFC Ground
Clubhouse
Glasshouse Experience

ROAD
B9085
GRICOR
323
NORTH
Fettes College Prep Sch
KINNEAR ROAD
Inverleith
Newfield Recreation Ground
Pav
INVERLEITH PLACE
Royal Botanic Garden Edinburgh

BA   BB   26   BC   BD

4

5

6

7

8

9

RTH

O F

F O R T H

Works

FIELD
ATION
UND

Pavilon

ouse

SEAFIELD

FILYSIDE ROAD

FILYSIDE TER

FILYSIDE AV

STAPELEY AVENUE

CRAIGENTINNY AVENUE

NAN DRIVE

SEAFIELD WAY

SEAFIELD ROAD

CYCLE TRACK

A199

PROMENADE

CYCLE TRACK

EAST A199

KING'S PLACE

CRAIGENTINNY ROAD

WAKEFIELD AVENUE

VANDELUER DRIVE

KERCHUR GRO

BRYCE GRO

GOFF AVENUE

VANDEL AVENUE

Seafield
Industrial
Estate

CHRISTIEMILLER AVENUE

SYDNEY PL

SYDNEY PK

VANDELEUR PL

BRYCE AVENUE

VANDELAVE

INCHVIEW TERR

KING'S ROAD

KING'S PLACE

GENTINNY CRESCENT

CRAIG GRO

E CHRIST. GRO

CHRIST. TERRACE

A1140

⁶75

Portobello Indoor
Bowls & Leisure
Centre

PORTOBELLO

20
AA
AB
AC
AD

Dundas
Loch

EH30

Craigend

8

A8000

(Due open early 200?

Carmelhill
Wood

7

hill

Humbie
Cottages

Wester
Humbie

Humbie

Almondhill
Steadings

Almondh

8

Queensferry Road

KIRKL Pk
GLENDINNING WAY
GLENDINNING RD
KIRKLANDS PK CRES
KIRKLANDS PK GDNS
KIRKLANDS PK GONS
ALLAN PK
ALLAN PK
STIRLING ROAD
BUIE RIGG

Kirkliston
Leisure
Centre

HUMBIE RD
NEWMAINS ROAD
NEWMAINS FARM LA
MAITLAND RD
Comm Cem
ALMONDHILL
ALLISON
STEWART PL
DUNDAS PL
DUNDAS PL
DUDDGE PL
B800

MAIN STREET
MAIN STREET

KIRKL

ALMONDSIDE
Health Cen
STATION RD
Bowling GRN
Bowl Club
AULDGATE
STATION
WELTRATS RD

B9080

9

M9

WEST LOTHIAN
EDINBURGH

harles's
ridge

BUIE BRAE
BUIE BRAE
Kirkliston
Prim Sch
ALLISON PARK
Pav
Waterfall
Swine Burn
CARMEL PL
MARSHALL
CARM AV
LISTON RD
LIST PL
GLEBE
MANSE
The
Distillery
KIRKLISTON CEM
BRAE ST
HIGH
PATH ROAD

Junction 1a

10

verton
ottages

Overton

Niddry Burn

COTLAWS
GATESIDE ROAD
KING EDWARDS WAY
MAITLAND
HROG LA
CLERIC'S HILL

NEW LISTON ROAD

Maitland
Bridge

LOCHEND

Hallyards

FB

HALLYARDS RD

11

Newliston

Inner
Lodge

Milrig
Cottages

Milrig

B800

ROAD

HALLYARDS ROAD

Hally
Cotte
HALLYARDS

M9

12

Home
Farm

The
Gardens

South
Lodge

Lawn Park
Cottage

EH28

Poultry
Farm

LOCHEND ROAD

Sewage
Works

673

311

AA

Brox Burn

KIRKLISTON RD

AB

36

EDINBURG

Poultry
Packing
Station

Newbridge

AC

AD

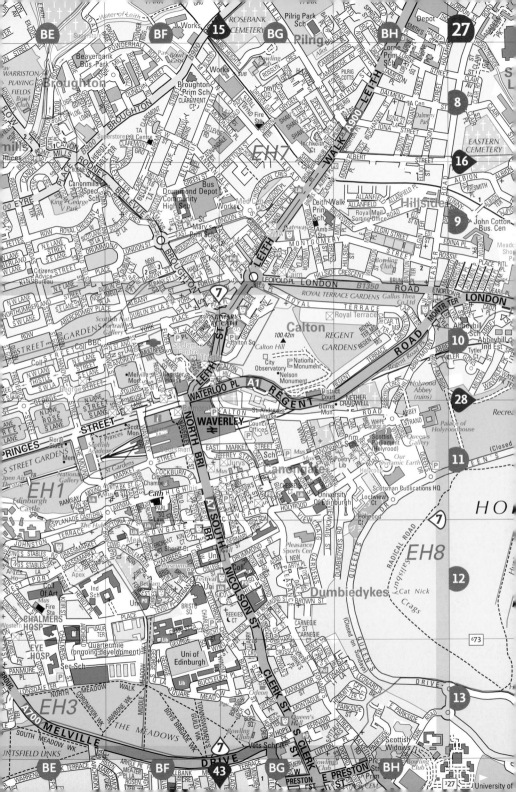

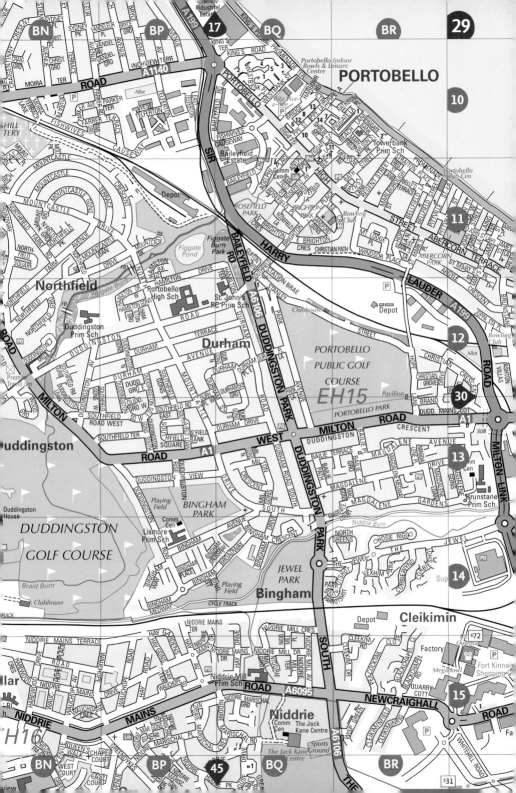

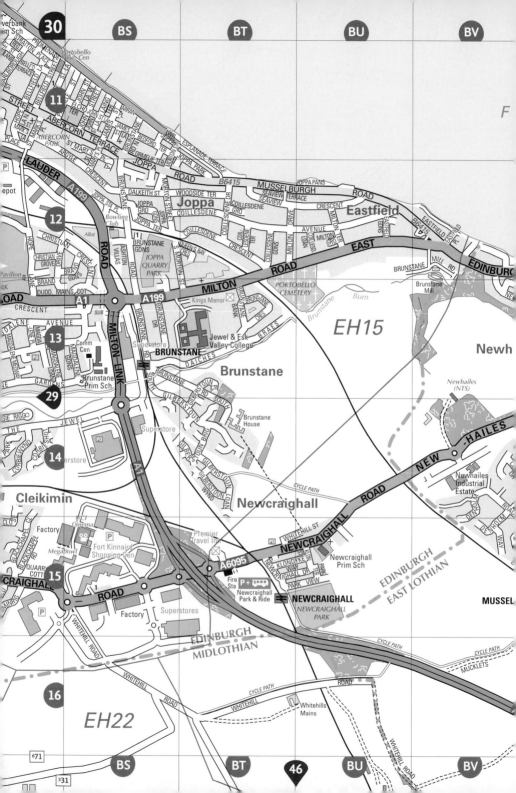

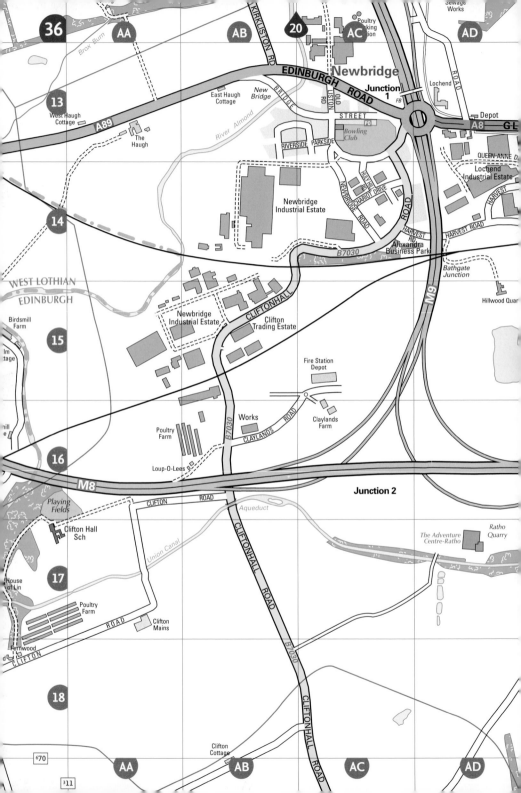

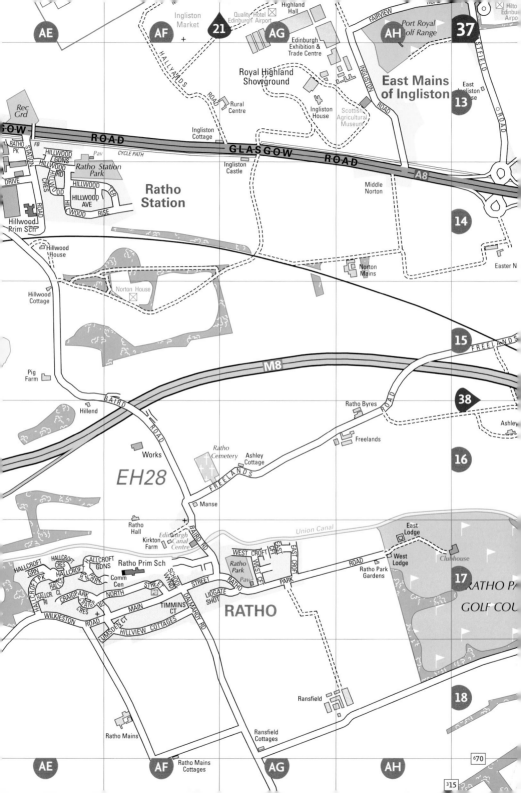

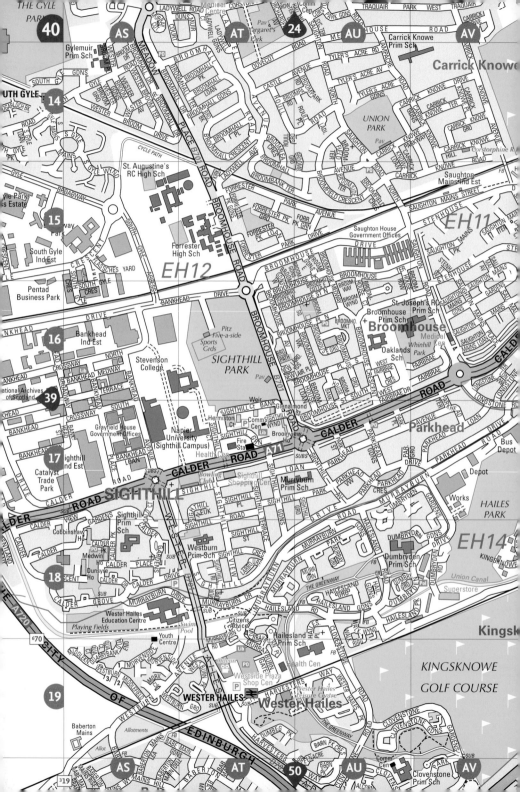

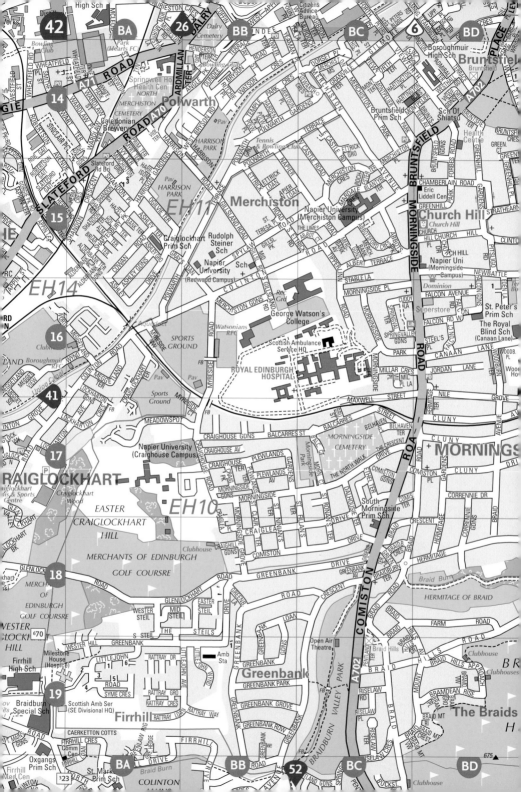

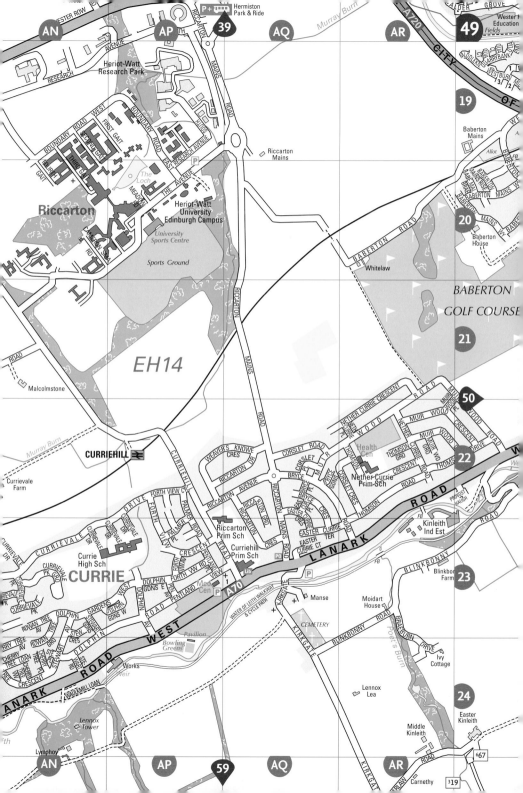

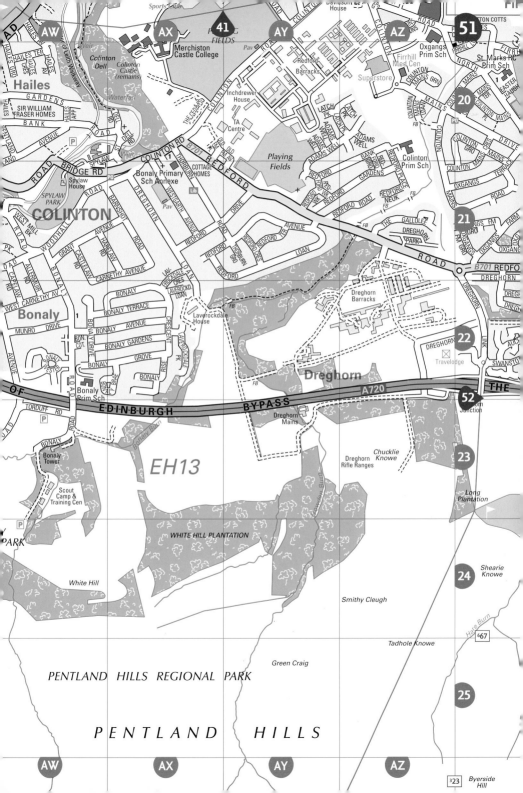

Lennox Tower

Middle Kinleith

Kinleith

AN

AP

49

AQ

AR

59

KIRKGATE

HARLAW ROAD

Carnethy

25

Wester Kinleith

26

BLACK WOOD

EH14

HARLAW ROAD

27

White

Reservoir (Covered)

Harlaw Farm

HARLAW ROAD

HARLAW ROAD

Balleny Farm

P

28

Visitor Centre

Harlaw Reservoir

29

Weir

30

Threipmuir Reservoir

AN

AP

AQ

AR

⁶64

³19

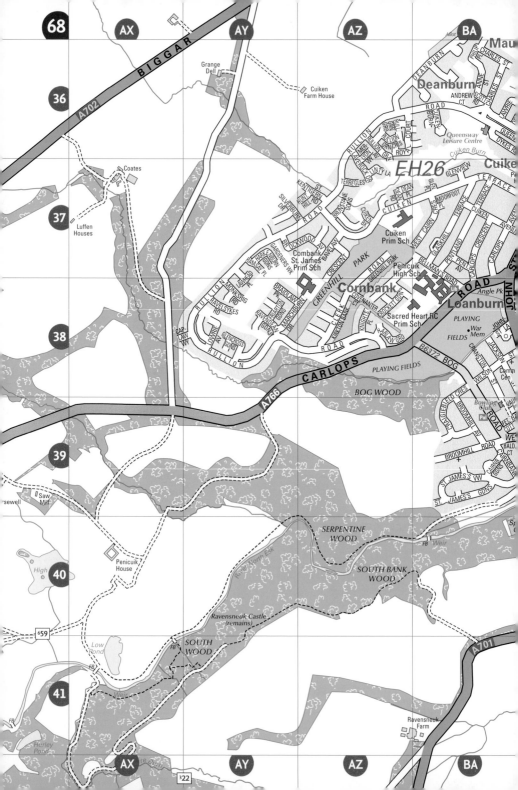

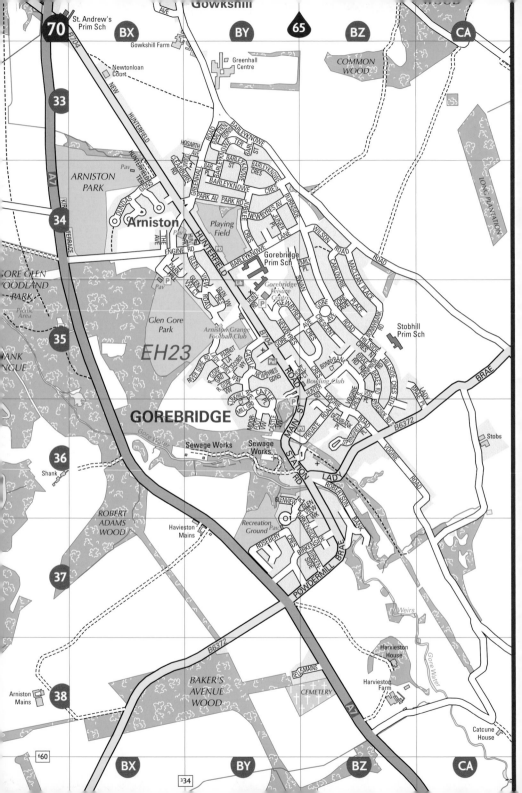

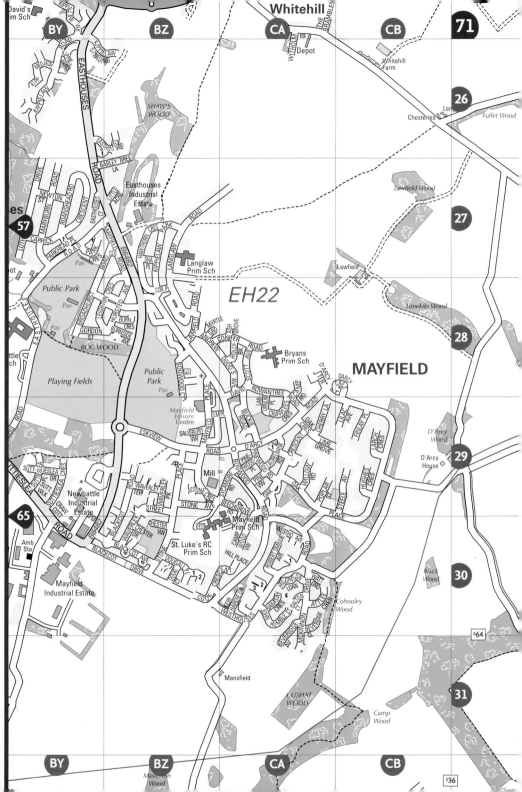

74

Bridge of Allan
Menstrie
Alva
Tillicoultry
Dollar
Dollarbeg
Cairngone
Solsgirth
Balgor

Mill Trail Visitor Centre
Sterling Mills
Devonside
Coalsnaughton
Fishcross
Gartmorn Dam
Forest Mill
Blairlogie
Causewayhead
Wallace National
Wallace Monument
Tullibody
Sauchie

M9
A84
A91
A91
A908
A91
A977
A907

Nyadd
Ochtertyre
Keir House
Satan Park

Gargunnock
Leckie
Gargunnock House
Drip Moss
Smith Art Gallery & Museum
Stirling Castle
Cambuskenneth Abbey
Cambus
Clackmannan
Tower
Kennet
Bogside
Blair

STIRLING
Argyll & Sutherland Highlanders Museum
Cambusbarron
Royal Burgh of Stirling Visitor Centre
St Ninians
Bannockburn Heritage Cen (NTS)
Fallin
South Alloa
Dunmore
Airth
Kincardine
Town House (NTS)
Culross Palace (NTS)
Culross

Gargunnock Hills
Ling Hill
Hart Hill
Earl's Hill
North Third
North Third Reservoir
Bannockburn
Cowie
The Pineapple (NTS)
Bowtrees
Letham
South Bellsdyke

FIRTH OF

M80
A872
M876
M9
A905
A985
A907

Loch Coulter Reservoir
Plean
Torwood
Glenbervie
Stenhousemuir
Carronshore
Skinflats
Grangemouth
Bo'ness & Kinneil Railway
Bo'ness

Cairnoch Hill
Easter Buckieburn
Dunipace
Denny
Larbert
Carron
Bainsford
Bonnybridge
FALKIRK
Laurieston
Polmont
Linlithgow Bridge
Linlith

Muirmill
Carron Bridge
Fankerton
Tomtain
Banton
Banknock
Dennyloanhead
Longcroft
Haggs
High Bonnybridge
Falkirk Wheel
Camelon
Callendar House
Glen Village
Hallglen
Reddingmuirhead
Brightons
Maddiston
Whitecross
Linlith

Kilsyth
Queenzieburn
Kilsyth Hills
Colzium House
Dullatur
Abronhill
Old Shields
Roman Fort
Shieldhill
Blackbraes
California
Standburn
Muiravonside
Belsyde
Cockleroy
Torpichen

Twechar
Croy
Balloch
Carbrain
Greenfaulds
Cumbernauld
Luggiebank
Slamannan
Avonbridge
Westfield
Cairnpapple Hill

Waterside
Westfield
Condorrat
Mollinsburn
Riggend
Binniehill
Limerigg
Drumtassie Burn

Glenboig
Greengairs
Wattston
Longriggend
Armadale
Bathgate
Whiteside
Seafield
Blackburn

Chryston
Muirhead
Glenmavis
Summerlee Heritage Park
Stand
Caldercruix
Plains
Rawyards
Hillend
Hillend Reservoir
Westrigg
Almond
East Whitburn
Addiewell
Loganlea

Airdrie
Coatbridge
Whifflet
Calderbank
Chapelhall
Newhouse
Blackridge
Harthill
Whitburn
Eastfield
Polkemmet
Stoneyburn
Longridge
Fauldhouse
Breich

M73
A89
A73
M8
A71
A706
A704

Easterhouse
Baillieston
Bargeddie
Tannochside
Viewpark
Holytown
Salsburgh
Kirk of Shotts
Shotts
Polkemmet Moor
Woolfords Cottages

Uddingston
Bothwell
Blantyre
Bellshill
Carfin
Cleland
Newarthill
Hareshaw
Hartwood
Dykehead
Stane
Torbothie
Bowhousebog
Gladsmuir Hills
Worm Law
Rootpark

MOTHERWELL
Craigneuk
Coltness
Cambusnethan
Morningside
Bonkle
Newmains
Allanton
Murdostoun
Black Hill
Hare Hill
Climpy
Forth
Stobwood
Braehead

HAMILTON
Wishaw
Shieldmuir Sta
Gowkthrapple
Waterloo
Law
Overtown
Springfield Reservoir
Netherton

Larkhall
Quarter
Dalserf
Machan
Ashgill
Rosebank
Milton-Lockhart
Yieldshields
Kilncadzow
Harelaw
Carnwath

Carluke
Braidwood
West Port

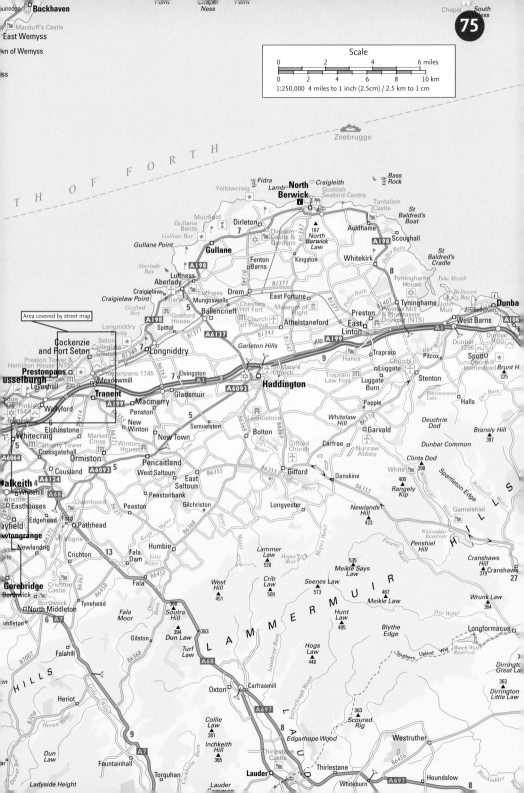

General abbreviations

Acad	Academy	Ex	Exchange	Pav	Pavilion
All	Alley	Exhib	Exhibition	Pk	Park
Allot	Allotments	FB	Footbridge	Pl	Place
Amb	Ambulance	FC	Football Club	Pol	Police
App	Approach	Fld	Field	Prec	Precinct
Arc	Arcade	Flds	Fields	Prim	Primary
Av	Avenue	Fm	Farm	Prom	Promenade
Ave	Avenue	Gall	Gallery	Pt	Point
Bdy	Broadway	Gar	Garage	Quad	Quadrant
Bk	Bank	Gdn	Garden	RC	Roman Catholic
Bldgs	Buildings	Gdns	Gardens	Rbt	Roundabout
Boul	Boulevard	Govt	Government	Rd	Road
Bowl	Bowling	Gra	Grange	Rds	Roads
Br	Bridge	Grd	Ground	Rec	Recreation
Bri	Bridge	Grds	Grounds	Res	Reservoir
Cath	Cathedral	Grn	Green	Ri	Rise
Cem	Cemetery	Grns	Greens	S	South
Cen	Central, Centre	Gro	Grove	Sch	School
Cft	Croft	Gros	Groves	Sec	Secondary
Cfts	Crofts	Gt	Great	Shop	Shopping
Ch	Church	Ho	House	Sq	Square
Chyd	Churchyard	Hosp	Hospital	St.	Saint
Cin	Cinema	Hts	Heights	St	Street
Circ	Circus	Ind	Industrial	Sta	Station
Cl	Close	Int	International	Sts	Streets
Clo	Close	Junct	Junction	Sub	Subway
Co	County	La	Lane	Swim	Swimming
Coll	College	Las	Lanes	TH	Town Hall
Comm	Community	Lib	Library	Tenn	Tennis
Conv	Convent	Ln	Loan	Ter	Terrace
Cor	Corner	Lo	Lodge	Thea	Theatre
Coron	Coroners	Lwr	Lower	Twr	Tower
Cors	Corners	Mag	Magistrates	Twrs	Towers
Cotts	Cottages	Mans	Mansions	Uni	University
Cov	Covered	Med	Medical, Medicine	Vet	Veterinary
Crem	Crematorium	Mem	Memorial	Vil	Villas
Cres	Crescent	Mkt	Market	Vil	Villa
Ct	Court	Mkts	Markets	Vw	View
Cts	Courts	Ms	Mews	W	West
Ctyd	Courtyard	Mt	Mount	Wd	Wood
Dep	Depot	Mus	Museum	Wds	Woods
Dev	Development	N	North	Wf	Wharf
Dr	Drive	NTS	National Trust for Scotland	Wk	Walk
Dws	Dwellings			Wks	Works
E	East	Nat	National	Yd	Yard
Ed	Education	PO	Post Office		
Embk	Embankment	Par	Parade		
Est	Estate	Pas	Passage		

Post town and locality abbreviations

Auch.	Auchendinny	Gowks.	Gowkshill	Polt.	Polton
Bal.	Balerno	Inglis.	Ingliston	Port S.	Port Seton
Bils.	Bilston	Inv.	Inveresk	Pres.	Prestonpans
Bonny.	Bonnyrigg	Jun. Grn	Juniper Green	Ratho Sta	Ratho Station
Cock.	Cockenzie	K'lis.	Kirkliston	Ricc.	Riccarton
Craig.	Craigiehall	Lass.	Lasswade	Ros.	Roslin
Cram.	Cramond	Lnhd	Loanhead	Rose.	Rosewell
Dalk.	Dalkeith	Mayf.	Mayfield	Silv.	Silverburn
Dalm.	Dalmeny	Milt.Br	Milton Bridge	S Q'fry	South Queensferry
Dand.	Danderhall	Monk.	Monktonhall		
David.M.	Davidsons Mains	Muss.	Musselburgh	Strait.	Straiton
		Newbr.	Newbridge	Tran.	Tranent
Easth.	Easthouses	Newcr.	Newcraighall	Wall.	Wallyford
Gilm.	Gilmerton	Newt.	Newtongrange	White.	Whitecraig
Gore.	Gorebridge	Pen.	Penicuik	Wool.	Woolmet

There are street names in the index which are followed by a number in **bold**. These numbers can be found on the map where there is insufficient space to show the street name in full. For example Affleck Ct (*EH12*, **1**   21 AQ11) will be found by a number **1** in the square AQ11 on page 21.

Place names are indicated in CAPITAL LETTERS, schools and hospitals are shown in red type and other places of interest are shown by blue type.

A

Abbeygrange (Newt.), Dalk. *EH22*	65	BW29
ABBEYHILL	28	BJ10
Abbeyhill *EH8*	7	BH11
Abbeyhill Cres *EH8*	7	BH11
Abbeyhill Ind Est *EH8*	28	BJ10
Abbeyhill Prim Sch *EH7*	28	BJ10
Abbey La *EH8*	28	BJ10
Abbeymount *EH8*	7	BH10
Abbey Rd, Dalk. *EH22*	56	BV25
Abbey Strand *EH8*	7	BH11
Abbey St *EH8*	28	BJ10
Abbotsford Ct *EH10*	42	BC15
Abbotsford Cres *EH10*	42	BC15
Abbotsford Pk *EH10*	42	BC15
Abercorn Av *EH8*	28	BM11
Abercorn Cotts *EH15*	28	BM13
Abercorn Ct *EH8* **1**	28	BM12
Abercorn Cres *EH8*	28	BL11
Abercorn Dr *EH8*	28	BL11
Abercorn Gdns *EH8*	28	BM10
Abercorn Gro *EH8*	28	BL11
Abercorn Rd *EH8*	28	BL11
Abercorn Ter *EH15*	29	BR11
Abercromby Pl *EH3*	6	BE10
Abinger Gdns *EH12*	25	AZ12
Academy La, Lnhd *EH20*	54	BL27
Academy Pk *EH6*	16	BJ7
Academy St *EH6*	16	BJ7
Acheson Dr, Pres. *EH32*	34	CG11
Acklam Path, Lnhd *EH20*	61	BH28
Adams Well *EH13*	51	AZ20
Addiston Cres, Bal. *EH14*	48	AL24
Addistone Br (Ratho), Newbr. *EH28*	48	AL19
Addiston Fm Rd (Ratho), Newbr. *EH28*	38	AK18
Addiston Gro, Bal. *EH14*	48	AL24
Addiston Pk, Bal. *EH14*	48	AK24
Adelphi Gro *EH15*	29	BQ11
Adelphi Pl *EH15*	29	BQ11
Admiral Ter *EH10*	42	BD14
Admiralty St *EH6*	15	BH5
Adventure Centre - Ratho *EH28*	36	AD17
Advocates Cl *EH1* **1**	7	BF11
Affleck Ct *EH12* **1**	23	AQ11
Afton Pl *EH5*	14	BC6
Afton Ter *EH5*	14	BC6
Agnew Ter *EH6*	15	BF6
Ainslie Pl *EH3*	6	BC10
Aird's Cl *EH1*	6	BE12
Aitchison's Pl *EH15* **11**	29	BQ11
Aitkenhill *EH11*	41	AX15
Alan Breck Gdns *EH4*	24	AT10
Albany La *EH1*	7	BF10
Albany St *EH1*	7	BF10
Albany St La *EH1*	7	BF10
Albert Cl (Wall.), Muss. *EH21* **2**	33	CD14
Albert Cres (Wall.), Muss. *EH21*	33	CD14
Albert Dock *EH6*	16	BJ5
Albert Pl *EH7*	27	BG9
Albert Pl (Wall.), Muss. *EH21*	33	CD14
Albert Rd *EH6*	16	BK6
Albert St *EH7*	27	BH8
Albert Ter *EH10*	42	BC15
Albert Ter, Muss. *EH21*	32	CA13
Albion Business Cen *EH7*	16	BJ9
Albion Gdns *EH7*	16	BJ9
Albion Pl *EH7*	16	BJ9
Albion Rd *EH7*	16	BJ9
Albion Ter *EH7*	16	BJ9
Albyn Pl *EH2*	6	BD10
Alcorn Rigg *EH14* **1**	50	AU20
Alcorn Sq *EH14*	50	AU20
Alderbank, Pen. *EH26*	68	BA39

Alderbank Gdns *EH11*	42	BA16
Alderbank Pl *EH11*	42	BA15
Alderbank Ter *EH11*	42	BA15
Alder Rd (Port S.), Pres. *EH32*	19	CL8
Alemoor Cres *EH7*	16	BK8
Alemoor Pk *EH7*	16	BK8
Alexander Dr *EH11*	41	AZ14
Alexander Dr, Pres. *EH32*	34	CG11
Alexandra Business Pk, Newbr. *EH28*	36	AC14
Alfred Pl *EH9*	43	BH14
Allanfield *EH7*	27	BH9
Allanfield Pl *EH7*	27	BH9
Allan Pk, K'lis. *EH29*	20	AC9
Allan Pk Cres *EH14*	41	AY16
Allan Pk Dr *EH14*	41	AY17
Allan Pk Gdns *EH14*	41	AY17
Allan Pk Ln *EH14*	41	AZ17
Allan Pk Rd *EH14*	41	AY17
Allan St *EH4*	26	BC9
Allan Ter, Dalk. *EH22*	57	BX24
Allermuir Av (Bils.), Ros. *EH25*	61	BG30
Allermuir Rd *EH13*	51	AW21
Allison Pl, K'lis. *EH29*	20	AD9
Alloway Ln *EH16*	44	BJ19
Almond Av *EH12*	21	AH12
Almond Bk Cotts *EH4* **1**	11	AR5
Almondbank Ter *EH11*	42	BA15
Almond Ct *EH16*	45	BN16
Almond Cres, Bonny. *EH19*	63	BR29
Almond Dr *EH12*	21	AH12
Almond Grn *EH12*	23	AQ11
Almond Gro, S Q'fry *EH30*	9	AE3
Almondhill Rd, K'lis. *EH29*	20	AD9
Almondhill Steadings, K'lis. *EH29*	20	AD8
Almond Rd *EH12*	21	AH12
Almondside, K'lis. *EH29*	20	AD10
Almond Sq *EH12*	23	AQ11
ALNWICKHILL	53	BH21
Alnwickhill Ct *EH16*	53	BH21
Alnwickhill Cres *EH16*	53	BH21
Alnwickhill Dr *EH16*	53	BH21
Alnwickhill Gdns *EH16*	53	BH21
Alnwickhill Gro *EH16*	53	BH21
Alnwickhill Ln *EH16*	53	BH21
Alnwickhill Pk *EH16*	44	BJ21
Alnwickhill Rd *EH16*	44	BJ20
Alnwickhill Ter *EH16*	53	BH21
Alnwickhill Vw *EH16*	53	BH21
Alvanley Ter *EH9* **1**	42	BD14
Alva Pl *EH7*	28	BJ10
Alva St *EH2*	6	BC11
Ambassador Ct, Muss. *EH21*	31	BZ13
Amos Path, Lnhd *EH20*	61	BG28
Anchor Cl *EH1* **11**	7	BF11
Anchorfield *EH6*	15	BF5
Ancrum Bk, Dalk. *EH22*	56	BV26
Ancrum Rd, Dalk. *EH22*	56	BV26
Anderson Av (Newt.), Dalk. *EH22*	65	BX29
Anderson Pl *EH6*	15	BG6
Andrew Ct, Pen. *EH26*	68	BA36
Andrew Dodd's Av (Mayf.), Dalk. *EH22*	57	BZ28
Andrew Wd Ct *EH6*	15	BE5
Angle Pk Ter *EH11*	42	BB14
Angres Ct (Dand.), Dalk. *EH22*	46	BS19
Annandale St *EH7*	27	BF8
Annandale St La *EH7*	27	BG9
Anne St, Pen. *EH26*	68	BA36
Annfield *EH6*	15	BF5
Annfield, Tran. *EH33*	35	CN14
Annfield St *EH6*	15	BF5
Ann St *EH4*	6	BC10
Ann Ter *EH8*	28	BJ10
Antigua St *EH1* **1**	27	BG9

Apex City Hotel *EH1*	6	BE12
Apex European Hotel *EH12*	26	BB12
Apex International Hotel *EH1*	6	BE12
Appin Dr, Pres. *EH32*	18	CJ9
Appin St *EH14*	41	AZ16
Appin Ter *EH14*	41	AZ15
Arboretum Av *EH4*	26	BC9
Arboretum Pl *EH3*	26	BC8
Arboretum Rd *EH3*	14	BC7
Arbuthnot Rd, Lnhd *EH20*	62	BL28
Archibald Pl *EH3*	6	BE12
Arden St *EH9*	43	BE14
Ardmillan Pl *EH11*	42	BB14
Ardmillan Ter *EH11*	42	BA14
Ardmillan Ter La *EH11* **1**	42	BB14
Ardshiel Av *EH4*	24	AT11
Argyle Cres *EH15*	29	BR11
Argyle Pk Ter *EH9*	43	BF14
Argyle Pl *EH9*	43	BF14
Argyle Pl, Bonny. *EH19*	63	BP29
Argyle St *EH6*	15	BG5
Argyll Ter *EH11* **2**	6	BC12
Armine Pl, Pen. *EH26*	69	BD36
ARNISTON	70	BX34
Arniston Pl, Bonny. *EH19* **2**	63	BR28
Arnott Gdns *EH14*	41	AW18
Arnprior Rd, Gore. *EH23*	70	BZ35
Arran Pl *EH15*	30	BS11
Arras Gro, Pen. *EH26*	66	BC35
Arrol Pl, S Q'fry *EH30*	9	AE3
Arthur's Seat *EH8*	28	BK13
Arthur St *EH6*	27	BH8
Arthur St La *EH6*	27	BH8
Arthur Vw Cres (Dand.), Dalk. *EH22*	45	BR19
Arthur Vw Ter (Dand.), Dalk. *EH22*	45	BR19
Ashburnham Gdns, S Q'fry *EH30*	9	AF2
Ashburnham Ln, S Q'fry *EH30*	9	AF2
Ashburnham Rd, S Q'fry *EH30*	9	AF3
Ash Gro (Mayf.), Dalk. *EH22*	71	CA28
Ashgrove, Muss. *EH21*	32	CA13
Ashgrove Pl, Muss. *EH21*	32	CB13
Ashgrove Vw, Muss. *EH21*	32	CB13
Ash La, Lnhd *EH20*	61	BG28
Ashley Dr *EH11*	42	BA16
Ashley Gdns *EH11*	42	BA16
Ashley Gra, Bal. *EH14*	58	AL25
Ashley Gro *EH11*	42	BA15
Ashley Pl *EH6*	15	BG7
Ashley Ter *EH11*	42	BA15
Ashton Gro *EH16*	44	BK18
Ashton Vil *EH15*	30	BS12
Ashville Ter *EH6*	16	BK8
Ashy Path *EH11* **1**	42	BB19
Assembly Rooms Theatre *EH2*	6	BE11
Assembly St *EH6*	16	BJ6
Assynt Bk, Pen. *EH26*	69	BC37
Astley Ainslie Hosp *EH9*	43	BE16
Atheling Gro, S Q'fry *EH30*	9	AE3
Atholl Cres *EH3*	6	BC12
Atholl Cres La *EH3*	6	BC12
Atholl Pl *EH3*	6	BC12
Atholl Ter *EH11* **3**	6	BC12
Atholl Vw, Pres. *EH32*	18	CJ9
Attlee Cres (Mayf.), Dalk. *EH22*	71	CA30
AUCHENDINNY	67	BE34
Auchingane *EH10*	52	BA22
Auchinleck Ct *EH6*	15	BF5
Auchinleck's Brae *EH6* **1**	15	BE5
Auldgate, K'lis. *EH29*	20	AD10
Auld Orchard, Bonny. *EH19*	56	BS28

Entry		
Avenue, The (Ricc.), Currie EH14	49	AP20
Avenue, The, Gore. EH23	70	BX34
Avenue Rd, Dalk. EH22	56	BV25
Avenue Rd (Cock.), Pres. EH32	19	CL8
Avenue Vil EH4	26	BB9
Avondale Pl EH3	26	BD9
Avon Gro EH4	23	AQ7
Avon Gro, Pen. EH26	69	BC37
Avon Pl EH4	23	AQ7
Avon Rd EH4	23	AQ7
Ayres Wynd, Pres. EH32 3	18	CH10

B

Entry		
BABERTON	50	AS20
Baberton Av, Jun. Grn EH14	50	AT21
Baberton Cres, Jun. Grn EH14	50	AT21
Baberton Golf Course EH14	50	AS21
Baberton Ln, Jun. Grn EH14	50	AT22
Baberton Mains Av EH14	50	AT20
Baberton Mains Bk EH14	50	AT20
Baberton Mains Brae EH14	50	AS20
Baberton Mains Ct EH14	50	AT20
Baberton Mains Cres EH14	50	AS20
Baberton Mains Dell EH14	50	AS20
Baberton Mains Dr EH14	50	AS20
Baberton Mains Gdns EH14	40	AS19
Baberton Mains Grn EH14	50	AT20
Baberton Mains Gro EH14	50	AT20
Baberton Mains Hill EH14	40	AS19
Baberton Mains Lea EH14	50	AS20
Baberton Mains Ln EH14	50	AU20
Baberton Mains Pk EH14	50	AT20
Baberton Mains Pl EH14	50	AS20
Baberton Mains Ri EH14	50	AS20
Baberton Mains Row EH14	50	AT20
Baberton Mains Ter EH14	50	AT20
Baberton Mains Vw EH14	50	AT20
Baberton Mains Way EH14	50	AS20
Baberton Mains Wd EH14	50	AS20
Baberton Mains Wynd EH14	50	AT20
Baberton Pk, Jun. Grn EH14	50	AT21
Baberton Rd, Currie EH14	49	AR20
Baberton Sq, Jun. Grn EH14	50	AT21
Back Dean EH4	26	BB11
Backdean Rd, Dalk. EH22	45	BQ19
Backlee EH16	53	BH21
Back Sta Rd EH16 1	28	BM15
Baileyfield Cres EH15	29	BQ11
Baileyfield Rd EH15	29	BP10
Bailie Gro EH15	29	BR13
Bailie Path EH15	29	BQ13
Bailie Pl EH15	29	BR13
Bailie Ter EH15	29	BQ13
Baird Av EH12	25	AY13
Baird Dr EH12	41	AX14
Baird Gdns EH12	25	AY13
Baird Gro EH12	25	AY13
Baird Rd (Ratho), Newbr. EH28	37	AF15
Baird Ter EH12	25	AY13
Bakehouse Cl EH8	7	BG11
Baker's Pl EH3 1	26	BD9
Balbirnie Pl EH12	26	BA12
Balcarres Ct EH10	42	BC17
Balcarres Pl, Muss. EH21	31	BZ12
Balcarres Rd, Muss. EH21	31	BZ12
Balcarres St EH10	42	BC17
Balderston Gdns EH16	44	BK18
Balderston Gdns N EH16	44	BK18
Baldwin Ct, Pen. EH26	68	BA39
BALERNO	58	AM26
Balerno Comm High Sch EH14	58	AL25
Balfour Pl EH6	27	BG8
Balfour Sq, Tran. EH33	35	CM13

Entry		
Balfour St EH6	15	BH7
Balfour Ter, Pen. EH26	66	BD34
Balfron Ln EH4	24	AS10
Balgreen Av EH12	25	AW13
Balgreen Gdns EH12	25	AW13
Balgreen Pk EH12	25	AW13
Balgreen Prim Sch EH11	41	AY14
Balgreen Rd EH11	41	AY15
Balgreen Rd EH12	25	AX13
Ballantyne La EH6 1	15	BH6
Ballantyne Rd EH6	15	BH6
Balmoral Hotel EH2	7	BF11
Balmoral Pl EH3	26	BD9
Balm Well Av EH16	54	BK22
Balm Well Gro EH16	54	BK22
Balmwell Pk EH16 1	54	BK22
Balm Well Ter EH16	54	BJ22
Baltic St EH6	16	BJ6
Bangholm Av EH5	14	BD6
Bangholm Bower Av EH5	14	BD6
Bangholm Gro EH5	15	BE6
Bangholm Ln EH5	15	BE6
Bangholm Pk EH5	14	BD6
Bangholm Pl EH5	14	BD6
Bangholm Rd EH5	14	BD6
Bangholm Ter EH3	14	BD7
Bangholm Vw EH5	15	BE6
Bangor Rd EH6	15	BG6
Bankhead Av EH11	40	AS16
Bankhead Bdy EH11	39	AR16
Bankhead Crossway N EH11	39	AR16
Bankhead Crossway S EH11	39	AR17
Bankhead Dr EH11	40	AS16
Bankhead Gro (Dalm.), S Q'fry EH30	9	AF2
Bankhead Ind Est EH11	40	AS16
Bankhead Ln EH11	40	AS17
Bankhead Medway EH11	40	AS16
Bankhead Pl EH11	40	AS16
Bankhead Rd (Dalm.), S Q'fry EH30	9	AG2
Bankhead St EH11	40	AS17
Bankhead Ter EH11	39	AR17
Bankhead Way EH11	39	AR17
Bankmill, Pen. EH26	69	BB39
Bankmill Vw, Pen. EH26 1	69	BB39
Bankpark Brae, Tran. EH33	34	CK12
Bankpark Cres, Tran. EH33	34	CK12
Bankpark Gro, Tran. EH33	34	CK12
Bank St EH1	7	BF11
Bank St, Pen. EH26	68	BA39
Bankton Ct, Tran. EH33	35	CM13
Bankton Ter, Pres. EH32	18	CK10
Barclay Pl EH10	6	BD13
Barclay Ter EH10	42	BD14
Barley Bree La, Dalk. EH22	57	BY27
Barleyknowe Cres, Gore. EH23	70	BY34
Barleyknowe Gdns, Gore. EH23	70	BY33
Barleyknowe La, Gore. EH23	70	BY34
Barleyknowe Pl, Gore. EH23	70	BY34
Barleyknowe Rd, Gore. EH23	70	BY33
Barleyknowe St, Gore. EH23	70	BY33
Barleyknowe Ter, Gore. EH23	70	BY34
Barn Pk EH14	50	AU20
Barn Pk Cres EH14	40	AU20
Barnshot Rd EH13	51	AX21
Barntalloch Ct EH12 4	23	AR12
BARNTON	23	AR9
Barnton Av EH4	12	AU7
Barnton Av W EH4	23	AR7
Barnton Brae EH4	23	AR7
Barnton Ct EH4	23	AR8
Barnton Gdns EH4	12	AU7
Barntongate Av EH4	23	AR9
Barntongate Dr EH4	23	AR9
Barntongate Ter EH4	23	AR9
Barnton Gro EH4	23	AR8

Entry		
Barnton Hotel EH4	23	AR9
Barnton Ln EH4	12	AT7
Barnton Pk EH4	12	AU7
Barnton Pk Av EH4	24	AS8
Barnton Pk Cres EH4	24	AS8
Barnton Pk Dell EH4	24	AT8
Barnton Pk Dr EH4	24	AS8
Barnton Pk Gdns EH4	24	AS8
Barnton Pk Gro EH4	24	AS8
Barnton Pk Pl EH4	24	AT8
Barnton Pk Vw EH4	23	AR8
Barnton Pk Wd EH4	23	AR9
Baroncourt Rd EH8	28	BL10
Baroncourt Ter EH8	28	BM10
Barony Pl EH3 3	27	BF9
Barony St EH3	27	BF9
Barony Ter EH12	24	AT12
Barracks St (Port S.), Pres. EH32	19	CM7
Barrie's Cl EH1 14	7	BF11
Basil Paterson Coll EH3	6	BD10
Bathfield EH6	15	BG5
Bath Pl EH15 2	29	BR10
Bath Rd EH6	16	BK6
Bath St EH15	29	BR11
Bath St La EH15	29	BR11
Bavelaw Cres, Pen. EH26	68	AZ37
Bavelaw Gdns, Bal. EH14	58	AL26
Bavelaw Grn, Bal. EH14	58	AL25
Bavelaw Rd, Bal. EH14	58	AL26
Baxter's Pl EH1 1	7	BG10
Bayview (Port S.), Pres. EH32 1	19	CM7
Beach La, Muss. EH21	31	BX12
Beauchamp Gro EH16	44	BJ19
Beauchamp Rd EH16	44	BJ19
Beaufort Rd EH9	43	BF15
Beaverbank Business Pk EH7	27	BE8
Beaverbank Pl EH7	27	BF8
Beaverhall Rd EH7	27	BF8
Bedford Ct EH4	26	BC9
Bedford St EH4	26	BC9
Bedford Ter EH15	30	BS11
Bedlam Paintball EH29	9	AE6
Bedlam Theatre EH1	7	BF12
Beeches, The (Newt.), Dalk. EH22	57	BW28
Beech Gro Av, Dalk. EH22	56	BT26
Beechgrove Rd (Mayf.), Dalk. EH22	71	CA29
Beech Ln, Bonny. EH19	63	BR29
Beechmount Cres EH12	25	AX12
Beechmount Pk EH12	25	AX13
Beech Pl, Pen. EH26	69	BB39
Beechwood Mains EH12	25	AX12
Beechwood (Newt.), Dalk. EH22	65	BX29
Beechwood Ter EH6	16	BK8
BEESLACK	69	BC36
Beeslack Comm High Sch EH26	69	BC36
Belford Av EH4	26	BA10
Belford Br EH4	26	BB11
Belford Gdns EH4	26	BA10
Belford Ms EH4	26	BB11
Belford Pk EH4	26	BB11
Belford Pl EH4	26	BA11
Belford Rd EH4	26	BB11
Belford Ter EH4 1	26	BB11
Belgrave Cres EH4	26	BB10
Belgrave Cres La EH4	26	BB10
Belgrave Gdns EH12	24	AU13
Belgrave Ms EH4	26	BB10
Belgrave Pl EH4	26	BB10
Belgrave Rd EH12	24	AU12
Belgrave Ter EH12	24	AU13
Belhaven Pl EH10	42	BC17
Belhaven Ter EH10	42	BC17
Bellenden Gdns EH16	44	BL18
Bellerophon Dr, Pen. EH26	69	BB39
Bellevue EH7	27	BF9
Bellevue Cres EH3	27	BF9
Bellevue Gdns EH7	27	BF8
Bellevue Gro EH7	27	BF9

Bellevue La EH7	27	BF9
Bellevue Pl EH7	27	BF9
Bellevue Rd EH7	27	BF9
Bellevue St EH7	27	BF9
Bellevue Ter EH7	27	BF8
Bellfield Av, Dalk. EH22	56	BU25
Bellfield Av, Muss. EH21	31	BX13
Bellfield Ct, Muss. EH21	31	BX14
Bellfield La EH15	29	BR11
Bellfield Sq, Pres. EH32 1	34	CG11
Bellfield St EH15	29	BR11
Bellfield Ter EH15	29	BR11
Bellfield Vw, Bonny. EH19 1	56	BT27
Bellman's Rd, Pen. EH26	68	BA37
Bell Pl EH3	26	BD9
Bells Brae EH4	6	BC11
Bellsmains, Gore. EH23	70	BY38
Bell's Mills EH4	26	BB11
Bellstane, S Q'fry EH30 1	8	AD2
Bell's Wynd EH1 2	7	BF11
Belmont Av EH12	25	AX12
Belmont Cres EH12	25	AX12
Belmont Dr EH12	25	AX12
Belmont Gdns EH12	25	AX12
Belmont Pk EH12	25	AX12
Belmont Rd,		
Jun. Grn EH14	50	AS21
Belmont Ter EH12	25	AX12
Belmont Vw EH12	25	AX12
Belvedere Pk EH6	15	BE5
Belwood Cres (Milt.Br),		
Pen. EH26	66	BD34
Belwood Rd (Milt.Br),		
Pen. EH26	66	BA34
Beresford Av EH5	15	BE5
Beresford Gdns EH5	15	BE6
Beresford Pl EH5	14	BD6
Beresford Ter EH5	14	BD6
Bernard St EH6	16	BJ5
Bernard Ter EH8	7	BG13
Best Western Bruntsfield		
Hotel EH10	42	BD14
Best Western Edinburgh		
City Hotel EH3	6	BE12
Best Western Kings		
Manor Hotel EH15	30	BT13
Bethlehem Way EH7	16	BK8
Beulah, Muss. EH21	32	CA13
Bevan Lee Ct, Dalk. EH22	57	BX23
Bevan Rd (Mayf.),		
Dalk. EH22 2	65	BZ30
Beveridge Av (Mayf.),		
Dalk. EH22	71	CA31
Beveridge Cl (Mayf.),		
Dalk. EH22	71	CA30
Big Brae, Bonny. EH19	55	BR27
Big Brigs Way (Newt.),		
Dalk. EH22	64	BV31
Biggar Rd EH10	52	BD22
Biggar Rd (Silv.),		
Pen. EH26	66	BB32
BILSTON	61	BF29
Bilston Cotts, Ros. EH25	61	BG29
Bilston Glen Ind Est,		
Lnhd EH20	61	BH28
BINGHAM	29	BQ14
Bingham Av EH15	29	BP14
Bingham Bdy EH15	29	BP14
Bingham Cres EH15	29	BQ14
Bingham Crossway EH15	29	BP14
Bingham Dr EH15	29	BQ14
Bingham Medway EH15	29	BP14
Bingham Pl EH15	29	BP14
Bingham St EH15	29	BP14
Bingham Way EH15	29	BP14
BioCampus, Ros. EH25	61	BE31
Birch Ct EH4	23	AR9
Birch Cres, Lnhd EH20	61	BH28
Birkenside, Gore. EH23	70	BZ37
Birnies Ct EH4	13	AW6
Birsley Brae, Tran. EH33	34	CJ13
Birsley Rd, Tran. EH33	35	CL13
Blackadder Pl EH5	14	BA5
Blackbarony Rd EH16	44	BJ17
Blackburn Crag EH17	44	BM19
Blackchapel Cl EH15	29	BR15
Blackchapel Rd EH15	29	BR15
Blackcot Av (Mayf.),		
Dalk. EH22	65	BZ30
Blackcot Dr (Mayf.),		
Dalk. EH22	65	BY30
Blackcot Pl (Mayf.),		
Dalk. EH22 1	65	BZ29
Blackcot Rd (Mayf.),		
Dalk. EH22	65	BZ30
Blacket Av EH9	43	BH14
Blacket Pl EH9	43	BH14
BLACKFORD	43	BF17
Blackford Av EH9	43	BF16
Blackford Bk EH9	43	BF16
Blackford Gate EH9	43	BE16
Blackford Glen Cotts EH16	44	BJ18
Blackford Glen Rd EH16	43	BG18
Blackford Hill EH9	43	BF17
Blackford Hill Gro EH9	43	BF17
Blackford Hill Ri EH9	43	BF17
Blackford Hill Vw EH9	43	BF17
Blackford Rd EH9	43	BE15
Blackfriars St EH1	7	BG11
BLACKHALL	25	AW9
Blackhall Prim Sch EH4	25	AW10
Blackie Rd EH6	16	BK7
Blackthorn Ct EH4	23	AR9
Blackwood Cres EH9	43	BG14
Blaeberry Gdns EH4	23	AR9
Blair St EH1	7	BF11
Blandfield EH7	27	BF8
Blantyre Ter EH10	42	BC15
Blawearie Rd, Tran. EH33	35	CM14
Bleachfield EH6	15	BF7
Blenheim Ct, Pen. EH26	66	BC35
Blenheim Pl EH7	7	BG10
Blinkbonny Av EH4	25	AY10
Blinkbonny Cres EH4	25	AY10
Blinkbonny Gdns EH4	25	AZ10
Blinkbonny Gro EH4	25	AZ10
Blinkbonny Gro W EH4	25	AZ10
Blinkbonny Rd EH4	25	AZ10
Blinkbonny Rd, Currie		
EH14	49	AR23
Blinkbonny Ter EH4	25	AY10
Boat Grn EH3	27	BE8
Boathouse Br, K'lis. EH29	21	AG10
BOGHALL	60	BC28
Bogpark Rd, Muss. EH21	31	BW13
Bog Rd, Pen. EH26	68	BA38
Bogsmill Rd EH14	41	AX18
Bogwood Ct (Mayf.),		
Dalk. EH22	57	BZ28
Bogwood Rd (Mayf.),		
Dalk. EH22	57	BZ28
BONALY	51	AW22
Bonaly Av EH13	51	AW22
Bonaly Brae EH13	51	AW22
Bonaly Cotts EH13	51	AW22
Bonaly Cres EH13	51	AX22
Bonaly Dr EH13	51	AW22
Bonaly Gdns EH13	51	AW22
Bonaly Gro EH13	51	AW22
Bonaly Prim Sch EH13	51	AW22
Bonaly Ri EH13	51	AX22
Bonaly Rd EH13	51	AW21
Bonaly Steading EH13 1	51	AW22
Bonaly Ter EH13	51	AW22
Bonaly Wester EH13	51	AW22
Bonar Pl EH6	15	BF6
Bo'ness Rd, S Q'fry EH30	8	AB2
BONNINGTON	15	BF7
Bonnington Av EH6	15	BF6
Bonnington Gait EH6 1	15	BG7
Bonnington Gro EH6	15	BF6
Bonnington Ind Est EH6	15	BG7
Bonnington Prim Sch EH6	15	BG7
Bonnington Rd EH6	15	BG7
Bonnington Rd La EH6	15	BG7
Bonnington Ter EH6	15	BF6
Bonnybank Ct, Gore.		
EH23	70	BZ35
Bonnybank Rd, Gore.		
EH23	70	BZ35
Bonnyhaugh EH6	15	BF7
Bonnyhaugh La EH6	15	BF7
BONNYRIGG & LASSWADE	56	BT28
Bonnyrigg Prim Sch EH19	64	BS29
Bonnyrigg Rd, Dalk. EH22	56	BU26
Boothacre Cotts EH6 2	16	BL7
Boothacre La EH6	16	BL7
Boroughloch EH8	7	BG13
Boroughloch Sq EH8	7	BG13
Boroughmuir High Sch		
EH10	42	BD14
Borthwick Pl EH12	26	BA12
Borthwick's Cl EH1 3	7	BF11
Borthwick Vw, Lnhd		
EH20	62	BJ28
Boswall Av EH5	14	BB6
Boswall Cres EH5	14	BB6
Boswall Dr EH5	14	BB5
Boswall Gdns EH5	14	BB6
Boswall Grn EH5	14	BC6
Boswall Gro EH5	14	BB6
Boswall Ln EH5	14	BB5
Boswall Ms EH5	14	BB5
Boswall Parkway EH5	14	BA5
Boswall Pl EH5	14	BB6
Boswall Quad EH5	14	BB6
Boswall Rd EH5	14	BC5
Boswall Sq EH5	14	BB6
Boswall Ter EH5	14	BB6
Bothwell St EH7	27	BH9
Boundary Rd E (Ricc.),		
Currie EH14	49	AP19
Boundary Rd W (Ricc.),		
Currie EH14	49	AN19
Bowhill Ter EH3	14	BD7
Bowie's Cl EH6 1	16	BJ6
Bowling Grn, The EH6	15	BH6
Bowling Grn Rd, K'lis.		
EH29	20	AC9
Bowling La EH6 8	15	BH6
Bowmont Pl EH8	7	BG13
Boyd-Orr Dr, Pen. EH26	66	BB35
Boyd's Entry EH1 2	7	BG11
Boy's Brigade Wk EH3	7	BF13
Brae, The (Auch.),		
Pen. EH26	67	BE34
Braeburn Dr, Currie EH14	49	AR23
Braefoot Ter EH16	44	BJ18
Braehead Av EH4	23	AQ8
Braehead Bk EH4	23	AQ8
Braehead Cres EH4	23	AQ8
Braehead Dr EH4	23	AQ8
Braehead Gro EH4	23	AQ8
Braehead Ln EH4	23	AQ8
Braehead Pk EH4	23	AQ8
Braehead Rd EH4	23	AQ8
Braehead Row EH4 1	23	AQ8
Braehead Vw EH4	23	AQ8
Brae Pk EH4	23	AQ7
Braepark Rd EH4	23	AQ7
Braeside Rd, Gore. EH23	70	BZ35
Braeside Rd, Lnhd EH20	54	BM27
Braeside Rd N, Gore. EH23	70	BZ35
Braeside Rd S, Gore. EH23	70	BZ36
Braid Av EH10	42	BD18
Braidburn Cres EH10	42	BC18
Braidburn Spec Sch EH14	41	AZ19
Braidburn Ter EH10	42	BC18
Braid Cres EH10	42	BC18
Braid Fm Rd EH10	42	BC18
Braid Hills App EH10	42	BD19
Braid Hills Av EH10	42	BC18
Braid Hills Cres EH10	42	BC19
Braid Hills Dr EH10	43	BE18
Braid Hills Dr EH16	43	BF19
Braid Hills Golf Course		
EH10	42	BD19
Braid Hills Golf		
Driving Range EH16	53	BG20
Braid Hills Hotel EH10	42	BC19
Braid Hills Rd EH10	42	BC19
Braidlaw Pk, Pen. EH26	68	AY38
Braid Mt EH10	42	BC19
Braid Mt Crest EH10	42	BD19
Braid Mt Ri EH10	42	BD19
Braid Mt Vw EH10	42	BD19
Braid Rd EH10	42	BC18
BRAIDS, THE	42	BD19

Bramble Dr *EH4*	23	AR9
Bramdean Gro *EH10*	42	BD19
Bramdean Pl *EH10*	42	BD19
Bramdean Ri *EH10*	42	BD19
Bramdean Vw *EH10*	42	BD19
Brand Dr *EH15*	29	BR13
Brandfield St *EH3*	6	BC13
Brand Gdns *EH15*	30	BS12
Brandon St *EH3*	27	BE9
Brandon Ter *EH3*	27	BE9
Brass Rubbing Centre *EH1* 10	7	BG11
Breadalbane St *EH6*	15	BG6
Breadalbane Ter *EH11* 5	6	BC12
Bread St *EH3*	6	BD12
Bread St La *EH3*	6	BD12
Breck Ter, Pen. *EH26*	66	BC35
Brewery Cl, S Q'fry *EH30*	8	AD2
Brewery La *EH6* 2	15	BH6
Briarbank Ter *EH11*	42	BA15
Brickfield St *EH15* 12	29	BQ10
Brickworks Rd, Tran. *EH33*	34	CK12
Bridge End *EH16*	44	BK16
Bridgend, Dalk. *EH22* 1	56	BV23
Bridgend Ct, Dalk. *EH22*	56	BV23
Bridge Pl *EH3*	26	BC9
Bridge Rd *EH13*	51	AW21
Bridge Rd, Bal. *EH14*	58	AL25
Bridge St *EH15*	29	BQ10
Bridge St, Muss. *EH21*	31	BY13
Bridge St, Newbr. *EH28*	36	AB13
Bridge St, Pen. *EH26*	69	BB39
Bridge St, Tran. *EH33*	35	CL13
Bridge St La *EH15* 6	29	BQ10
Briery Bauks *EH8*	7	BG12
Brighouse Pk Ct *EH4*	12	AS5
Brighouse Pk Cres *EH4*	12	AS5
Brighouse Pk Dr *EH4*	12	AS6
Brighouse Pk Gait *EH4*	12	AS5
Brighouse Pk Rigg *EH4*	12	AS5
Brighton Pl *EH15*	29	BQ11
Brighton St *EH1*	7	BF12
Bright's Cres *EH9*	43	BH15
Bright Ter *EH11* 8	6	BC12
Bristo Pl *EH1*	7	BF12
Bristo Port *EH1*	7	BF12
Bristo Sq *EH8*	7	BF12
Britwell Cres *EH7*	28	BM10
Brixwold Bk, Bonny. *EH19*	64	BT29
Brixwold Castle Hotel *EH19*	64	BT30
Brixwold Dr, Bonny. *EH19*	64	BT29
Brixwold Neuk, Bonny. *EH19*	64	BT29
Brixwold Pk, Bonny. *EH19*	64	BT29
Brixwold Ri, Bonny. *EH19*	64	BT29
Brixwold Vw, Bonny. *EH19*	64	BT29
Broadhurst Rd (Easth.), Dalk. *EH22*	57	BY28
Broadway Pk *EH12*	39	AR15
Broad Wynd *EH6* 7	16	BJ6
Brockwood Av, Pen. *EH26*	68	AY37
Brookfield Ter (Bils.), Ros. *EH25*	61	BG29
Broombank Ter *EH12*	40	AT15
Broomburn Gro *EH12*	40	AU14
Broomfield Cres *EH12*	40	AU15
Broomfield Ter *EH12*	40	AU14
Broomhall Av *EH12*	40	AT14
Broomhall Bk *EH12*	40	AT14
Broomhall Cres *EH12*	40	AT14
Broomhall Dr *EH12*	40	AS14
Broomhall Gdns *EH12*	40	AT14
Broomhall Ln *EH12*	40	AT14
Broomhall Pk *EH12*	40	AT14
Broomhall Pl *EH12*	40	AT14
Broomhall Rd *EH12*	40	AS14
Broomhall Ter *EH12*	40	AS14
Broomhill Av, Pen. *EH26*	68	BA39
Broomhill Dr, Dalk. *EH22*	56	BU25
Broomhill Pk, Dalk. *EH22*	56	BU26
Broomhill Rd, Pen. *EH26*	68	BA39
BROOMHOUSE	40	AU16
Broomhouse Av *EH11*	40	AT16
Broomhouse Bk *EH11*	40	AU16
Broomhouse Cotts E *EH11*	40	AU16
Broomhouse Cotts W *EH11*	40	AT16
Broomhouse Ct *EH11*	40	AU16
Broomhouse Cres *EH11*	40	AU16
Broomhouse Dr *EH11*	40	AT15
Broomhouse Gdns *EH11*	40	AU15
Broomhouse Gdns E *EH11*	40	AU15
Broomhouse Gdns W *EH11*	40	AT15
Broomhouse Gro *EH11*	40	AU16
Broomhouse Ln *EH11*	40	AU16
Broomhouse Mkt *EH11*	40	AU16
Broomhouse Medway *EH11*	40	AU15
Broomhouse Pk *EH11*	40	AT16
Broomhouse Path *EH11*	40	AU16
Broomhouse Pl N *EH11*	40	AT16
Broomhouse Pl S *EH11*	40	AT16
Broomhouse Prim Sch *EH11*	40	AU16
Broomhouse Rd *EH11*	40	AT16
Broomhouse Rd *EH12*	40	AT15
Broomhouse Row *EH11*	40	AV15
Broomhouse Sq *EH11*	40	AU16
Broomhouse St N *EH11*	40	AT16
Broomhouse St S *EH11*	40	AU17
Broomhouse Ter *EH11*	40	AU15
Broomhouse Wk *EH11*	40	AU16
Broomhouse Way *EH11*	40	AU16
Broomhouse Wynd *EH11*	40	AU16
BROOMIEKNOWE	55	BQ27
Broomieknowe, Lass. *EH18*	55	BQ27
Broomieknowe Gdns, Bonny. *EH19*	55	BR27
Broomieknowe Golf Course *EH19*	56	BS26
Broomieknowe Pk, Bonny. *EH19*	55	BR26
Broomlea Cres *EH12*	40	AT14
Broompark Rd *EH12*	40	AU14
Broomside Ter *EH12*	40	AU15
Broomview Ho *EH11*	40	AT17
Broomyknowe *EH14*	41	AX19
Brougham Pl *EH3*	6	BE13
Brougham St *EH3*	6	BD13
BROUGHTON	27	BE8
Broughton High Sch *EH4*	26	BB9
Broughton Mkt *EH3*	27	BF9
Broughton Pl *EH1*	27	BF9
Broughton Pl La *EH1*	27	BF9
Broughton Prim Sch *EH7*	27	BF8
Broughton Rd *EH7*	27	BF8
Broughton St *EH1*	27	BF9
Broughton St La *EH1*	7	BF10
Brown's Cl *EH8*	7	BH11
Brown's Pl *EH1* 4	6	BE12
Brown St *EH8*	7	BG12
Brown St La *EH8* 8	7	BG12
Bruce Gdns, Dalk. *EH22*	57	BX25
Bruce St *EH10*	42	BC17
BRUNSTANE	30	BT13
Brunstane Bk *EH15*	30	BT13
Brunstane Cres *EH15*	30	BT13
Brunstane Dr *EH15*	30	BS13
Brunstane Gdns *EH15*	30	BS12
Brunstane Gdns, Pen. *EH26*	68	AZ37
Brunstane Gdns Ms *EH15* 1	30	BS12
Brunstane Mill Rd *EH15*	30	BU12
Brunstane Prim Sch *EH15*	30	BS13
Brunstane Rd *EH15*	30	BS12
Brunstane Rd N *EH15*	30	BS11
Brunstane Rd S *EH15*	30	BS13
Brunstane Sta *EH15*	30	BS13
Brunswick Pl *EH7*	27	BG9
Brunswick Rd *EH7*	27	BG9
Brunswick St *EH7*	27	BG9
Brunswick St La *EH7*	27	BG9
Brunswick Ter *EH7* 1	27	BH9
Brunton Ct, Muss. *EH21*	31	BY13
Brunton Gdns *EH7* 2	27	BH9
Brunton Pl *EH7*	27	BH9
Brunton's Cl, Dalk. *EH22*	57	BW24
Brunton Ter *EH7*	27	BH9
Brunton Theatre *EH21*	31	BY13
BRUNTSFIELD	42	BD14
Bruntsfield Av *EH10*	42	BD14
Bruntsfield Cres *EH10*	42	BD14
Bruntsfield Gdns *EH10*	42	BD15
Bruntsfield Links Golf Course *EH4*	12	AS6
Bruntsfield Pl *EH10*	42	BC15
Bruntsfield Prim Sch *EH10*	42	BC14
Bruntsfield Ter *EH10*	42	BD14
Bryans Av (Newt.), Dalk. *EH22*	65	BX29
Bryans Prim Sch *EH22*	71	CA28
Bryans Rd (Newt.), Dalk. *EH22*	65	BW29
Bryce Av *EH7*	17	BP9
Bryce Cres, Currie *EH14*	49	AQ22
Bryce Gdns, Currie *EH14*	49	AQ22
Bryce Gro *EH7*	17	BP9
Bryce Pl, Currie *EH14*	49	AQ22
Bryce Rd, Currie *EH14*	49	AQ22
Bryson Rd *EH11*	42	BB14
Buccleuch Pl *EH8*	7	BF13
Buccleuch St *EH8*	7	BG13
Buccleuch St, Dalk. *EH22*	57	BW24
Buccleuch Ter *EH8*	7	BG13
Buchanan St *EH6*	27	BH8
Buckie Rd (Mayf.), Dalk. *EH22*	71	CA29
Buckingham Ter *EH4*	26	BB10
Buckstane Pk *EH10*	52	BC20
Buckstone Av *EH10*	52	BD21
Buckstone Bk *EH10*	52	BD20
Buckstone Circle *EH10*	53	BE21
Buckstone Cl *EH10*	52	BE21
Buckstone Ct *EH10*	52	BD21
Buckstone Cres *EH10*	52	BD20
Buckstone Crook *EH10*	53	BE22
Buckstone Dell *EH10*	52	BD20
Buckstone Dr *EH10*	52	BD20
Buckstone Gdns *EH10*	52	BD21
Buckstone Gate *EH10*	53	BE21
Buckstone Grn *EH10*	52	BE21
Buckstone Gro *EH10*	52	BD20
Buckstone Hill *EH10*	53	BE21
Buckstone Howe *EH10*	53	BE21
Buckstone Lea *EH10*	53	BE21
Buckstone Ln *EH10*	52	BD21
Buckstone Ln E *EH10*	53	BE21
Buckstone Neuk *EH10*	53	BE20
Buckstone Pl *EH10*	52	BD21
Buckstone Prim Sch *EH10*	53	BE21
Buckstone Ri *EH10*	52	BD21
Buckstone Rd *EH10*	52	BD21
Buckstone Row *EH10*	53	BE21
Buckstone Shaw *EH10*	53	BE22
Buckstone Ter *EH10*	52	BD21
Buckstone Vw *EH10*	52	BD20
Buckstone Way *EH10*	52	BD20
Buckstone Wd *EH10*	52	BD21
Buckstone Wynd *EH10*	53	BE21
BUGHTLIN	23	AR10
Bughtlin Dr *EH12*	23	AQ10
Bughtlin Gdns *EH12*	23	AQ11
Bughtlin Grn *EH12*	23	AQ10
Bughtlin Ln *EH12*	23	AQ11
Bughtlin Mkt *EH12*	23	AR11
Bughtlin Pk *EH12*	23	AR10
Bughtlin Pl *EH12*	23	AQ10
Buie Brae, K'lis. *EH29*	20	AB9
Buie Haugh, K'lis. *EH29*	20	AB9
Buie Rigg, K'lis. *EH29*	20	AB9
Builyeon Rd, S Q'fry *EH30*	8	AA3
Bull's Cl *EH8* 5	7	BH11
BUPA Murrayfield Hosp *EH12*	25	AW12
BURDIEHOUSE	54	BJ24
Burdiehouse Av *EH17*	54	BK23
Burdiehouse Cres *EH17*	54	BK23
Burdiehouse Crossway *EH17* 2	54	BK23
Burdiehouse Dr *EH17*	54	BK24
Burdiehouse Ln *EH17*	54	BK23
Burdiehouse Medway *EH17*	54	BK23
Burdiehouse Pl *EH17*	54	BK23
Burdiehouse Prim Sch *EH17*	54	BK23
Burdiehouse Rd *EH17*	54	BJ22
Burdiehouse Sq *EH17*	54	BJ24
Burdiehouse St *EH17*	54	BK23

Burdiehouse Ter *EH17* 54 BK23
Burgess Rd, S Q'fry *EH30* 8 AD2
Burgess St *EH6* 16 BJ6
Burgess Ter *EH9* 28 BJ15
Burghlee Cres, Lnhd *EH20* 62 BK28
Burghlee Ter, Lnhd *EH20* 62 BL28
Burghtoft *EH17* 55 BN22
Burlington St *EH6* 15 BH6
Burnbank, Lnhd *EH20* 54 BJ27
Burnbank Cres, Lnhd *EH20* 54 BJ26
Burnbank Gro, Lnhd *EH20* 54 BJ26
Burnbank Ter (Bils.), Ros. *EH25* 61 BG29
Burnbrae *EH12* 23 AQ11
Burndene Dr (Strait.), Lnhd *EH20* 61 BH26
Burndene Pk (Strait.), Lnhd *EH20* 61 BH26
Burnhead Cres *EH16* 44 BJ20
Burnhead Gro *EH16* 44 BK21
Burnhead Ln *EH16* 44 BK21
Burnhead Path E *EH16* 44 BK21
Burnhead Path W *EH16* 44 BK21
Burnside *EH12* 23 AQ11
Burnside, Pres. *EH32* 1 18 CG10
Burnside Av (Easth.), Dalk. *EH22* 57 BZ28
Burnside Cres (Easth.), Dalk. *EH22* 57 BZ28
Burnside Pk, Bal. *EH14* 58 AL26
Burnside Rd *EH12* 22 AJ11
Burnside Rd, Gore. *EH23* 70 BY34
Burns St *EH6* 16 BJ7
BUSH 60 BD31
Bush Ln, Pen. *EH26* 67 BE32
Bush St, Muss. *EH21* 31 BX12
Bush Ter, Muss. *EH21* 1 31 BX13
Bus Sta *EH1* 7 BF10
Butlerfield, Dalk. *EH22* 64 BV30
Butlerfield Ind Est, Bonny. *EH19* 65 BW31
Butterfly & Insect World *EH18* 56 BS23

C

Cables Wynd *EH6* 15 BH6
Cables Wynd Ho *EH6* 15 BH6
Caddell's Row *EH4* 11 AR6
Cadell Pl (Cock.), Pres. *EH32* 19 CL7
Cadell Sq, Tran. *EH33* 3 35 CM13
Cadiz St *EH6* 16 BJ6
Cadogan Rd *EH16* 44 BJ20
Cadzow Pl *EH7* 28 BJ10
Caerketton Av (Bils.), Ros. *EH25* 61 BG29
Caerketton Cotts *EH13* 42 BA19
Caerlaverock Ct *EH12* 3 23 AR12
Caesar Rd, Tran. *EH33* 35 CL13
Caesar Way, Tran. *EH33* 1 35 CL13
Caird's Row, Muss. *EH21* 31 BX12
Cairnbank Gdns, Pen. *EH26* 68 BA39
Cairnbank Rd, Pen. *EH26* 68 BA39
Cairn Hotel *EH7* 27 BG9
Cairnmuir Rd *EH12* 24 AU11
Cairnpark Sch *EH14* 41 AY18
Cairns Dr, Bal. *EH14* 58 AK27
Cairns Gdns, Bal. *EH14* 58 AK27
Cairntows Cl *EH16* 28 BM15
Caithness Pl *EH5* 14 BD6
Caiyside *EH10* 52 BC23
Caiystane Av *EH10* 52 BC22
Caiystane Cres *EH10* 52 BC21
Caiystane Dr *EH10* 52 BB22
Caiystane Gdns *EH10* 52 BB21
Caiystane Hill *EH10* 52 BC21
Caiystane Ter *EH10* 52 BB22
Caiystane Vw *EH10* 52 BC22
Calder Ct *EH11* 40 AS18
Calder Cres *EH11* 39 AR18
Calder Dr *EH11* 40 AS18
Calder Gdns *EH11* 40 AS18
Calder Gro *EH11* 39 AR18

Calder Pk *EH11* 40 AS18
Calder Pl *EH11* 40 AS18
Calder Rd *EH11* 40 AV16
Calder Rd (Ratho), Newbr. *EH28* 48 AJ19
Calder Rd Gdns *EH11* 41 AW16
Calder Vw *EH11* 39 AR18
Caledonian Cres *EH11* 26 BB13
Caledonian Hilton Hotel *EH1* 6 BD11
Caledonian Pl *EH11* 6 BC13
Caledonian Rd *EH11* 6 BC12
CALTON 7 BG10
Calton Hill *EH1* 7 BG10
Calton Hill *EH7* 7 BG10
Calton Rd *EH8* 7 BG11
Calton Sq *EH7* 7 BG10
Cambridge Av *EH6* 27 BG8
Cambridge Gdns *EH6* 27 BG8
Cambridge St *EH1* 6 BD12
Cambridge St La *EH1* 3 6 BD12
Cambusnethan St *EH7* 28 BK10
Cameo Cinema *EH3* 6 BD13
Camera Obscura & World of Illusions *EH1* 4 6 BE11
Cameron Br *EH16* 44 BK16
Cameron Cres *EH16* 44 BK16
Cameron Cres, Bonny. *EH19* 63 BP30
Cameron Ho Av *EH16* 28 BK15
Cameron March *EH16* 44 BJ16
Cameron Pk *EH16* 44 BJ16
Cameron Smail Rd (Ricc.), Currie *EH14* 49 AN20
Cameron Ter *EH16* 44 BK16
Cameron Toll *EH16* 44 BJ16
Cameron Toll Gdns *EH16* 44 BK16
Cameron Toll Lade *EH16* 44 BK16
Cameron Toll Shopping Centre *EH16* 44 BJ16
Cameron Way, Pres. *EH32* 18 CJ9
CAMMO 23 AP9
Cammo Bk *EH4* 23 AQ9
Cammo Brae *EH4* 23 AQ9
Cammo Cres *EH4* 23 AQ9
Cammo Gdns *EH4* 23 AQ9
Cammo Gro *EH4* 23 AP9
Cammo Hill *EH4* 23 AP9
Cammo Parkway *EH4* 23 AQ9
Cammo Pl *EH4* 23 AQ9
Cammo Rd *EH4* 23 AP9
Cammo Rd *EH12* 23 AN9
Cammo Wk *EH4* 23 AP10
Campbell Av *EH12* 25 AY12
Campbell Pk Cres *EH13* 50 AV21
Campbell Pk Dr *EH13* 50 AV21
Campbell Rd *EH12* 25 AY11
Campbell's Cl *EH8* 7 BG11
Campie Gdns, Muss. *EH21* 31 BX13
Campie Ho, Muss. *EH21* 31 BX13
Campie La, Muss. *EH21* 31 BX13
Campie Prim Sch *EH21* 31 BX13
Campie Rd, Muss. *EH21* 31 BX13
Camp Rd (Mayf.), Dalk. *EH22* 71 CA28
Campview (Dand.), Dalk. *EH22* 45 BR20
Campview Av (Dand.), Dalk. *EH22* 45 BR20
Campview Cres (Dand.), Dalk. *EH22* 45 BR20
Campview Gdns (Dand.), Dalk. *EH22* 45 BR20
Campview Gro (Dand.), Dalk. *EH22* 46 BS20
Campview Rd, Bonny. *EH19* 63 BR20
Campview Ter (Dand.), Dalk. *EH22* 45 BR20
Camp Wd Vw (Mayf.), Dalk. *EH22* 71 CA30
Camus Av *EH10* 52 BC21
Camus Pk *EH10* 52 BC21
Canaan La *EH9* 43 BE16
Canaan La *EH10* 43 BE16

Candlemaker Row *EH1* 7 BF12
Candlemaker's Cres *EH17* 45 BP20
Candlemaker's Pk *EH17* 45 BP21
Canmore St, S Q'fry *EH30* 8 AD3
Canning St *EH3* 6 BC11
Canning St La *EH3* 6 BC12
Cannon Wynd *EH6* 15 BG5
Canon Ct *EH3* 3 27 BE8
CANONGATE 7 BG11
Canongate *EH8* 7 BG11
Canon La *EH3* 27 BE9
CANONMILLS 26 BD8
Canonmills *EH3* 27 BE8
Canonmills Br *EH3* 2 27 BE8
Canonmills Spec Sch *EH7* 27 BE9
Canon St *EH3* 27 BE9
Capelaw Rd *EH13* 51 AW22
Caplaw Way, Pen. *EH26* 68 AX38
Caponhall Ct, Tran. *EH33* 35 CL14
Caponhall Dr, Tran. *EH33* 34 CK14
Caponhall Rd, Tran. *EH33* 35 CL14
Captain's Dr *EH16* 44 BK21
Captain's Ln *EH16* 44 BK21
Captain's Rd *EH17* 54 BK22
Captain's Row *EH16* 54 BK22
Carberry Cl (Inv.), Muss. *EH21* 32 CA16
Carberry Gro (Inv.), Muss. *EH21* 31 BZ16
Carberry Pl *EH12* 26 BA12
Carberry Rd (Inv.), Muss. *EH21* 31 BZ15
Carfrae Gdns *EH4* 25 AW9
Carfrae Gro *EH4* 25 AW9
Carfrae Pk *EH4* 25 AW9
Carfrae Rd *EH4* 25 AW9
Cargil Ct *EH5* 14 BC6
Cargilfield Sch *EH4* 23 AR7
Cargilfield Vw *EH4* 23 AR7
Cargil Ter *EH5* 14 BD6
Carlaverock Av, Tran. *EH33* 35 CM14
Carlaverock Cl, Tran. *EH33* 35 CN15
Carlaverock Ct, Tran. *EH33* 35 CN14
Carlaverock Cres, Tran. *EH33* 35 CM14
Carlaverock Dr, Tran. *EH33* 35 CM14
Carlaverock Gro, Tran. *EH33* 35 CM14
Carlaverock Ter, Tran. *EH33* 35 CN15
Carlaverock Vw, Tran. *EH33* 35 CM15
Carlaverock Wk, Tran. *EH33* 35 CM14
Carlops Av, Pen. *EH26* 68 BA37
Carlops Cres, Pen. *EH26* 68 BA37
Carlops Rd, Pen. *EH26* 68 AZ38
Carlowrie Av (Dalm.), S Q'fry *EH30* 9 AG4
Carlowrie Cres (Dalm.), S Q'fry *EH30* 9 AG4
Carlowrie Pl, Gore. *EH23* 70 BZ34
Carlton Hotel, The *EH1* 7 BF11
Carlton St *EH4* 6 BC10
Carlton Ter *EH7* 7 BH10
Carlton Ter Brae *EH7* 7 BH10
Carlton Ter La *EH7* 7 BH10
Carlton Ter Ms *EH7* 7 BH10
Carlyle Pl *EH7* 28 BJ10
Carlyle Pl, Muss. *EH21* 31 BY13
Carmel Av, K'lis. *EH29* 20 AC9
Carmelite Rd, S Q'fry *EH30* 8 AD3
Carmel Rd, K'lis. *EH29* 20 AC10
Carnbee Av *EH16* 44 BL21
Carnbee Cres *EH16* 44 BL21
Carnbee Dell *EH16* 1 44 BL21
Carnbee End *EH16* 44 BL20
Carnbee Pk *EH16* 44 BL21
Carnegie Ct *EH8* 7 BG12
Carnegie St *EH8* 7 BG12
Carnethie St, Rose. *EH24* 63 BN33
Carnethy Av *EH13* 51 AW21
Carnethy Av, Pen. *EH26* 68 BA37
Carnethy Ct, Pen. *EH26* 69 BB38
Caroline Gdns *EH12* 24 AU12
Caroline Pk Av *EH5* 13 AZ4
Caroline Pk Gro *EH5* 13 AZ5
Caroline Pl *EH12* 24 AU12

Caroline Ter EH12   24   AT11
Carpet La EH6   16   BJ6
Carrick Cres (Easth.), Dalk. EH22   57   BY27
CARRICK KNOWE   40   AV14
Carrick Knowe Av EH12   24   AV13
Carrick Knowe Dr EH12   40   AU14
Carrick Knowe Gdns EH12   40   AV14
Carrick Knowe Golf Course EH12   41   AW14
Carrick Knowe Gro EH12   40   AV14
Carrick Knowe Hill EH12   40   AV14
Carrick Knowe Ln EH12   40   AU14
Carrick Knowe Parkway EH12   40   AU14
Carrick Knowe Pl EH12   40   AV14
Carrick Knowe Prim Sch EH12   40   AV14
Carrick Knowe Rd EH12   40   AU15
Carrick Knowe Ter EH12   40   AV14
Carrington Rd EH4   26   BA9
Carrington Rd, Bonny. EH19   64   BT31
Carron Pl EH6   16   BK6
Carrubber's Cl EH1 5   7   BF11
Casselbank St EH6   15   BH7
Cassel's La EH6   15   BH7
Cast, The, Lass. EH18   62   BM29
Castle Av EH12   40   AT14
Castle Av, Gore. EH23   70   BY35
Castle Av (Port S.), Pres. EH32   19   CN7
Castlebrae Comm High Sch EH16   45   BN16
Castlebrae Glebe EH16   28   BM15
Castlebrae Gro EH16   44   BM16
Castlebrae Pl EH16   28   BM15
Castlebrae Rigg EH16   28   BM15
Castlehill EH1   6   BE11
Castlelaw Ct, Pen. EH26   69   BB37
Castlelaw Cres (Bils.), Ros. EH25   61   BG30
Castlelaw Rd EH13   51   AW21
Castlepark Gait EH16   28   BM15
Castlepark Glade EH16   44   BM16
Castlepark Grn EH16   44   BM16
Castle Pl, Gore. EH23   70   BY35
Castle Rd (Port S.), Pres. EH32   19   CN7
Castle Rd, Tran. EH33   34   CK15
Castle St EH2   6   BD11
Castle Ter EH1   6   BD12
Castle Ter EH3   6   BE12
Castle Ter (Port S.), Pres. EH32   19   CN7
Castle Vw, Gore. EH23   70   BY36
Castle Vw (Port S.), Pres. EH32   19   CN7
Castleview Dr EH16   44   BM16
Castleview Gro EH16   44   BM16
Castleview Ho EH17   44   BM18
Castleview Prim Sch EH16   45   BN16
Castleview Ter EH16   28   BM15
Castle Wk (Port S.), Pres. EH32   19   CN7
Castle Wynd N EH1 11   6   BE12
Castle Wynd S EH1 6   6   BE12
Catalyst Trade Pk EH11   39   AR17
Cathcart Pl EH11   26   BB13
Cathedral La EH1   7   BF10
Catherine Pl EH7   28   BE8
Catriona Ter, Pen. EH26   66   BD34
Causeway, The EH15   28   BL13
Causewayside EH9   43   BG14
Cavalry Pk Dr EH15   28   BM13
Cedar Dr (Port S.), Pres. EH32   19   CL8
Cedar Rd, Lnhd EH20   61   BH28
Cedars, The EH13   51   AX20
Cemetery Rd, Dalk. EH22   56   BV24
Chalmers Bldgs EH3 2   6   BD13
Chalmers Cl EH1 4   7   BG11
Chalmers Cres EH9   43   BF14
Chalmers Hosp EH3   6   BE12
Chalmers St EH3   6   BE12
Chamberlain Rd EH10   42   BD15

Chambers St EH1   7   BF12
Champigny Ct, Muss. EH21   32   CA14
Chancelot Cres EH6   15   BE6
Chancelot Gro EH5   15   BE6
Chancelot Ter EH6   15   BF6
Chapel Ct EH16   29   BN15
Chapel La EH6 2   16   BJ6
Chapel Ln, Ros. EH25   62   BJ32
Chapel St EH8   7   BG12
Chapel Wynd EH1 7   6   BE12
Chariot Dr EH28   36   AC14
Charlesfield EH8 1   7   BF12
Charles St EH8   7   BF12
Charles St, Pen. EH26   68   BA36
Charles St La EH8   7   BF12
Charlotte La EH2   6   BD11
Charlotte Sq EH2   6   BD11
Charlton Gro, Ros. EH25   67   BH32
Charterhall Gro EH9   43   BF16
Charterhall Rd EH9   43   BF17
Chatterrig EH13   52   BB20
Cherry La (Mayf.), Dalk. EH22   71   CA29
Cherry Rd, Bonny. EH19   63   BR29
Cherry Tree Av, Bal. EH14   49   AN24
Cherry Tree Cres, Bal. EH14   48   AM24
Cherry Tree Cres, Currie EH14   48   AM24
Cherry Tree Gdns, Bal. EH14   48   AM24
Cherry Tree Gro, Bal. EH14   48   AM24
Cherry Tree Ln, Bal. EH14   49   AN24
Cherry Tree Pk, Bal. EH14   48   AM24
Cherry Tree Pl, Currie EH14   49   AN24
Cherry Tree Vw, Bal. EH14   49   AN24
Chessels Ct EH8   7   BG11
Chesser Av EH14   41   AX15
Chesser Cotts EH11 1   41   AY15
Chesser Ct EH14   41   AX15
Chesser Cres EH14   41   AX16
Chesser Gdns EH14   41   AX15
Chesser Gro EH14   41   AX16
Chesser Ln EH14   41   AX16
Chester Ct, Bonny. EH19   63   BR29
Chester Dr (Mayf.), Dalk. EH22   65   BZ30
Chester Gro, Bonny. EH19   63   BR29
Chester St EH3   6   BC11
Chesters Vw, Bonny. EH19   63   BR29
Chester Vw (Mayf.), Dalk. EH22   65   BZ30
Chestnut Gro, Bonny. EH19   63   BR29
Chestnut Gro (Port S.), Pres. EH32   19   CM8
Chestnut St EH5   14   BA4
Cheyne St EH4   26   BC9
Chisholm Ter, Pen. EH26   69   BB36
Christian Cres EH15   29   BR12
Christian Gro EH15   29   BR12
Christian Path EH15   29   BQ11
Christiemiller Av EH7   17   BN9
Christiemiller Gro EH7   29   BN10
Christiemiller Pl EH7   17   BN9
Chuckie Pend EH3   6   BD12
CHURCH HILL   42   BD15
Church Hill EH10   42   BD15
Church Hill Dr EH10   42   BD15
Church Hill Pl EH10   42   BD15
Church Hill Theatre EH10   42   BD15
Church La, Muss. EH21   31   BY14
Church Rd, Lass. EH18   55   BP26
Church St, Lnhd EH20   62   BL28
Church St, Tran. EH33   35   CL12
Cineworld Cinema (Fountain Park) EH11   6   BC13
Circle, The (Dand.), Dalk. EH22   45   BR19
Circus Gdns EH3   6   BD10
Circus La EH3   26   BD9
Circus Pl EH3   6   BD10
Citadel Ct EH6   15   BH5
Citadel Pl EH6   15   BH5
Citadel St EH6 2   15   BH5
City Art Centre EH1   7   BF11

City of Edinburgh Bypass, The EH10   52   BA22
City of Edinburgh Bypass, The EH12   39   AP15
City of Edinburgh Bypass, The EH13   50   AU21
City of Edinburgh Bypass, The EH14   39   AR18
City of Edinburgh Bypass, The EH17   53   BH24
City of Edinburgh Bypass, The, Dalk. EH22   46   BV21
City of Edinburgh Bypass, The, Lass. EH18   55   BQ23
City of Edinburgh Bypass, The, Muss. EH21   46   BV21
Civic Sq, Tran. EH33 1   35   CM13
Clackmae Gro EH16   43   BH19
Clackmae Rd EH16   43   BH19
Clan Tartan Centre EH6   15   BG6
Clapper La EH16   44   BJ17
Clarebank Cres EH6   16   BK7
Claremont Bk EH7   27   BF9
Claremont Ct EH7   27   BF8
Claremont Cres EH7   27   BF8
Claremont Gdns EH6   16   BK7
Claremont Gro EH7   27   BF8
Claremont Pk EH6   16   BK7
Claremont Rd EH6   16   BK7
Clarence St EH3   26   BD9
Clarendon Cres EH4   6   BC10
Clarendon Hotel EH2   6   BD11
Clarinda Gdns, Dalk. EH22   57   BZ24
Clarinda Ter EH16   44   BJ18
Clark Av EH5   15   BE6
Clark Pl EH5   14   BD6
Clark Rd EH5   14   BD6
Claverhouse Dr EH16   44   BJ19
Clayhills Gro, Bal. EH14   58   AK26
Clayhills Pk, Bal. EH14   58   AK26
Clayknowes Av, Muss. EH21   31   BW14
Clayknowes Ct, Muss. EH21   31   BW14
Clayknowes Dr, Muss. EH21   30   BV14
Clayknowes Pl, Muss. EH21   30   BV14
Clayknowes Rd, Muss. EH21   31   BW14
Clayknowes Way, Muss. EH21   31   BW14
Claylands Rd, Newbr. EH28   36   AB16
Clearburn Cres EH16   28   BK15
Clearburn Gdns EH16   28   BK15
Clearburn Rd EH16   28   BK15
Clearburn Rd, Gore. EH23   70   BX33
Cleekim Dr EH15   29   BR15
Cleekim Rd EH15   29   BR15
CLEIKIMIN   29   BR14
Cleikiminfield EH15   29   BR15
Cleikiminrig EH15   29   BR15
Cleric's Hill, K'lis. EH29   20   AC10
Clerk Rd, Pen. EH26   68   AZ38
Clerk St EH8   7   BG13
Clerk St, Lnhd EH20   54   BL27
CLERMISTON   24   AS9
Clermiston Av EH4   24   AT9
Clermiston Cres EH4   24   AT9
Clermiston Dr EH4   24   AT9
Clermiston Gdns EH4   24   AT10
Clermiston Grn EH4   24   AT9
Clermiston Gro EH4   24   AT10
Clermiston Hill EH4   24   AT9
Clermiston Ln EH4   24   AT9
Clermiston Medway EH4   24   AT9
Clermiston Pk EH4   24   AT9
Clermiston Pl EH4   24   AT10
Clermiston Prim Sch EH4   24   AS9
Clermiston Rd EH12   24   AU13
Clermiston Rd N EH4   24   AU9
Clermiston Ter EH12 1   24   AU12
Clermiston Vw EH4   24   AU10
Clerwood Bk EH12   24   AT11

Name	Page	Grid
Clerwood Gdns EH12	24	AT11
Clerwood Gro EH12	24	AU11
Clerwood Ln EH12	24	AT11
Clerwood Pk EH12	24	AU11
Clerwood Pl EH12	24	AU11
Clerwood Row EH12	24	AT11
Clerwood Ter EH12	24	AU11
Clerwood Vw EH12	24	AU11
Clerwood Way EH12	24	AT11
Cliftonhall Rd, Newbr. EH28	36	AB15
Clifton Rd, Newbr. EH28	36	AA16
Clifton Sq EH15	29	BQ11
Clifton Ter EH12	6	BC12
Clifton Trd Est, Newbr. EH28	36	AB15
Clinton Rd EH9	42	BD15
Clockmill La EH8	28	BK10
Clovenstone Dr EH14	50	AU20
Clovenstone Gdns EH14	40	AU18
Clovenstone Pk EH14	50	AU20
Clovenstone Prim Sch EH14	50	AU20
Clovenstone Rd EH14	40	AU18
Cloverfoot EH16	45	BQ17
Clufflat, S Q'fry EH30	8	AB1
Clufflat Brae, S Q'fry EH30	8	AB1
Cluny Av EH10	42	BD17
Cluny Dr EH10	42	BD17
Cluny Gdns EH10	42	BD17
Cluny Pl EH10	43	BE17
Cluny Ter EH10	42	BD16
Coalgate Av, Tran. EH33	35	CL13
Coalgate Rd, Tran. EH33	35	CM12
Coalhill EH6	15	BH6
Coal Neuk, Tran. EH33	35	CL13
Coal Neuk Cor, Tran. EH33 7	35	CL13
Coal Neuk Ct, Tran. EH33	35	CL13
COATES	26	BA11
Coates Cres EH3	6	BC12
Coates Gdns EH12	26	BB12
Coates Pl EH3	6	BC12
Coatfield La EH6	16	BJ6
Cobbinshaw Ho EH11	40	AS18
Cobden Cres EH9	43	BH15
Cobden Rd EH9	43	BH15
Cobden Ter EH11 7	6	BC12
Coburg St EH6	15	BH6
Cochrane Pl EH6 1	16	BJ7
Cochran Pl EH7	27	BF9
Cochran Ter EH7	27	BF9
Cochrina Pl, Rose. EH24	62	BM33
Cockburn Cres, Bal. EH14	58	AL28
Cockburnhill Rd, Bal. EH14	58	AK27
Cockburn St EH1	7	BF11
COCKENZIE	19	CM8
Cockenzie Prim Sch EH32	19	CL8
Cockmylane EH10	52	BB21
Cockpen Av, Bonny. EH19	63	BQ30
Cockpen Cres, Bonny. EH19	63	BQ30
Cockpen Dr, Bonny. EH19	63	BQ30
Cockpen Pl, Bonny. EH19 1	63	BQ30
Cockpen Rd, Bonny. EH19	64	BS29
Cockpen Rd Rbt, Bonny. EH19	64	BT30
Cockpen Ter, Bonny. EH19	63	BQ30
Cockpen Vw, Bonny. EH19	63	BQ30
Coffin La EH11	26	BB13
Coillesdene Av EH15	30	BS12
Coillesdene Cres EH15	30	BT12
Coillesdene Dr EH15	30	BT12
Coillesdene Gdns EH15	30	BT12
Coillesdene Gro EH15	30	BT12
Coillesdene Ln EH15	30	BU12
Coillesdene Ter EH15	30	BT12
Coinyie Ho Cl EH1 1	7	BG11
COLINTON	51	AW21
Colinton Gro EH14	41	AZ17
Colinton Gro W EH14	41	AZ17
Colinton Mains Cres EH13	51	AZ21
Colinton Mains Dr EH13	41	AZ19
Colinton Mains Gdns EH13	41	AZ19
Colinton Mains Grn EH13	51	AZ20
Colinton Mains Gro EH13	52	BA20
Colinton Mains Ln EH13	51	AZ20
Colinton Mains Pl EH13	52	BA20
Colinton Mains Rd EH13	52	BA20
Colinton Mains Ter EH13	52	BA20
Colinton Prim Sch EH13	51	AZ20
Colinton Rd EH10	42	BB16
Colinton Rd EH13	41	AY19
Colinton Rd EH14	42	BA16
College Wynd EH1 2	7	BF12
Colliery Cres (Newt.), Dalk. EH22	65	BW31
Colliery Vw (Newt.), Dalk. EH22	65	BX31
Collins Pl EH3	26	BD9
Colmestone Gate EH10	52	BC21
Coltbridge Av EH12	25	AZ12
Coltbridge Gdns EH12	26	BA12
Coltbridge Millside EH12	26	BA12
Coltbridge Ter EH12	25	AZ12
Coltbridge Vale EH12	26	BA12
Columba Av EH4	25	AX9
Columba Rd EH4	25	AX9
Colville Pl EH3	26	BD9
COMELY BANK	26	BB9
Comely Bk EH4	26	BB9
Comely Bk Av EH4	26	BC9
Comely Bk Gro EH4	26	BB10
Comely Bk Pl EH4	26	BC9
Comely Bk Pl Ms EH4 2	26	BC9
Comely Bk Rd EH4	26	BC9
Comely Bk Row EH4	26	BC9
Comely Bk St EH4	26	BB9
Comely Bk Ter EH4	26	BB9
Comely Grn Cres EH7	28	BJ10
Comely Grn Pl EH7	28	BJ10
COMISTON	52	BC21
Comiston Dr EH10	42	BB18
Comiston Gdns EH10	42	BC17
Comiston Gro EH10	52	BC20
Comiston Pl EH10	42	BC17
Comiston Prim Sch EH13	52	BB21
Comiston Ri EH10	52	BC20
Comiston Rd EH10	42	BC18
Comiston Springs Av EH10	52	BC20
Comiston Ter EH10	42	BC17
Comiston Vw EH10	52	BC20
Commercial St EH6	15	BH5
Commercial Wf EH6 1	16	BJ5
Conference Sq EH3	6	BD12
Conifer Rd (Mayf.), Dalk. EH22	71	CA28
Connaught Pl EH6	15	BF6
Considine Gdns EH8	28	BL10
Considine Ter EH8	28	BL10
Constitution St EH6	15	BH7
Convening Ct EH4 1	6	BC11
Cook Cres (Mayf.), Dalk. EH22	65	BZ30
Cookies Wynd, Pres. EH32 2	18	CG10
Cooper's Cl EH8 3	7	BH11
Cope La (Port S.), Pres. EH32	19	CM7
Corbiehill Av EH4	25	AW8
Corbiehill Cres EH4	24	AV8
Corbiehill Gdns EH4	25	AW8
Corbiehill Gro EH4	25	AW8
Corbiehill Pk EH4	24	AV8
Corbiehill Pl EH4	24	AV8
Corbiehill Rd EH4	24	AV8
Corbiehill Ter EH4	24	AV8
Corbieshot EH15	29	BR14
Corbiewynd EH15	29	BR14
CORNBANK	68	AZ38
Cornbank St. James' Prim Sch EH26	68	AZ38
Cornhill Ter EH6	16	BK7
Cornwallis Pl EH3	27	BE9
Cornwall St EH1	6	BD12
Coronation Pl (Mayf.), Dalk. EH22	57	BZ28
Coronation Pl, Tran. EH33	35	CL13
Coronation Wk EH3	6	BE13
Corrennie Dr EH10	42	BD17
Corrennie Gdns EH10	42	BD18
Corrie Ct (Newt.), Dalk. EH22	65	BX31
Corslet Cres, Currie EH14	49	AR22
Corslet Pl, Currie EH14	49	AQ22
Corslet Rd, Currie EH14	49	AQ22
CORSTORPHINE	24	AT12
Corstorphine Bk Av EH12	24	AS12
Corstorphine Bk Dr EH12	24	AS12
Corstorphine Bk Ter EH12	24	AS12
Corstorphine High St EH12	24	AT13
Corstorphine Hill Av EH12	24	AU12
Corstorphine Hill Cres EH12	24	AU12
Corstorphine Hill Gdns EH12	24	AU12
Corstorphine Hill Rd EH12	24	AU12
Corstorphine Hosp EH12	24	AV13
Corstorphine Ho Av EH12	24	AU13
Corstorphine Ho Ter EH12	24	AU13
Corstorphine Pk Gdns EH12	24	AU13
Corstorphine Prim Sch EH12	24	AT13
Corstorphine Rd EH12	25	AY12
Cortleferry Dr, Dalk. EH22	56	BU26
Cortleferry Gro, Dalk. EH22	56	BU26
Cortleferry Pk, Dalk. EH22	56	BU26
Cortleferry Ter, Dalk. EH22	56	BU26
Corunna Pl EH6	15	BH6
Corunna Ter, Pen. EH26	66	BC35
Costkea Way, Lnhd EH20	54	BJ27
Cotlaws, K'lis. EH29	20	AB10
Cottage Grn EH4	23	AR7
Cottage Homes EH13	51	AX21
Cottage La, Muss. EH21	32	CA14
Cottage Pk EH4	25	AW10
County Hotel EH22	57	BW24
County Rd, Pres. EH32	18	CG10
County Sq, Pres. EH32	18	CG10
Couper Fld EH6	15	BH5
Couper St EH6	15	BH5
Cousland Rd, Dalk. EH22	57	BZ23
Covenanter Ct, Pen. EH26	68	AZ38
Covenanters La, S Q'fry EH30	8	AD2
Cowan Rd EH11	42	BA15
Cowan's Cl EH8	7	BG13
Cowan Ter, Pen. EH26	69	BB36
Cowden Cres, Dalk. EH22	57	BZ24
Cowden Gro, Dalk. EH22	57	BZ24
Cowden La, Dalk. EH22	57	BZ24
Cowden Pk, Dalk. EH22	57	BY24
Cowden Ter, Dalk. EH22	57	BZ24
Cowden Vw, Dalk. EH22	57	BZ24
Cowgate EH1	7	BF12
Cowgatehead EH1	7	BF12
Cowpits Ford Rd, Muss. EH21	31	BY16
Cowpits Rd (White.), Muss. EH21	47	BZ18
Coxfield EH11	41	AY15
Coxfield La EH11 2	41	AY15
Craigcrook Av EH4	25	AW9
Craigcrook Gdns EH4	25	AX10
Craigcrook Gro EH4	25	AW10
Craigcrook Pk EH4	25	AW10
Craigcrook Pl EH4 1	25	AY9
Craigcrook Rd EH4	25	AX10
Craigcrook Sq EH4	25	AW9
Craigcrook Ter EH4	25	AX9
Craigend Pk EH16	44	BL18
CRAIGENTINNY	16	BM8
Craigentinny Av EH7	29	BN10
Craigentinny Av N EH6	16	BM7
Craigentinny Cres EH7	29	BN10
Craigentinny Golf Course EH7	16	BM8
Craigentinny Gro EH7	29	BN10
Craigentinny Pl EH7	29	BN10
Craigentinny Prim Sch EH7	16	BM9
Craigentinny Rd EH7	16	BM9
Craighall Av EH6	15	BE5
Craighall Bk EH6	15	BE5
Craighall Cres EH6	15	BE5
Craighall Gdns EH6	15	BE6
Craighall Rd EH6	15	BE5
Craighall Ter EH6	15	BE6
Craighall Ter, Muss. EH21	32	CB13
Craighill Gdns EH10	42	BB18

Craighouse Av EH10   42   BB17
Craighouse Gdns EH10   42   BB17
Craighouse Pk EH10   42   BB17
Craighouse Rd EH10   42   BB17
Craighouse Ter EH10   42   BB17
Craigiebield Cres, Pen.
  EH26   68   BA39
Craigievar Sq EH12   23   AR11
Craigievar Wynd EH12   23   AQ12
Craiglea Dr EH10   42   BB18
Craiglea Pl EH10   42   BB17
CRAIGLEITH   25   AZ9
Craigleith Av N EH4   25   AY11
Craigleith Av S EH4   25   AY11
Craigleith Bk EH4   25   AY10
Craigleith Cres EH4   25   AY10
Craigleith Dr EH4   25   AY10
Craigleith Gdns EH4   25   AY10
Craigleith Gro EH4   25   AY10
Craigleith Hill EH4   25   AZ10
Craigleith Hill Av EH4   25   AY9
Craigleith Hill Cres EH4   25   AZ9
Craigleith Hill Gdns EH4   25   AZ9
Craigleith Hill Grn EH4   25   AZ9
Craigleith Hill Gro EH4   25   AZ9
Craigleith Hill Ln EH4   25   AZ9
Craigleith Hill Pk EH4   25   AZ9
Craigleith Hill Row EH4   25   AZ9
Craigleith Retail Park EH4   25   AZ9
Craigleith Ri EH4   25   AY11
Craigleith Rd EH4   25   AZ10
Craigleith Vw EH4   25   AY11
CRAIGLOCKHART   41   AZ17
Craiglockhart Av EH14   41   AY17
Craiglockhart Bk EH14   41   AY18
Craiglockhart Cres EH14   41   AY18
Craiglockhart Dell Rd EH14   41   AY17
Craiglockhart Dr N EH14   41   AY17
Craiglockhart Dr S EH14   41   AY19
Craiglockhart Gdns EH14   41   AY17
Craiglockhart Gro EH14   41   AY19
Craiglockhart Ln EH14   41   AY18
Craiglockhart Pk EH14   41   AY18
Craiglockhart Pl EH14   41   AZ17
Craiglockhart Prim Sch
  EH11   42   BA15
Craiglockhart Quad EH14   41   AY18
Craiglockhart Rd EH14   41   AY19
Craiglockhart Rd N EH14   41   AZ17
Craiglockhart Ter EH14   42   BA17
Craiglockhart Vw EH14   41   AZ17
CRAIGMILLAR   28   BM15
Craigmillar Castle EH1   44   BM17
Craigmillar Castle Av EH16   44   BM16
Craigmillar Castle Gdns
  EH16   28   BM15
Craigmillar Castle Ln EH16   28   BM15
Craigmillar Castle Rd EH16   44   BM17
Craigmillar Ct EH16   44   BL16
Craigmillar Pl EH16   43   BH16
Craigmillar Park
  Golf Course EH9   43   BG17
Craigmount App EH12   24   AS12
Craigmount Av EH12   24   AS12
Craigmount Av N EH4   23   AR10
Craigmount Av N EH12   24   AS10
Craigmount Bk EH4   23   AR10
Craigmount Bk W EH4   23   AR10
Craigmount Brae EH12   23   AR10
Craigmount Ct EH4   23   AR10
Craigmount Cres EH12   23   AR11
Craigmount Dr EH12   23   AR11
Craigmount Gdns EH12   23   AR12
Craigmount Gro EH12   23   AR11
Craigmount Gro N EH12   23   AR11
Craigmount High Sch
  EH12   23   AR12
Craigmount Hill EH4   23   AR10
Craigmount Ln EH12   23   AR11
Craigmount Pk EH12   23   AR12
Craigmount Pl EH12   23   AR11
Craigmount Ter EH12   23   AR12
Craigmount Vw EH12   23   AR11
Craigmount Way EH12   24   AS10
Craigmuir Pl EH13   13   AY6
Craigour Av EH17   45   BN19

Craigour Cres EH17   45   BN19
Craigour Dr EH17   44   BM18
Craigour Gdns EH17   45   BN19
Craigour Grn EH17   44   BM19
Craigour Gro EH17   45   BN19
Craigour Ln EH17   45   BN19
Craigour Pk Prim Sch EH17   45   BN20
Craigour Pl EH17   44   BM19
Craigour Ter EH17   45   BN19
Craigpark Av (Ratho),
  Newbr. EH28   37   AE17
Craigpark Cres (Ratho),
  Newbr. EH28   37   AE17
Craigroyston Comm
  Ed Cen EH4   13   AX7
Craigroyston Gro EH4   13   AW7
Craigroyston Pl EH4   13   AW6
Craigroyston Prim Sch
  EH4   13   AX7
Craigs Av EH12   39   AR13
Craigs Bk EH12   23   AR12
Craigs Cres EH12   23   AR12
Craigs Dr EH12   23   AR12
Craigs Gdns EH12   23   AR12
Craigs Gro EH12   24   AS12
Craigs Ln EH12   24   AS12
Craigs Pk EH12   23   AR12
Craigs Rd EH12   23   AR12
Crame Ter, Dalk. EH22   56   BU25
CRAMOND   11   AQ5
Cramond Av EH4   11   AR5
Cramond Bk EH4   11   AR6
CRAMOND BRIDGE   23   AP8
Cramond Br Cotts EH4   23   AP7
Cramond Brig Toll EH4   23   AP7
Cramond Cres EH4   11   AR6
Cramond Gdns EH4   11   AR6
Cramond Glebe Gdns EH4   12   AS5
Cramond Glebe Rd EH4   11   AR5
Cramond Glebe Ter EH4   11   AR5
Cramond Grn EH4   11   AR5
Cramond Gro EH4   11   AR6
Cramond New Br EH4   23   AP8
Cramond Pk EH4   11   AR6
Cramond Pl EH4   12   AS6
Cramond Prim Sch EH4   11   AR6
Cramond Regis EH4   23   AR7
Cramond Rd N EH4   12   AS5
Cramond Rd S EH4   12   AT6
Cramond Ter EH4   11   AR6
Cramond Vale EH4   11   AQ6
Cramond Village EH4   11   AR5
Cranston St EH8   7   BG11
Cranston St, Pen. EH26   68   BA38
Crarae Av EH4   25   AZ11
Craufurdland EH4   23   AQ8
Crawford Br EH7 1   16   BJ9
Crawford Rd EH16   43   BH16
Crawlees Cotts (Newt.),
  Dalk. EH22   65   BY29
Crawlees Cres (Mayf.),
  Dalk. EH22   71   CA29
Crescent, The EH10   42   BC17
Crescent, The (Gowks.),
  Gore. EH23   65   BY32
Crewe Bk EH5   14   BA6
Crewe Cres EH5   13   AZ6
Crewe Gro EH5   14   BA6
Crewe Ln EH5   13   AZ6
Crewe Path EH5   13   AZ6
Crewe Pl EH5   13   AZ6
Crewe Rd Gdns EH5   13   AZ6
Crewe Rd N EH5   13   AZ6
Crewe Rd S EH4   13   AZ7
Crewe Rd W EH5   13   AZ6
Crewe Ter EH5   13   AZ6
Crewe Toll EH4   13   AZ7
Crichton's Cl EH8 4   7   BH11
Crichton St EH8   7   BF12
Crighton Pl EH7   27   BH8
Croall Pl EH7   27   BG9
Crockett Gdns, Pen.
  EH26   68   AZ38
Croft-an-righ EH8   7   BH10
Croft St, Dalk. EH22   57   BW24
Croft St, Pen. EH26   68   BA39

Cromwell Pl EH6   15   BH5
Crookston Ct (Inv.),
  Muss. EH21   32   CA15
Crookston Rd (Inv.),
  Muss. EH21   31   BZ15
Cross Cotts, Pres. EH32 2   18   CJ10
Cross Rd, Lnhd EH20   61   BH27
Crosswood Av, Bal. EH14   58   AK27
Crosswood Cres, Bal. EH14   58   AK27
Crown Ct, Tran. EH33   35   CM13
Crown Pl EH6   15   BH7
Crown St EH6   15   BH7
Cruachan Ct, Pen. EH26   69   BC37
Crusader Dr, Ros. EH25   67   BH32
Cuddies Ln EH13 1   51   AW21
Cuddy La EH10   42   BC16
Cuguen Pl, Lass. EH18   55   BR26
CUIKEN   68   BA37
Cuiken Av, Pen. EH26   68   BA37
Cuiken Bk, Pen. EH26   68   AZ37
Cuiken Br, Pen. EH26   69   BB37
Cuikenburn, Pen. EH26   68   BA36
Cuiken Prim Sch EH26   68   AZ37
Cuiken Ter, Pen. EH26   68   AZ37
Cultins Rd EH11   39   AR16
Cumberland St EH3   27   BE9
Cumberland St N E La EH3   27   BE9
Cumberland St N W La EH3   27   BE9
Cumberland St S E La EH3   27   BE9
Cumberland St S W La EH3   27   BE9
Cumin Pl EH9   43   BG14
Cumlodden Av EH12   25   AY11
Cumnor Cres EH16   44   BJ18
Cunningham Pl EH6 1   15   BH7
CURRIE   49   AN23
Currie Comm High Sch
  EH14   49   AP23
Curriehill Castle Dr, Bal.
  EH14   48   AM23
Curriehill Prim Sch EH14   49   AQ23
Curriehill Rd, Currie EH14   49   AP22
Curriehill Sta EH14   49   AP22
Currievale Dr, Currie EH14   49   AP22
Currievale Pk, Currie
  EH14   49   AN23
Currievale Pk Gro, Currie
  EH14   49   AN23
CUTHILL   34   CG11

D

Daiches Braes EH15   30   BT13
Daisy Ter EH11 3   42   BA15
Dalgety Av EH7   16   BK9
Dalgety Rd EH7   16   BK9
Dalgety St EH7   28   BK10
Dalhousie Av, Bonny.
  EH19   63   BQ29
Dalhousie Av W, Bonny.
  EH19   63   BP29
Dalhousie Bk, Dalk.
  EH22   56   BV25
Dalhousie Castle Hotel
  EH19   64   BU31
Dalhousie Chesters Ct,
  Bonny. EH19   63   BQ31
Dalhousie Cres, Dalk.
  EH22   56   BV26
Dalhousie Dr, Bonny. EH19   63   BQ29
Dalhousie Gdns, Bonny.
  EH19   63   BQ29
Dalhousie Pl, Bonny. EH19   63   BP29
Dalhousie Rd, Dalk. EH22   56   BV25
Dalhousie Rd E, Bonny.
  EH19   63   BQ29
Dalhousie Rd W, Bonny.
  EH19   63   BQ29
Dalhousie Ter EH10   42   BC17
DALKEITH   57   BX25
Dalkeith Country Park
  Visitor Centre EH22   47   BX22
Dalkeith High Sch EH22   47   BZ22
Dalkeith Rd EH16   7   BH13
Dalkeith St EH15   30   BS12
Dalkeith Western Bypass,
  Dalk. EH22   56   BT26

Dalkeith Western Bypass, Lass. *EH18* 56 BT24
Dalmahoy Cres, Bal. *EH14* 48 AK24
DALMENY 9 AH4
Dalmeny House *EH30* 10 AM2
Dalmeny Prim Sch *EH30* 9 AG4
Dalmeny Rd *EH6* 15 BF6
Dalmeny Sta *EH30* 9 AF3
Dalmeny St *EH6* 27 BH8
DALRY 26 BA13
Dalry Gait *EH11* 26 BB12
Dalrymple Cres *EH9* 43 BG15
Dalrymple Cres, Muss. *EH21* 31 BW13
Dalrymple Ln, Muss. *EH21* 31 BY13
Dalry Pl *EH11* 6 BC12
Dalry Prim Sch *EH11* 26 BB13
Dalry Rd *EH11* 26 BB13
Dalton Ct (Mayf.), Dalk. *EH22* 71 CA30
Dalum Ct, Lnhd *EH20* 54 BJ27
Dalum Dr, Lnhd *EH20* 54 BJ27
Dalum Gro, Lnhd *EH20* 54 BJ27
Dalum Ln, Lnhd *EH20* 54 BJ27
Dalziel Pl *EH7* 1 28 BJ10
Dambrae, Muss. *EH21* 1 31 BZ13
Damhead Holdings *EH10* 61 BF26
Damside *EH4* 26 BB11
Dance Base *EH1* 6 BE12
DANDERHALL 46 BS20
Danderhall Cres (Dand.), Dalk. *EH22* 45 BR20
Danderhall Prim Sch *EH22* 45 BR19
Dania Ct *EH11* 40 AV15
Danube St *EH4* 6 BC10
D'Arcy Cres (Mayf.), Dalk. *EH22* 71 CB28
D'Arcy Rd (Mayf.), Dalk. *EH22* 71 CA29
D'Arcy Ter (Mayf.), Dalk. *EH22* 71 CA28
Darnaway St *EH3* 6 BD10
Darnell Rd *EH5* 14 BC6
David Scott Av (Mayf.), Dalk. *EH22* 71 CA28
Davidson Gdns *EH4* 25 AW8
Davidson Pk *EH4* 25 AZ8
Davidson Rd *EH4* 25 AZ8
DAVIDSONS MAINS 24 AU8
Davidson's Mains Prim Sch *EH4* 24 AV8
Davies Row *EH12* 24 AT13
Davie St *EH8* 7 BG12
Dean Bk La *EH3* 26 BD9
Deanbank Pl, Gore. *EH23* 70 BZ36
Dean Br *EH3* 6 BC10
Dean Br *EH4* 6 BC10
DEANBURN 68 BA36
Deanburn, Pen. *EH26* 68 BA36
Deanery Cl *EH7* 1 28 BL10
Dean Gallery *EH4* 26 BB11
Deanhaugh St *EH4* 26 BD9
Dean Pk (Newt.), Dalk. *EH22* 65 BW30
Deanpark Av, Bal. *EH14* 58 AK26
Deanpark Bk, Bal. *EH14* 58 AL26
Deanpark Brae, Bal. *EH14* 58 AL26
Deanpark Ct, Bal. *EH14* 58 AK27
Deanpark Ct (Newt.), Dalk. *EH22* 1 65 BW30
Dean Pk Cres *EH4* 6 BC10
Deanpark Cres, Bal. *EH14* 58 AL26
Deanpark Gdns, Bal. *EH14* 58 AL26
Deanpark Gro, Bal. *EH14* 58 AL26
Dean Pk Ms *EH4* 26 BC9
Deanpark Pl, Bal. *EH14* 58 AL26
Dean Pk Pl (Newt.), Dalk. *EH22* 65 BW30
Dean Pk Prim Sch *EH14* 58 AL27
Deanpark Sq, Bal. *EH14* 58 AL26
Dean Pk St *EH4* 26 BC9
Dean Path *EH4* 26 BB10

Dean Path Bldgs *EH4* 2 6 BC11
Dean Pl, Pen. *EH26* 68 AZ37
Dean Rd, Pen. *EH26* 68 AZ37
Dean St *EH4* 26 BC9
Dean Ter *EH4* 6 BC10
DEAN VILLAGE 26 BB11
Dechmont Rd *EH12* 23 AQ12
Delhaig *EH11* 41 AY15
Dell Rd *EH13* 51 AX20
Delta Av, Muss. *EH21* 32 CC14
Delta Cres, Muss. *EH21* 32 CC14
Delta Dr, Muss. *EH21* 32 CC13
Delta Gdns, Muss. *EH21* 32 CC14
Delta Pl (Inv.), Muss. *EH21* 31 BZ15
Delta Rd, Muss. *EH21* 32 CC14
Delta Vw, Muss. *EH21* 32 CC13
Denham Grn Av *EH5* 14 BD6
Denham Grn Pl *EH5* 14 BD6
Denham Grn Ter *EH5* 14 BD6
Denholm Av, Muss. *EH21* 30 BV15
Denholm Dr, Muss. *EH21* 31 BW15
Denholm Rd, Muss. *EH21* 30 BV14
Denholm Way, Muss. *EH21* 30 BV15
De Quincey Path, Lass. *EH18* 63 BN29
De Quincey Rd, Lass. *EH18* 63 BN29
Dequincey Wk, Tran. *EH33* 1 35 CL14
Derby St *EH6* 15 BF5
Devon Pl *EH12* 26 BB12
Dewar Pl *EH3* 6 BC12
Dewar Pl La *EH3* 6 BC12
Dick Pl *EH9* 43 BF15
Dicksonfield *EH7* 27 BG9
Dickson Gro, Bonny. *EH19* 1 64 BS29
Dickson's Cl *EH1* 5 7 BG11
Dickson St *EH6* 27 BH8
Dick Ter, Pen. *EH26* 69 BB37
Dinmont Dr *EH16* 44 BK18
Distillery La *EH11* 26 BB12
Dobbie's Rd, Bonny. *EH19* 63 BQ28
Dobbie's Rd, Lass. *EH18* 63 BQ28
Dochart Dr *EH4* 24 AS10
Dock Pl *EH6* 15 BH5
Dock St *EH6* 15 BH5
Dolphin Av, Currie *EH14* 49 AP23
Dolphin Gdns E, Currie *EH14* 49 AP23
Dolphin Gdns W, Currie *EH14* 49 AP23
Dolphin Rd, Currie *EH14* 49 AN24
Dominion Cinema *EH10* 42 BD16
Donaldson's Coll *EH12* 26 BB13
Doo'Cot Pl, Pres. *EH32* 1 34 CJ11
Dorset Pl *EH11* 42 BC14
Double Dykes (Inv.), Muss. *EH21* 31 BZ15
Double Hedges Pk *EH16* 44 BJ18
Double Hedges Rd *EH16* 44 BJ18
Dougall Ct (Mayf.), Dalk. *EH22* 65 BZ30
Dougall Pl (Mayf.), Dalk. *EH22* 65 BZ30
Dougall Rd (Mayf.), Dalk. *EH22* 1 65 BZ30
Douglas Cres *EH12* 26 BB11
Douglas Cres, Bonny. *EH19* 63 BR28
Douglas Gdns *EH4* 26 BB11
Douglas Gdns Ms *EH4* 3 26 BB11
Douglas Ter *EH11* 1 6 BC12
Doune Ter *EH3* 6 BD10
Dovecot Brae, Tran. *EH33* 35 CL12
Dovecot Gro *EH14* 41 AW18
Dovecot Ln *EH14* 41 AW18
Dovecot Pk *EH14* 41 AW19
Dovecot Rd *EH12* 40 AT14
Dowie's Mill Cotts *EH4* 23 AP7
Dowie's Mill La *EH4* 23 AP7
Downfield Pl *EH11* 26 BB13
Downie Gro *EH12* 24 AV13
Downie Pl, Muss. *EH21* 31 BY13
Downie Ter *EH12* 24 AV13
Downing Ct, Ros. *EH25* 62 BJ32

DREGHORN 51 AY22
Dreghorn Av *EH13* 52 BA22
Dreghorn Cotts *EH13* 51 AZ22
Dreghorn Dr *EH13* 52 BA22
Dreghorn Gdns *EH13* 52 BA21
Dreghorn Gro *EH13* 52 BA22
Dreghorn Junct *EH10* 52 BA23
Dreghorn Junct *EH13* 52 BA23
Dreghorn Link *EH13* 52 BA22
Dreghorn Ln *EH13* 51 AX21
Dreghorn Pl *EH13* 51 AZ21
Dreghorn Pl *EH13* 52 BA22
Drum Av *EH17* 45 BN21
DRUMBRAE 24 AS10
Drum Brae Av *EH12* 24 AS11
Drum Brae Cres *EH4* 24 AS10
Drum Brae Dr *EH4* 24 AT10
Drum Brae Gdns *EH12* 24 AS11
Drum Brae Gro *EH4* 24 AS10
Drum Brae Neuk *EH12* 24 AS11
Drum Brae N *EH4* 23 AR9
Drum Brae Pk *EH12* 24 AS11
Drum Brae Pk App *EH12* 24 AS11
Drum Brae Pl *EH12* 24 AS11
Drumbrae Prim Sch *EH4* 24 AS11
Drum Brae S *EH12* 24 AS10
Drum Brae Ter *EH4* 24 AS10
Drum Brae Wk *EH4* 24 AS10
Drum Cotts *EH17* 55 BP22
Drum Cres *EH17* 45 BP21
Drumdryan St *EH3* 6 BD13
Drummohr Av (Wall.), Muss. *EH21* 32 CC14
Drummohr Gdns (Wall.), Muss. *EH21* 33 CD14
Drummond Comm High Sch *EH7* 27 BF9
Drummond Pl *EH3* 27 BE9
Drummond St *EH8* 7 BG12
Drummore Dr, Pres. *EH32* 34 CG11
Drum Pl *EH17* 45 BP21
Drumsheugh Gdns *EH3* 6 BC11
Drumsheugh Pl *EH3* 3 6 BC11
Drum St *EH17* 45 BN21
Drum Ter *EH7* 16 BJ9
Drum Vw Av (Dand.), Dalk. *EH22* 45 BR20
Drybrough Cres *EH16* 28 BM15
Dryden Av, Lnhd *EH20* 62 BJ28
Dryden Cres, Lnhd *EH20* 62 BJ28
Dryden Gait *EH7* 27 BG8
Dryden Gdns *EH7* 27 BG8
Dryden Glen, Lnhd *EH20* 61 BH28
Dryden Gro, Ros. *EH25* 62 BJ31
Dryden Ln, Lnhd *EH20* 61 BH28
Dryden Pk, Lnhd *EH20* 61 BH28
Dryden Pl *EH9* 43 BH14
Dryden Pl, Lnhd *EH20* 61 BH28
Dryden Rd, Lnhd *EH20* 61 BH28
Dryden St *EH7* 27 BG8
Dryden Ter *EH7* 27 BG8
Dryden Ter, Lnhd *EH20* 62 BJ28
Dryden Vale, Lnhd *EH20* 61 BH28
Dryden Vw, Lnhd *EH20* 62 BJ28
DRYLAW 25 AX8
Drylaw Av *EH4* 25 AY9
Drylaw Cres *EH4* 25 AX9
Drylaw Gdns *EH4* 25 AX8
Drylaw Grn *EH4* 25 AX9
Drylaw Gro *EH4* 25 AX9
Drylaw Ho Gdns *EH4* 25 AX8
Drylaw Ho Paddock *EH4* 25 AX8
Duart Cres *EH4* 24 AS10
Dublin Meuse *EH3* 7 BF10
Dublin St *EH1* 27 BF9
Dublin St *EH3* 27 BF9
Dublin St La N *EH3* 27 BF9
Dublin St La S *EH1* 7 BF10
DUDDINGSTON 29 BN13
Duddingston Av *EH15* 29 BN13
Duddingston Cres *EH15* 29 BQ13
Duddingston Gdns N *EH15* 29 BP12
Duddingston Gdns S *EH15* 29 BP13
Duddingston Golf Course *EH15* 29 BN14
Duddingsto Gro E *EH15* 29 BP12

Duddingston Gro W EH15   29   BP13
Duddingston Ln EH15   29   BN12
Duddingston Mains Cotts
   EH15   29   BR13
Duddingston Mills EH8   29   BN12
Duddingston Pk EH15   29   BQ12
Duddingston Pk S EH15   29   BQ13
Duddingston Prim Sch
   EH15   29   BN12
Duddingston Ri EH15   29   BP13
Duddingston Rd EH15   29   BN12
Duddingston Rd W EH15   28   BM13
Duddingston Rd W EH16   28   BM14
Duddingston Row EH15   29   BP13
Duddingston Sq E EH15   29   BP12
Duddingston Sq W EH15   29   BP12
Duddingston Vw EH15   29   BP13
Duddingston Yards EH15 1   29   BQ14
Dudgeon Pl, K'lis. EH29   20   AD9
Dudley Av EH6   15   BF5
Dudley Av S EH6   15   BG6
Dudley Bk EH6   15   BF5
Dudley Cres EH6   15   BF5
Dudley Gdns EH6   15   BF5
Dudley Gro EH6   15   BF5
Dudley Ter EH6   15   BF5
Duff Rd EH11   26   BB13
Duff St EH11   26   BB13
Duff St La EH11   26   BB13
Duke Pl EH6   16   BJ7
Duke St EH6   16   BJ7
Duke St, Dalk. EH22   57   BW24
Duke St Glebe EH6   16   BJ7
Duke's Wk EH8   28   BK11
Dumbeg Pk EH14   40   AT19
DUMBIEDYKES   7   BG12
Dumbiedykes Rd EH8   7   BH12
Dumbryden Dr EH14   40   AU18
Dumbryden Gdns EH14   40   AU17
Dumbryden Gro EH14   40   AU18
Dumbryden Prim Sch
   EH14   40   AU18
Dumbryden Rd EH14   40   AV18
Dun-ard Gdn EH9   43   BF16
Dunbar St EH3   6   BD12
Duncan Gdns, Tran. EH33   35   CL12
Duncan Pl EH6   16   BJ7
Duncans Gait EH14   40   AV17
Duncan St EH9   43   BG15
Dundas Av, S Q'fry EH30   9   AE3
Dundas Cres, Dalk. EH22   56   BU26
Dundas Gdns, Gore. EH23   70   BX34
Dundas Gro, Dalk. EH22   56   BU25
Dundas Pk, Bonny. EH19   56   BS28
Dundas Parks Golf Course
   EH30   8   AC5
Dundas Pl, K'lis. EH29   20   AD9
Dundas Rd, Dalk. EH22   56   BU25
Dundas St EH3   27   BE9
Dundas St, Bonny. EH19   63   BR28
Dundee St EH11   26   BB13
Dundee Ter EH11   42   BB14
Dundonald St EH3   27   BE9
Dundrennan Cotts EH16   44   BL17
Dunedin St EH7   27   BF8
Dunlop's Ct EH1 12   6   BE12
Dunlop Ter, Pen. EH26   69   BC38
Dunollie Ct EH12 2   23   AR12
Dunrobin Rd EH3   26   BD9
Dunsmuir Ct EH12   24   AS13
Dunsyre Ho EH11   40   AS18
Dunvegan Ct EH4   23   AR7
Durar Dr EH4   24   AS11
DURHAM   29   BP12
Durham Av EH15   29   BP12
Durham Bk, Bonny. EH19   64   BS29
Durham Dr EH15   29   BQ13
Durham Gdns N EH15   29   BQ12
Durham Gdns S EH15   29   BQ13
Durham Gro EH15   29   BQ12
Durham Gro, Bonny. EH19   64   BS29
Durham Pl, Bonny. EH19   63   BR29
Durham Pl E EH15   29   BQ12
Durham Pl La EH15   29   BQ12
Durham Pl W EH15   29   BP12
Durham Rd EH15   29   BQ12

Durham Rd S EH15   29   BQ13
Durham Sq EH15   29   BP12
Durham Ter EH15   29   BP12
Durward Gro EH16   44   BK17
Dykes Rd, Pen. EH26   68   BA36

E

Earl Grey St EH3   6   BD12
Earl Haig Gdns EH5   14   BD6
Earl Haig Homes EH11   41   AW15
Earlston Pl EH7   28   BJ10
East Adam St EH8   7   BG12
East Barnton Av EH4   12   AU7
East Barnton Gdns EH4   24   AU8
East Brighton Cres EH15   29   BQ11
East Broughton Pl EH1 1   27   BF9
East Caiystane Pl EH10   52   BC22
East Caiystane Rd EH10   52   BD22
East Camus Pl EH10   52   BC21
East Camus Rd EH10   52   BC21
East Castle Rd EH10   42   BC14
East Champanyie EH9   43   BG16
East Clapperfield EH16   44   BJ18
East Claremont St EH7   27   BF9
East Comiston EH10   52   BC21
East Ct EH4 2   25   AY10
East Ct EH16   45   BP16
EAST CRAIGS   23   AR11
East Craigs Prim Sch EH12   23   AR11
East Craigs Rigg EH12   23   AQ12
East Craigs Wynd EH12   23   AQ12
East Cft (Ratho),
   Newbr. EH28   37   AG17
East Cromwell St EH6   15   BH5
East Crosscauseway EH8   7   BG13
Easter Auchendinny Br, Pen.
   EH26   67   BE35
Easter Belmont Rd EH12   25   AX12
Easter Currie Ct, Currie
   EH14   49   AQ23
Easter Currie Cres, Currie
   EH14   49   AQ22
Easter Currie Pl, Currie
   EH14   49   AQ22
Easter Currie Ter, Currie
   EH14   49   AQ23
Easter Dalry Dr EH11   26   BB13
Easter Dalry Pl EH11 1   26   BB12
Easter Dalry Rigg EH11 3   26   BB13
Easter Dalry Rd EH11   26   BB12
Easter Dalry Wynd EH11   26   BB12
Easter Drylaw Av EH4   25   AY8
Easter Drylaw Bk EH4   13   AY7
Easter Drylaw Dr EH4   25   AZ8
Easter Drylaw Gdns EH4   25   AY8
Easter Drylaw Gro EH4   25   AY8
Easter Drylaw Ln EH4   13   AY7
Easter Drylaw Pl EH4   13   AY7
Easter Drylaw Vw EH4   13   AY7
Easter Drylaw Way EH4   25   AY8
Easter Haugh EH13   52   BA20
Easter Hermitage EH6   16   BK8
EASTER HOWGATE   60   BC30
Eastern Gen Hosp EH6   16   BM8
Easter Pk Dr EH4   12   AU7
Easter Pk Ho EH4 5   12   AU7
Easter Rd EH6   16   BJ8
Easter Rd EH7   27   BH9
Easter Road Stadium
   (Hibernian FC) EH7   16   BJ9
Easter Steil EH10   42   BB18
Easter Warriston EH7   15   BE7
East Fm of Gilmerton
   EH17   45   BN21
East Fettes Av EH4   26   BB8
Eastfield EH15   30   BV12
EASTFIELD, Penicuik   69   BB36
EASTFIELD, Portobello   30   BU12
Eastfield Dr, Pen. EH26   69   BB37
Eastfield Fm Rd, Pen.
   EH26   69   BB36
Eastfield Gdns EH15   30   BU12
Eastfield Ind Est, Pen.
   EH26   69   BB37
Eastfield Ln, Tran. EH33   35   CM12

Eastfield Pk Rd, Pen.
   EH26   69   BB37
Eastfield Pl EH15   30   BV12
Eastfield Prim Sch EH26   69   BB37
Eastfield Rd, Newbr. EH28   22   AJ12
East Fountainbridge EH3   6   BD12
East Hannahfield, Bal.
   EH14   58   AJ25
East Hermitage Pl EH6   16   BJ7
EASTHOUSES   57   BX27
Easthouses Ct, Dalk. EH22   57   BY27
Easthouses Ind Est (Easth.),
   Dalk. EH22   57   BZ27
Easthouses Pl (Easth.),
   Dalk. EH22 1   57   BY26
Easthouses Rd (Easth.),
   Dalk. EH22   57   BY26
Easthouses Way (Easth.),
   Dalk. EH22   57   BY26
East Kilngate Pl EH17   54   BM22
East Kilngate Rigg EH17   54   BM22
East Kilngate Wynd EH17   54   BM22
East Lillypot EH5   14   BD6
East Ln, Pres. EH32   18   CH9
East London St EH7   27   BF9
East Lorimer Pl (Cock.),
   Pres. EH32 3   19   CL7
EAST MAINS OF
   INGLISTON   37   AH13
East Mkt St EH8   7   BF11
East Mayfield EH9   43   BH15
East Montgomery Pl EH7   27   BH9
East Newington Pl EH9   43   BG14
East Norton Pl EH7   7   BH10
East Parkside EH16   7   BH13
EAST PILTON   14   BA6
East Pilton Fm Av EH5   14   BA6
East Pilton Fm Rigg EH5   14   BA6
East Preston St EH8   43   BG14
East Preston St La EH8 3   43   BG14
East Queensway, Pen.
   EH26   69   BB36
East Restalrig Ter EH6   16   BK7
East Savile Rd EH16   43   BH16
East Sciennes St EH9   43   BG14
East Scotland St La EH3   27   BF9
East Sea Side, Pres. EH32 2   18   CH9
East Silvermills La EH3   26   BD9
East Suffolk Pk EH16   44   BJ16
East Suffolk Rd EH16   44   BJ16
East Telferton EH7   29   BP10
East Ter, S Q'fry EH30 4   9   AE2
East Trinity Rd EH5   14   BD6
East Way, The EH8   29   BN11
East Werberside EH4   14   BA7
East Werberside Pl EH4   14   BA7
Echline, S Q'fry EH30 2   8   AB3
Echline Av, S Q'fry EH30   8   AB2
Echline Dr, S Q'fry EH30   8   AB3
Echline Gdns, S Q'fry EH30   8   AB2
Echline Grn, S Q'fry EH30   8   AB2
Echline Pk, S Q'fry EH30   8   AB3
Echline Pl, S Q'fry EH30   8   AC3
Echline Prim Sch EH30   8   AC2
Echline Rigg, S Q'fry EH30   8   AC2
Echline Steadings,
   S Q'fry EH30 1   8   AB3
Echline Ter, S Q'fry EH30   8   AC3
Echline Vw, S Q'fry EH30   8   AC2
Edenhall Bk, Muss. EH21   32   CA14
Edenhall Cres, Muss. EH21   32   CA14
Edenhall Hosp EH21   32   CA15
Edenhall Rd, Muss. EH21   32   CA14
Eden La EH10   42   BD16
Eden Ter EH10 1   42   BD16
Edgefield Ind Est, Lnhd
   EH20   54   BL26
Edgefield Pl, Lnhd EH20   54   BL27
Edgefield Rd, Lnhd EH20   54   BL27
Edina Pl EH7   27   BH9
Edina St EH7   27   BH9
Edinburgh Acad EH3   26   BD9
Edinburgh Acad Jun Sch
   EH3   14   BC7
Edinburgh Airport EH12   22   AJ11

Edinburgh Canal Centre
 EH28   37   AF17
Edinburgh Capital Hotel
 EH12   24   AU10
Edinburgh Castle EH1   6   BE11
Edinburgh Coll of Art EH3   6   BE12
Edinburgh Coll of Art
 (Inverleith) EH3   14   BD7
Edinburgh Crystal
 Visitor Centre EH26   69   BB37
Edinburgh Dock EH6   16   BK5
Edinburgh Dungeon EH1   7   BF11
Edinburgh International
 Conference Centre EH3   6   BD12
Edinburgh Marriott Hotel
 EH12   39   AQ13
Edinburgh Pk EH12   39   AP14
Edinburgh Pk Business Cen
 EH12   39   AP15
Edinburgh Pk Sta EH12   39   AQ16
Edinburgh Quay EH3   6   BD13
Edinburgh Rd, Dalk. EH22   57   BW24
Edinburgh Rd, Muss. EH21   30   BV12
Edinburgh Rd, Newbr.
 EH28   36   AB13
Edinburgh Rd, Pen. EH26   69   BB36
Edinburgh Rd (Cock.),
 Pres. EH32   18   CK8
Edinburgh Rd, S Q'fry EH30   9   AE2
Edinburgh Rd, Tran. EH33   34   CK13
Edinburgh Sch of Shiatsu
 EH10   42   BD14
Edinburgh Technopole,
 Pen. EH26   66   BD32
Edinburgh Tutorial Coll
 EH3   6   BC11
Edinburgh Zoo EH12   24   AV12
EDMONSTONE   45   BP18
Edmonstone Av (Dand.),
 Dalk. EH22   45   BR19
Edmonstone Dr (Dand.),
 Dalk. EH22   45   BR19
Edmonstone Rd (Dand.),
 Dalk. EH22   45   BQ19
Edmonstone Ter (Dand.),
 Dalk. EH22   45   BR19
Eglinton Cres EH12   26   BB12
Eglinton St EH12 3   26   BA12
Egypt Ms EH10   43   BE16
Eighth St (Newt.),
 Dalk. EH22   65   BX30
Eildon St EH3   27   BE8
Eildon Ter EH3   26   BD8
Elbe St EH6   16   BJ6
Elcho Pl (Port S.),
 Pres. EH32 2   19   CL7
Elcho Ter EH15   30   BS11
Elder St EH1   7   BF10
Elder St, Tran. EH33   35   CL12
Elder St E EH1 5   7   BF10
ELDINDEAN   56   BS27
Eldindean Pl, Bonny.
 EH19   55   BR27
Eldindean Rd, Bonny.
 EH19   55   BR27
Eldindean Ter, Bonny.
 EH19   55   BR27
Eldin Ind Est, Lnhd EH20   54   BL25
Electra Pl EH15 2   29   BQ10
Elgin Pl EH12   26   BB12
Elgin St EH7   27   BH9
Elgin St N EH7   27   BH9
Elgin Ter EH7   27   BH9
Elizafield EH6   15   BG7
Ellangowan Ter EH16   44   BL18
Ellen's Glen Ln EH17   44   BL20
Ellen's Glen Rd EH17   44   BL20
Ellersly Rd EH12   25   AX12
Elliot Gdns EH14   41   AY19
Elliot Pk EH14   41   AY19
Elliot Rd EH14   41   AY19
Elliot St EH7   27   BH9
Elmfield Ct, Dalk. EH22   57   BW24
Elmfield Pk, Dalk. EH22   57   BW24
Elmfield Rd, Dalk. EH22   57   BW24

Elm Pl EH6 2   16   BK7
Elm Pl (Mayf.), Dalk. EH22   65   BZ29
Elm Row EH7   27   BG9
Elm Row, Lass. EH18   55   BQ26
Elmwood Ter EH6   16   BK7
Elphinstone Ct, Tran.
 EH33 2   35   CL13
Elphinstone Rd, Tran.
 EH33   34   CK15
Elphinstone Wk EH33 6   35   CL14
Eltringham Gdns EH14   41   AY15
Eltringham Gro EH14   41   AY15
Eltringham Ter EH14   41   AY15
Emily Ct, Gore. EH23 1   70   BY34
Emily Pl, Gore. EH23   70   BY34
Engine Rd, Gore. EH23   70   BX34
Engine Rd, Lnhd EH20   54   BL27
Esdaile Bk EH9   43   BF15
Esdaile Gdns EH9   43   BF15
Esdaile Pk EH9 1   43   BF15
ESKBANK   56   BV25
Eskbank Ct, Dalk. EH22 2   56   BU25
Eskbank Rd, Bonny. EH19   56   BS27
Eskbank Rd, Dalk. EH22   56   BV25
Eskbank Rd Junct,
 Dalk. EH22   56   BT27
Eskbank Ter, Dalk. EH22   56   BV25
Eskbank Toll, Dalk. EH22   56   BV25
Esk Br, Pen. EH26   69   BD38
Eskdaill Ct, Dalk. EH22 4   57   BW24
Eskdaill St, Dalk. EH22   57   BW24
Eskdale Ct, Bonny. EH19   63   BQ28
Eskdale Dr, Bonny. EH19   63   BQ28
Eskdale Ms, Muss. EH21   31   BY13
Eskdale Ter, Bonny. EH19   63   BQ28
Eskfield Gro, Dalk. EH22   56   BT25
Esk Glades, Dalk. EH22   57   BX23
ESKGROVE   55   BP27
Eskgrove Dr (Bils.),
 Ros. EH25   61   BG29
Eskhill, Pen. EH26   69   BB38
Eskmill Ind Est, Pen.
 EH26   69   BC38
Eskmill Rd, Pen. EH26   69   BC38
Eskmills EH21   31   BX14
Eskmills Pk, Muss. EH21   31   BX14
Eskmill Vil, Muss. EH21   31   BX14
Esk Pl, Dalk. EH22   56   BV24
Eskside Ct, Dalk. EH22   56   BV23
Eskside E, Muss. EH21   31   BY13
Eskside W, Muss. EH21   31   BX13
Eskvale Ct, Pen. EH26   69   BC38
Eskvale Cres, Pen. EH26   69   BC38
Eskvale Dr, Pen. EH26   69   BC37
Eskvale Vw, Pen. EH26   69   BC37
Eskview Av, Muss. EH21   31   BX14
Eskview Cres, Muss. EH21   31   BX14
Eskview Gro, Dalk. EH22   56   BV24
Eskview Gro, Muss. EH21   31   BX14
Eskview Rd (Mayf.),
 Dalk. EH22   65   BZ29
Eskview Rd, Muss. EH21   31   BX14
Eskview Ter, Muss. EH21   31   BX14
Eskview Vil, Dalk. EH22   56   BU25
Esplanade EH1   6   BE12
Esplanade EH4   12   AS4
Esplanade EH15   30   BT11
Essendean Pl EH4   24   AT10
Essendean Ter EH4   24   AT10
Essex Brae EH4   23   AQ7
Essex Pk EH4   23   AQ7
Essex Rd EH4   23   AQ7
Esslemont Rd EH16   43   BH17
Ethel Ter EH10   42   BC17
Eton Ter EH4   6   BC10
Ettrickdale Pl EH3   26   BD8
Ettrick Gro EH10   42   BC14
Ettrick Ln EH10   42   BB15
Ettrick Rd EH10   42   BB15
Evans Gdns, Bonny. EH19   56   BT27
Eva Pl EH9   43   BG17
Evelyn Ter (Auch.),
 Pen. EH26   67   BE34
Everland EH4   23   AQ7
Ewing St, Pen. EH26   69   BB36
Eyre Cres EH3   27   BE9

Eyre Pl EH3   27   BE9
Eyre Pl La EH3   27   BE9
Eyre Ter EH3   27   BE9

F

Fair-a-Far EH4   11   AR6
Fair-a-Far Cotts EH4   11   AR6
Fair-a-Far Shot EH4   11   AR6
Fairbrae EH11   40   AV16
Fairford Gdns EH16   44   BK18
Fairhaven Vil, Dalk.
 EH22 1   56   BU26
Fairmile Av EH10   52   BD21
FAIRMILEHEAD   52   BD22
Fairview Rd, Newbr.
 EH28   21   AH12
Fairways (Monk.),
 Muss. EH21   31   BX16
Faith Mission Bible Coll
 EH17   45   BN21
Fala Ct EH16   44   BK21
Falcon Av EH10   42   BD16
Falcon Ct EH10   42   BD16
Falcon Gdns EH10   42   BD15
Falcon Rd EH10   42   BD16
Falcon Rd W EH10   42   BD16
Falkland Gdns EH12   24   AU10
Farm Av, Lass. EH18   63   BP29
Farquhar Ter, S Q'fry
 EH30   8   AC2
Farrer Gro EH7   29   BN10
Farrer Ter EH7   29   BN10
Fa'side Av, Tran. EH33 1   35   CM14
Fa'side Av Ct (Wall.),
 Muss. EH21   33   CD15
Fa'side Av N (Wall.),
 Muss. EH21   33   CD15
Fa'side Av S (Wall.),
 Muss. EH21   33   CD15
Fa'side Bldgs (Wall.),
 Muss. EH21   33   CD15
Fa'side Cres (Wall.),
 Muss. EH21   33   CD15
Fa'side Cres, Tran. EH33 2   35   CM14
Fa'side Dr (Wall.),
 Muss. EH21   33   CD15
Fa'side Gdns (Wall.),
 Muss. EH21   33   CD15
Fa'side Rd, Tran. EH33   35   CM14
Fa'side Ter (Wall.),
 Muss. EH21   33   CD15
Fa'side Vw, Tran. EH33   34   CK15
Fauldburn EH12   23   AR10
Fauldburn Pk EH12   23   AR10
Featherall Av EH12   24   AT13
Featherhall Cres EH12 1   24   AS13
Featherhall Cres N EH12   24   AS13
Featherhall Cres S EH12   24   AS13
Featherhall Gro EH12   24   AT13
Featherhall Pl EH12   24   AT13
Featherhall Rd EH12   24   AT13
Featherhall Ter EH12   24   AT13
Ferguson Ct, Muss. EH21   31   BY16
Ferguson Dr, Muss. EH21   31   BX16
Ferguson Gdns, Muss.
 EH21   31   BY16
Ferguson Grn, Muss. EH21   31   BX16
Ferguson Vw, Muss. EH21   31   BX16
Ferguson Way (Newt.),
 Dalk. EH22   65   BX31
FERNIEHILL   45   BP20
Ferniehill Av EH17   45   BN21
Ferniehill Dr EH17   45   BN21
Ferniehill Gdns EH17   45   BP20
Ferniehill Gro EH17 1   45   BP20
Ferniehill Pl EH17   45   BN21
Ferniehill Rd EH17   45   BP20
Ferniehill Sq EH17   45   BN21
Ferniehill St EH17   45   BN20
Ferniehill Ter EH17   45   BN21
Ferniehill Way EH17   45   BP20
Fernielaw Av EH13   51   AW22
Fernieside Av EH17   45   BN20
Fernieside Cres EH17   45   BN20
Fernieside Dr EH17   45   BN20

Fernieside Gdns *EH17* 45 BN20
Fernieside Gro *EH17* 45 BP20
Fernieside Pl *EH17* 45 BN20
Ferryburn, S Q'fry *EH30* 1 9 AE3
Ferryburn Grn, S Q'fry *EH30* 9 AE3
Ferryfield *EH5* 14 BB7
Ferry Gait Cres *EH4* 13 AW7
Ferry Gait Dr *EH4* 13 AW7
Ferry Gait Gdns *EH4* 13 AW7
Ferry Gait Pl *EH4* 13 AW7
Ferry Gait Wk *EH4* 13 AW7
Ferryhill Prim Sch *EH4* 25 AY8
Ferrylee *EH6* 15 BG5
Ferrymuir,
  S Q'fry *EH30* 8 AD3
Ferrymuir Gait,
  S Q'fry *EH30* 8 AD3
Ferrymuir La,
  S Q'fry *EH30* 8 AD3
Ferrymuir Rd,
  S Q'fry *EH30* 8 AD3
Ferry Rd *EH4* 13 AY7
Ferry Rd *EH5* 14 BD6
Ferry Rd *EH6* 15 BF6
Ferry Rd Av *EH4* 13 AZ7
Ferry Rd Dr *EH4* 13 AZ6
Ferry Rd Gdns *EH4* 13 AY7
Ferry Rd Gro *EH4* 13 AY7
Ferry Rd Pl *EH4* 13 AY7
Festival Sq *EH3* 1 6 BD12
Festival Theatre *EH8* 7 BG12
Fetteresk Cotts, Pen.
  EH26 68 BA39
Fettes Av *EH4* 26 BB9
Fettes Coll *EH4* 26 BB8
Fettes Ri *EH4* 14 BB7
Fettes Row *EH3* 27 BE9
Fidra Ct *EH4* 13 AW6
Fifth St (Newt.),
  Dalk. *EH22* 65 BW30
Figgate Bk *EH15* 29 BR10
Figgate La *EH15* 29 BR10
Figgate St *EH15* 29 BQ10
Fillyside Av *EH7* 17 BN9
Fillyside Rd *EH7* 17 BN8
Fillyside Ter *EH7* 17 BN8
Filmhouse Cinema *EH3* 6 BD12
Findhorn Pl *EH9* 43 BG14
Findlay Av *EH7* 16 BL8
Findlay Cotts *EH7* 16 BL8
Findlay Gdns *EH7* 16 BL8
Findlay Gro *EH7* 16 BL8
Findlay Medway *EH7* 16 BL8
Fingal Pl *EH9* 43 BF14
Fingzies Pl *EH6* 3 16 BK7
Finlaggan Ct *EH12* 2 23 AQ11
Finlay Pl (Mayf.),
  Dalk. *EH22* 71 CB29
FIRRHILL 42 BA19
Firrhill Cres *EH13* 41 AZ19
Firrhill Dr *EH13* 52 BA20
Firrhill High Sch *EH14* 41 AZ19
Firrhill Ln *EH13* 52 BA20
First Gait (Ricc.),
  Currie *EH14* 49 AN19
First St (Newt.),
  Dalk. *EH22* 65 BX31
Firth Br, Ros. *EH25* 67 BF35
Firth Cres (Auch.),
  Pen. *EH26* 67 BF34
Firth Rd (Auch.),
  Pen. *EH26* 67 BF34
Fir Vw, Lnhd *EH20* 1 61 BH28
Fishergate Rd (Port S.),
  Pres. *EH32* 19 CN8
FISHERROW 31 BY12
Fisherrow Ind Pk, Muss.
  EH21 31 BW13
Fishers Rd (Port S.),
  Pres. *EH32* 19 CM7
Fishers Wynd, Muss.
  EH21 31 BX13
Fishmarket Sq *EH6* 2 15 BF4
Fishwives' Causeway *EH7* 29 BN10
Fishwives' Causeway *EH15* 29 BQ10
Flassches Yd *EH12* 40 AS15

Fleets Gro, Tran. *EH33* 35 CM15
Fleets Ind Est, Tran. *EH33* 35 CL16
Fleets Rd, Tran. *EH33* 35 CL14
Fleets Vw, Tran. *EH33* 35 CM15
Fleshmarket Cl *EH1* 13 7 BF11
Fletcher Gro, Pen. *EH26* 66 BB35
Flora Stevenson Prim Sch
  EH4 26 BB9
Flotterstone Br, Pen.
  EH26 66 BA33
Forbes Rd *EH10* 42 BD15
Forbes St *EH8* 7 BG13
Ford's Rd *EH11* 41 AX15
Forester's Vw, Tran. *EH33* 35 CM13
Forkenford *EH16* 28 BM14
Forres St *EH3* 6 BD10
Forrester High Sch *EH12* 40 AT15
Forrester Pk Av *EH12* 40 AT15
Forrester Pk Dr *EH12* 40 AT15
Forrester Pk Gdns *EH12* 40 AT15
Forrester Pk Grn *EH12* 40 AU15
Forrester Pk Gro *EH12* 40 AT15
Forrester Pk Ln *EH12* 40 AT15
Forrester Rd *EH12* 24 AT12
Forrest Hill *EH1* 7 BF12
Forrest Rd *EH1* 7 BF12
Forteviot Ho *EH17* 44 BM19
Forth Ct (Port S.),
  Pres. *EH32* 19 CN7
Forth Gdns (Port S.),
  Pres. *EH32* 19 CN7
Forth Gro (Port S.),
  Pres. *EH32* 19 CN7
Forth Ind Est *EH5* 14 BA4
Fort Ho *EH6* 15 BG5
Forth Pk (Dalm.),
  S Q'fry *EH30* 9 AG3
Forth Pl, S Q'fry *EH30* 8 AB2
Forth St *EH1* 7 BF10
Forth Ter (Dalm.),
  S Q'fry *EH30* 9 AF3
Forth Vw Av, Currie *EH14* 49 AP23
Forthview Av (Wall.),
  Muss. *EH21* 32 CC14
Forthview Ct, Tran.
  EH33 35 CM12
Forth Vw Cres, Currie
  EH14 49 AP22
Forth Vw Cres (Dand.),
  Dalk. *EH22* 45 BR19
Forthview Cres (Wall.),
  Muss. *EH21* 32 CC14
Forthview Dr (Wall.),
  Muss. *EH21* 1 33 CD14
Forthview Prim Sch *EH4* 13 AZ7
Forth Vw Rd, Currie *EH14* 49 AP23
Forthview Ter *EH4* 25 AY9
Forthview Ter (Wall.),
  Muss. *EH21* 33 CD14
Forthview Wk, Tran. *EH33* 35 CM12
Forth Wynd (Port S.),
  Pres. *EH32* 19 CN7
Fort Kinnaird
  Shopping Centre *EH15* 30 BS15
Fort Prim Sch *EH6* 15 BG5
Foulis Cres, Jun. Grn *EH14* 50 AT21
Foundry La, Lnhd *EH20* 54 BM26
Fountainbridge *EH3* 6 BD13
Fountainhall Rd *EH9* 43 BG16
FountainPark *EH11* 6 BC13
Fountain Pl, Lnhd *EH20* 54 BK27
Fourth Gait (Ricc.),
  Currie *EH14* 49 AN20
Fourth St (Newt.),
  Dalk. *EH22* 65 BX30
Fowler Cres, Lnhd *EH20* 1 54 BM27
Fowlers Ct, Pres. *EH32* 3 18 CH9
Fowler Sq, Lnhd *EH20* 2 54 BM27
Fowler St, Tran. *EH33* 35 CL12
Fowler Ter *EH11* 42 BB14
Fox Covert Av *EH12* 24 AU10
Fox Covert Gro *EH12* 24 AU10
Fox Covert Prim Sch *EH12* 24 AU11
Fox Spring Cres *EH10* 52 BB20
Fox Spring Ri *EH10* 52 BC20

Fox St *EH6* 16 BK6
Fraser Av *EH5* 14 BC6
Fraser Cres *EH5* 14 BC6
Fraser Gdns *EH5* 14 BC6
Fraser Gro *EH5* 14 BC6
Frederick St *EH2* 6 BE10
Freelands Rd (Ratho),
  Newbr. *EH28* 38 AJ15
Friarton Gdns, Pen.
  EH26 68 AY38
Frogston Av *EH10* 52 BD22
Frogston Brae *EH17* 53 BG23
Frogston Gdns *EH10* 52 BD22
Frogston Gro *EH10* 53 BE22
Frogston Rd E *EH17* 53 BG23
Frogston Rd W *EH10* 52 BD22
Frogston Ter *EH10* 53 BE22
Fruitmarket Gallery *EH1* 7 BF11
Furcheons Pk *EH8* 29 BN11

G

Gabriel's Rd *EH2* 6 7 BF10
Gabriel's Rd *EH3* 6 26 BD9
Galachlawshot *EH10* 53 BE21
Galachlawside *EH10* 53 BE22
Galadale (Newt.),
  Dalk. *EH22* 65 BW29
Galadale Cres (Newt.),
  Dalk. *EH22* 65 BW29
Galadale Dr (Newt.),
  Dalk. *EH22* 65 BW29
Gallolee, The *EH13* 51 AZ21
Galt Av, Muss. *EH21* 32 CC14
Galt Cres, Muss. *EH21* 32 CC14
Galt Dr, Muss. *EH21* 32 CC14
Galt Rd, Muss. *EH21* 32 CC14
Galt Ter, Muss. *EH21* 32 CC14
Gamekeeper's Ln *EH4* 11 AR6
Gamekeeper's Pk *EH4* 11 AR6
Gamekeeper's Rd *EH4* 11 AR6
Gardener's Cl (Cock.),
  Pres. *EH32* 19 CL7
Gardeners Pl, Tran. *EH33* 2 35 CL12
Gardener's Wk, Pen. *EH26* 68 AY37
Garden Ter *EH4* 12 AT7
Gardiner Cres, Pres. *EH32* 18 CK10
Gardiner Gro *EH4* 25 AX9
Gardiner Pl (Newt.),
  Dalk. *EH22* 65 BW29
Gardiner Rd *EH4* 25 AX9
Gardiner Rd, Pres. *EH32* 18 CJ10
Gardiner Ter *EH4* 25 AX10
Gardiner Ter, Pres. *EH32* 34 CJ11
Gardner's Cres *EH3* 6 BC12
Garscube Ter *EH12* 25 AZ11
Garvald Ct *EH16* 44 BK21
Gateside Rd, K'lis. *EH29* 20 AC10
Gateway Theatre *EH7* 27 BG9
Gayfield Cl *EH1* 27 BG9
Gayfield Pl *EH7* 27 BG9
Gayfield Pl La *EH1* 27 BG9
Gayfield Sq *EH1* 27 BG9
Gayfield St *EH1* 27 BF9
Gayfield St La *EH1* 27 BF9
Gaynor Av, Lnhd *EH20* 54 BJ27
Gentle's Entry *EH8* 8 7 BH11
George Av, Lnhd *EH20* 54 BK27
George Cres, Lnhd *EH20* 1 54 BL27
George Dr, Lnhd *EH20* 54 BK27
George IV Br *EH1* 7 BF11
George Heriot's Sch *EH3* 6 BE10
George Intercontinental
  Hotel *EH2* 6 BE10
George Sq *EH8* 7 BF13
George Sq La *EH8* 7 BF13
George St *EH2* 6 BD11
George Ter, Lnhd *EH20* 54 BK27
George Wk, Tran. *EH33* 35 CL13
George Watson's Coll
  EH10 42 BB16
George Way, Tran. *EH33* 3 35 CL13
Georgian House (NTS)
  EH2 6 BD11
Gibbs Entry *EH8* 7 BG12
Gibraltar Ct, Dalk. *EH22* 57 BX24

Name	Page	Grid
Gibraltar Gdns, Dalk. EH22	57	BW24
Gibraltar Rd, Dalk. EH22	57	BW24
Gibraltar Ter, Dalk. EH22	57	BX24
Gibson Dr, Dalk. EH22	57	BY24
Gibson St EH7	15	BG7
Gibson Ter EH11	6	BC13
Gifford Pk EH8	7	BG13
Gilberstoun EH15	30	BS13
Gilberstoun Brig EH15	30	BT14
Gilberstoun Ln EH15	30	BT14
Gilberstoun Pl EH15	30	BT14
Gilberstoun Wynd EH15	30	BT14
Giles St EH6	15	BH6
Gillespie Cres EH10	6	BD13
Gillespie Pl EH10	6	BD13
Gillespie Rd EH13	50	AV21
Gillespie St EH3	6	BD13
Gillsland Pk EH10	42	BB15
Gillsland Rd EH10	42	BB15
GILMERTON	45	BP21
Gilmerton Dykes Av EH17	44	BM21
Gilmerton Dykes Cres EH17	44	BL21
Gilmerton Dykes Dr EH17	44	BM21
Gilmerton Dykes Gdns EH17	44	BL21
Gilmerton Dykes Gro EH17	44	BL21
Gilmerton Dykes Ln EH17	54	BL22
Gilmerton Dykes Pl EH17	44	BL21
Gilmerton Dykes Rd EH17	54	BM22
Gilmerton Dykes St EH17	44	BM21
Gilmerton Dykes Ter EH17	54	BM22
Gilmerton Dykes Vw EH17	54	BM22
Gilmerton Junct, Lass. EH18	55	BR23
Gilmerton Ms EH17	55	BN22
Gilmerton Pl EH17	54	BM22
Gilmerton Prim Sch EH17	44	BM21
Gilmerton Rd EH16	44	BJ17
Gilmerton Rd EH17	44	BL19
Gilmerton Rd (Gilm.) EH17	55	BP22
Gilmerton Rd, Dalk. EH22	56	BU24
Gilmerton Rd, Lass. EH18	56	BS23
Gilmerton Rd Rbt, Lass. EH18	56	BS23
Gilmerton Sta Rd EH17	55	BN24
Gilmore Pk EH3	6	BC13
Gilmore Pl EH3	42	BC14
Gilmore Pl La EH3	6	BD13
Gilmour Rd EH16	43	BH16
Gilmour's Entry EH8 7	7	BG12
Gilmour St EH8	7	BG12
Gladstone Pl EH6	16	BK7
Gladstone's Land (NTS) EH1 5	7	BF11
Gladstone Ter EH9	43	BG14
Glanville Pl EH3 5	26	BD9
Glasgow Rd EH12	39	AQ13
Glasgow Rd, Newbr. EH28	37	AG13
Glaskhill Ter, Pen. EH26	68	BA37
Glasshouse Experience EH3	14	BD7
Glasshouse Hotel, The EH1	7	BG10
Glebe, The EH4	11	AR5
Glebe, The, K'lis. EH29	20	AC10
Glebe, The (Dalm.), S Q'fry EH30	9	AG4
Glebe Gdns EH12	24	AU13
Glebe Gdns, Pres. EH32 4	18	CH10
Glebe Gro EH12	24	AT13
Glebe Pl, Lass. EH18	55	BP26
Glebe Rd EH12	24	AT13
Glebe St, Dalk. EH22	57	BW24
Glebe Ter EH12	24	AU13
Glenallan Dr EH16	44	BK17
Glenallan Ln EH16	44	BK17
Glenalmond Ct EH11	40	AT17
Glenbrook Rd, Bal. EH14	58	AJ26
Glencairn Cres EH12	26	BB12
Glencoe Path, Pres. EH32	18	CJ9
GLENCORSE	66	BD35
Glencorse Golf Course EH26	67	BE34
Glencorse Pk (Milt.Br), Pen. EH26	67	BE35
Glencorse Prim Sch EH26	66	BD34
Glencross Gdns, Pen. EH26	68	AY38
Glendevon Av EH12	25	AX13
Glendevon Gdns EH12	25	AX13
Glendevon Gro EH12	25	AX13
Glendevon Pk EH12	41	AX14
Glendevon Pl EH12	25	AX13
Glendevon Rd EH12	41	AX14
Glendevon Ter EH12	25	AX13
Glendinning Cres EH16	44	BJ19
Glendinning Dr, K'lis. EH29	20	AB9
Glendinning Pl, K'lis. EH29	20	AB9
Glendinning Rd, K'lis. EH29	20	AB9
Glendinning Way, K'lis. EH29	20	AB9
Glenesk Cres, Dalk. EH22	56	BV25
Glenfinlas St EH3	6	BD11
Glengarry Ter, Pres. EH32	18	CJ9
Glengyle Ter EH3	6	BD13
Glenisla Gdns EH9	43	BF16
Glenisla Gdns La EH9 1	43	BF16
Glenlea Cotts EH11	41	AY15
Glenlee Av EH8	28	BL11
Glenlee Gdns EH8	28	BL11
Glenlockhart Bk EH14	41	AZ18
Glenlockhart Rd EH10	42	BA18
Glenlockhart Rd EH14	41	AZ18
Glenlockhart Valley EH14	41	AZ17
Glennie Gdns, Tran. EH33	35	CM13
Glenogle Ct EH3	26	BD8
Glenogle Pl EH3 7	26	BD9
Glenogle Rd EH3	26	BD9
Glenogle Ter EH3	26	BD8
Glenorchy Pl EH1 4	7	BG10
Glenorchy Ter EH9	43	BH15
Glen Pl, Pen. EH26	68	BA37
Glen St EH3	6	BE12
Glenure Ln EH4	24	AT10
Glenvarloch Cres EH16	44	BJ18
Glenview, Pen. EH26	68	BA37
Glen Vw Ct, Gore. EH23	70	BY34
Glen Vw Cres, Gore. EH23	70	BY35
Glenview Pl, Gore. EH23	70	BY36
Glen Vw Rd, Gore. EH23	70	BY34
Glen Vw Wk, Gore. EH23	70	BZ36
Gloucester La EH3	6	BD10
Gloucester Pl EH3	6	BD10
Gloucester Sq EH3	6	BD10
Gloucester St EH3	6	BD10
Goff Av EH7	17	BP9
Gogarbank EH12	39	AN17
Gogar Br Rd EH12	22	AJ11
Gogarburn Golf Course EH12	38	AL14
Gogarloch Bk EH12	39	AR14
Gogarloch Haugh EH12	39	AR14
Gogarloch Muir EH12	39	AR14
Gogarloch Rd EH12	39	AQ14
Gogarloch Syke EH12	39	AQ14
Gogar Mains Fm Rd EH12	38	AL13
Gogar Rbt EH12	39	AN13
Gogar Sta Rd EH12	39	AQ17
Gogarstone Rd EH12	38	AK14
GOLDENACRE	14	BD7
Goldenacre Ter EH3	14	BD7
Goldie Ter, Lnhd EH20	62	BJ28
Golf Course Rd, Bonny. EH19	55	BR27
Golf Dr (Port S.), Pres. EH32	19	CM7
Goodtrees Gdns EH17	44	BM19
GOOSE GREEN	31	BZ12
Goose Grn Av, Muss. EH21	31	BZ12
Goose Grn Br, Muss. EH21	31	BZ12
Goose Grn Cres, Muss. EH21	31	BZ12
Goose Grn Pl, Muss. EH21	31	BZ12
Goose Grn Rd, Muss. EH21	31	BZ12
Gordon Av, Bonny. EH19	63	BP29
Gordon Ln EH12	24	AU12
Gordon Rd EH12	24	AU12
Gordon St EH6	16	BJ7
Gordon St (Easth.), Dalk. EH22	57	BY28
Gordon Ter EH16	44	BJ17
Gore Av, Gore. EH23	70	BZ35
GOREBRIDGE	70	BX36
Gorebridge Prim Sch EH23	70	BY34
GORGIE	41	AZ15
Gorgie Cotts EH11	41	AY15
Gorgie Pk Cl EH14	41	AZ15
Gorgie Pk Rd EH11	41	AZ14
Gorgie Pk Rd EH14	41	AZ15
Gorgie Rd EH11	41	AZ14
Gorton Ln, Rose. EH24	62	BM33
Gorton Pl, Rose. EH24	62	BM33
Gorton Rd, Rose. EH24	62	BM33
Gosford Pl EH6	15	BF6
Gosford Rd (Port S.), Pres. EH32	19	CL7
Gosford Wk (Port S.), Pres. EH32	19	CL7
Gote La, S Q'fry EH30	8	AD2
Gowanhill Rd, Currie EH14	48	AK22
GOWKSHILL	65	BY32
Gracefield Ct, Muss. EH21	31	BX13
GRACEMOUNT	44	BK21
Gracemount Av EH16	44	BK20
Gracemount Dr EH16	44	BK21
Gracemount High Sch EH16	54	BL22
Gracemount Pl EH16	44	BK21
Gracemount Prim Sch EH16	44	BK21
Gracemount Rd EH16	54	BJ22
Gracemount Sq EH16	44	BK20
Graham's Rd (Milt.Br), Pen. EH26	66	BD34
Graham St EH6	15	BG6
Granby Rd EH16	43	BH16
Grandfield EH6	15	BE6
Grandville EH6	15	BE5
GRANGE	43	BF15
Grange Ct EH9	43	BG14
Grange Cres EH9	43	BF15
Grange Cres E, Pres. EH32	18	CH10
Grange Cres W, Pres. EH32	18	CH10
Grange Gro, Pres. EH32	18	CH10
Grange Ln EH9	43	BE15
Grange Ln Gdns EH9	43	BF15
Grange Rd EH9	43	BF14
Grange Rd, Pres. EH32	18	CH10
Grange Ter EH9	43	BF16
Grannies Pk Ind Est, Dalk. EH22	57	BW23
Grannus Ms (Inv.), Muss. EH21	31	BZ14
Grant Av EH13	51	AW21
GRANTON	14	BA4
Granton Cres EH5	14	BB5
Granton Gdns EH5	14	BB5
Granton Gro EH5	14	BB5
Granton Harbour EH5	14	BB3
Granton Mains Av EH4	13	AY5
Granton Mains Bk EH4 1	13	AY5
Granton Mains Brae EH4	13	AY5
Granton Mains Ct EH4	13	AZ5
Granton Mains E EH4	13	AZ5
Granton Mains Gait EH4	13	AY5
Granton Mains Vale EH4	13	AY5
Granton Mains Wynd EH4	13	AY5
Granton Medway EH5	14	BA5
Granton Mill Cres EH4	13	AY5
Granton Mill Dr EH4	13	AX6
Granton Mill March EH4	13	AX6
Granton Mill Pk EH4	13	AX6
Granton Mill Pl EH4	13	AX5
Granton Mill Rd EH4	13	AX5
Granton Mill W EH4 1	13	AX5
Granton Pk Av EH5	14	BA4
Granton Pl EH5	14	BB5
Granton Prim Sch EH5	14	BB5
Granton Rd EH5	14	BB5
Granton Sq EH5	14	BB4
Granton Ter EH5	14	BB4
Granton Vw EH5	14	BB4
Grant Rd, Pres. EH32	18	CJ9
Grantully Pl EH9	43	BH15
Granville Ter EH10	42	BC14
Grassmarket EH1	6	BE12
Grays Ct EH8 6	7	BG12

Name		
Graysknowe EH14 1	41	AX17
Gray's Ln EH10	42	BA15
Great Cannon Bk EH15 3	29	BQ10
Great Carleton Pl EH16	45	BQ16
Great Carleton Sq EH16 1	45	BQ16
Great Junct St EH6	15	BH6
Great King St EH3	6	BE10
Great Michael Cl EH6 4	15	BF4
Great Michael Ri EH6	15	BF5
Great Michael Sq EH4 1	15	BF4
Great Stuart St EH3	6	BC11
Green, The EH4	12	AV7
Green, The, Bal. EH14	58	AM27
Green, The, Lnhd EH20 1	54	BL26
Greenacre EH14	50	AU20
GREENBANK	42	BB19
Greenbank Av EH10	42	BC18
Greenbank Cres EH10	42	BB19
Greenbank Dr EH10	42	BB18
Greenbank Gdns EH10	42	BB19
Greenbank Gro EH10	42	BB19
Greenbank La EH10	42	BB18
Greenbank Ln EH10	42	BB19
Greenbank Pk EH10	42	BB19
Greenbank Pl EH10	42	BC18
Greenbank Ri EH10	42	BB19
Greenbank Rd EH10	42	BB19
Greenbank Row EH10	42	BB19
Greenbank Ter EH10	42	BC18
Greendale Pk EH4	13	AW7
GREENDYKES	45	BP16
Greendykes Av EH16	45	BP16
Greendykes Dr EH16	45	BP16
Greendykes Gdns EH16	45	BP16
Greendykes Ho EH16	45	BP16
Greendykes Ln EH16	45	BP16
Greendykes Rd EH16	45	BN16
Greendykes Ter EH16	45	BP16
GREENEND	44	BL19
Greenend Dr EH17	44	BL20
Greenend Gdns EH17	44	BL19
Greenend Gro EH17	44	BL19
Greenfield Cres, Bal. EH14	58	AL27
Greenfield Pk (Monk.), Muss. EH21	31	BX16
Greenfield Rd, Bal. EH14	58	AL27
Greenhall Cres, Gore. EH23 1	70	BX34
Greenhall Rd, Gore. EH23	70	BY34
Greenhill Ct EH9	42	BD14
Greenhill Gdns EH10	42	BD14
Greenhill Pk EH10	42	BD15
Greenhill Pk, Pen. EH26	68	AZ38
Greenhill Pl EH10	42	BD15
Greenhill Ter EH10	42	BD14
Green La, Lass. EH18	55	BP27
Greenlaw Gro (Milt.Br), Pen. EH26	66	BC34
Greenlaw Hedge EH13	52	BA20
GREENLAW MAINS	66	BC35
Greenlaw Rig EH13	52	BA20
Greenmantle Ln EH16	44	BK18
Greenpark EH17	44	BL19
Greens Hotel EH12	26	BB11
Greenside End EH1 6	7	BG10
Greenside La EH1	7	BG10
Greenside Pl EH1 5	7	BG10
Greenside Pl, Rose. EH24	62	BM33
Greenside Row EH1	7	BG10
Green St EH7	27	BF9
Greenway, The EH14	40	AU18
Greyfriars Bobby EH1	7	BF12
Greyfriars Pl EH1	7	BF12
Grey Sch Cor, Pres. EH32	18	CH10
Grierson Av EH5	14	BC5
Grierson Cres EH5	14	BC5
Grierson Gdns EH5	14	BC5
Grierson Rd EH5	14	BB5
Grierson Sq EH5	14	BC5
Grierson Vil EH5	14	BC5
Grieve Ct, Pen. EH26	69	BB36
Grigor Av EH4	25	AZ8
Grigor Dr EH4	25	AZ8
Grigor Gdns EH4	25	AZ8
Grigor Ter EH4	25	AZ8
Grindlay St EH3	6	BD12
Grindlay St Ct EH3	6	BD12
Groathill Av EH4	25	AY9
Groathill Gdns E EH4	25	AY9
Groathill Gdns W EH4	25	AY9
Groathill Ln EH4	25	AY8
Groathill Rd N EH4	25	AY8
Groathill Rd S EH4	25	AY9
Grosvenor Cres EH12	26	BB12
Grosvenor Gdns EH12	26	BB12
Grosvenor St EH12	6	BC12
Grotto Br, S Q'fry EH30	23	AN8
Grove, The, Muss. EH21	32	CA14
Grove End, Lass. EH18	55	BR27
Grove Pl, Jun. Grn EH14	50	AT21
Grove St EH3	6	BC12
Grove St, Muss. EH21	31	BZ14
Grove Ter EH3 4	6	BC12
Grundie's Well Rd EH17	45	BN21
Guardianswood EH12	25	AY12
Guardwell Cres EH17	44	BL20
Gullan's Cl EH8	7	BG11
Gunnet Ct EH4	13	AW6
Guthrie St EH1	7	BF12
GYLE, THE	39	AR13
Gyle Av EH12 1	39	AP14
Gylemuir Prim Sch EH12	40	AS14
Gylemuir Rd EH12	24	AS13
Gyle Pk Gdns EH12	39	AQ13
Gyle Service La EH12	39	AQ13
Gyle Shopping Centre EH12	39	AQ14
Gypsy Brae EH5	13	AX5

H

Name		
Haddington Pl EH7	27	BG9
Haddington Rd, Muss. EH21	32	CC13
Haddington Rd, Tran. EH33	35	CN13
Haddon's Ct EH8	7	BG12
HAILES	51	AW20
Hailes App EH13	51	AW20
Hailes Av EH13	41	AW19
Hailes Bk EH13	51	AW20
Hailes Cres EH13	51	AW20
Hailes Gdns EH13	50	AV20
Hailes Gro EH13	51	AW20
Hailesland Gdns EH14	40	AU18
Hailesland Gro EH14	40	AU18
Hailesland Pk EH14	40	AU18
Hailesland Pl EH14	40	AU18
Hailesland Prim Sch EH14	40	AU19
Hailesland Rd EH14	40	AU18
Hailes Pk EH13	50	AV20
Hailes St EH3	6	BD13
Hailes Ter EH13	51	AW20
Hainburn Pk EH10	52	BB22
Hallcroft Cl (Ratho), Newbr. EH28	37	AE17
Hallcroft Cres (Ratho), Newbr. EH28	37	AE17
Hallcroft Gdns (Ratho), Newbr. EH28	37	AE17
Hallcroft Grn (Ratho), Newbr. EH28	37	AE17
Hallcroft Neuk (Ratho), Newbr. EH28	37	AE17
Hallcroft Pk (Ratho), Newbr. EH28	37	AE17
Hallcroft Ri (Ratho), Newbr. EH28	37	AE17
Hallhead Rd EH16	43	BH17
Hall Ter EH12	24	AU13
Hallyards Rd, K'lis. EH29	20	AD11
Hallyards Rd, Newbr. EH28	37	AF13
Halmyre St EH6	27	BH8
Hamburgh Pl EH6 1	15	BG5
Hamilton Cres (Newt.), Dalk. EH22	65	BX29
Hamilton Dr EH15	29	BP12
Hamilton Dr W EH15	29	BP12
Hamilton Gdns EH15	29	BP12
Hamilton Gro EH15	29	BP12
Hamilton Pk EH15	29	BP11
Hamilton Pl EH3	26	BD9
Hamilton's Cl, S Q'fry EH30 1	9	AE2
Hamilton's Folly Ms EH8 5	7	BG13
Hamilton Ter EH15	29	BQ11
Hamilton Wynd EH6	15	BG5
Hammermen's Entry EH8	7	BG11
Hampton Pl EH12 4	26	BA12
Hampton Ter EH12	26	BA12
Hanover St EH2	6	BE10
Harbour La, S Q'fry EH30 5	8	AD2
Harbour Pl EH15 13	29	BQ10
Harbour Rd EH15	29	BQ10
Harbour Rd, Muss. EH21	31	BW13
Harbour Vw, Muss. EH21	31	BX13
Hardengreen Business Pk, Dalk. EH22	56	BU26
Hardengreen Ind Est, Dalk. EH22	56	BU26
Hardengreen Junct, Dalk. EH22	56	BU28
Hardengreen La, Dalk. EH22	56	BU27
Harden Pl EH11	42	BB14
Hardwell Cl EH8	7	BG13
Harelaw, Dalk. EH22	46	BT19
Harelaw Rd EH13	51	AX21
Hares Cl (Cock.), Pres. EH32	19	CL7
Harewood Cres EH16	29	BN15
Harewood Dr EH16	29	BN15
Harewood Rd EH16	28	BM15
Harkenburn Gdns, Pen. EH26	68	AY37
Harkness Cres, Tran. EH33	35	CM13
Harlaw Bk, Bal. EH14	58	AL26
Harlaw Gait, Bal. EH14	58	AM26
Harlaw Gro, Pen. EH26	68	AZ38
Harlaw Hill, Pres. EH32	18	CH9
Harlawhill Gdns, Pres. EH32	18	CH10
Harlaw March, Bal. EH14	58	AM27
Harlaw Rd, Bal. EH14	59	AR25
Harmeny Sch EH14	58	AM27
Harmony Ct, Bonny. EH19	56	BT28
Harmony Cres, Bonny. EH19	56	BT28
Harmony St, Bonny. EH19	56	BT28
Harmony Wk, Bonny. EH19	56	BT28
Harnes Ct, Lnhd EH20 2	62	BL28
Harper's Brae, Pen. EH26	69	BD37
Harrismith Pl EH7	16	BJ9
Harrison Gdns EH11	42	BA15
Harrison La EH11	42	BB14
Harrison Pl EH11	42	BA15
Harrison Rd EH11	42	BA14
Hartington Gdns EH10	42	BC14
Hartington Pl EH10	42	BC14
Hart St EH1	27	BF9
Hart St La EH1	27	BF9
Harvest Dr, Newbr. EH28	36	AD14
Harvesters Way EH14	40	AT19
Harvest Rd, Newbr. EH28	36	AD14
Harvieston Vil, Gore. EH23 1	70	BZ36
Hatton Pl EH9	43	BF14
Haugh Pk EH14	41	AW17
Haugh St EH4	26	BD9
Hawes Brae, S Q'fry EH30	9	AF2
Hawes Pier, S Q'fry EH30	9	AF1
Hawkhead Cres EH16	44	BJ19
Hawkhead Gro EH16	44	BJ19
Hawkhill EH7	16	BK8
Hawkhill Av EH7	16	BJ8
Hawkhill Cl EH7	16	BJ8
Hawkhill Ct EH7	16	BK8
Hawkins Ter, Pen. EH26	66	BD34
Hawthorn (Cock.), Pres. EH32 1	18	CK7
Hawthorn Bk, S Q'fry EH30	8	AD2
Hawthornbank La EH4	6	BC11
Hawthornbank Pl EH6	15	BG5
Hawthornbank Ter EH6 2	15	BG5

Name	Page	Grid
Hawthorn Bldgs EH4 2	26	BB11
Hawthorn Cres (Mayf.), Dalk. EH22	57	BZ27
Hawthornden Av, Bonny. EH19	63	BQ29
Hawthornden Gdns, Bonny. EH19	63	BQ28
Hawthornden Pl EH7	27	BG8
Hawthornden Prim Sch EH19	63	BP29
Hawthorn Gdns, Lnhd EH20	54	BK26
Hawthorn Pl EH17	45	BN21
Hawthorn Rd, Pres. EH32	18	CK10
Hawthorn Ter EH4 5	6	BC11
Hawthorn Ter (Cock.), Pres. EH32	18	CK8
Hawthornvale EH6	15	BF5
Hay Av EH16	29	BP15
Hay Dr EH16	29	BQ15
Hayfield EH12	23	AQ11
Hay Gdns EH16	29	BP14
Haymarket EH12	6	BC12
Haymarket Sta EH12	26	BB12
Haymarket Ter EH12	26	BB12
Haymarket Yards EH12	26	BB12
Hay Rd EH16	29	BP15
Hay Ter EH16	29	BP15
Hazelbank Ter EH11	42	BA15
Hazeldean Ter EH16	44	BK18
Hazel Dr, Bonny. EH19	63	BR29
Hazel La, Lnhd EH20	61	BG28
Hazelwood Gro EH16	44	BL17
Headrigg Row EH16	44	BK18
Hedge Row, Lnhd EH20	61	BG28
Henderland Rd EH12	25	AZ12
Henderson Gdns EH6 4	15	BH6
Henderson Gdns, Tran. EH33	35	CM13
Henderson Pl EH3	27	BE9
Henderson Pl La EH3	26	BD9
Henderson Row EH3	26	BD9
Henderson St EH6	15	BH6
Henderson Ter EH11	42	BB14
Henry Ross Pl, S Q'fry EH30	8	AD2
Hepburn Dr, Dalk. EH22	57	BY25
Hercus Ln, Muss. EH21	31	BX13
Herd Ter, Lnhd EH20	62	BJ28
Heriot Br EH1	6	BE12
Heriot Cross EH1 1	6	BE12
Heriot Hill Ter EH7	27	BE8
Heriot Pl EH3	6	BE12
Heriot Row EH3	6	BD10
Heriot-Watt Research Pk (Ricc.), Currie EH14	49	AN19
Heriot-Watt Uni (Edinburgh Campus) EH14	49	AP20
Hermand Cres EH11	42	BA15
Hermand St EH11	41	AZ15
Hermand Ter EH11	41	AZ15
Hermiston Ct EH11	40	AT17
Hermiston Gait Retail Park EH11	39	AQ17
Hermiston Ho Rd EH12	38	AM17
Hermiston Ho Rd, Currie EH14	39	AN18
Hermiston Junct EH12	39	AQ16
Hermitage Dr EH10	42	BD18
Hermitage Gdns EH10	42	BD18
Hermitage Golf Course EH10	43	BE18
Hermitage Pk EH6	16	BK8
Hermitage Pk Gro EH6	16	BK8
Hermitage Pk Lea EH6	16	BK8
Hermitage Pk Prim Sch EH6	16	BK8
Hermitage Pk S EH6	16	BK8
Hermitage Pl EH6	16	BJ7
Hermitage Ter EH10	42	BD17
Hermits Cft EH8	7	BH13
Heugh, The, Tran. EH33	35	CL12
Higginson Ln (Mayf.), Dalk. EH22	71	CA30
High Buckstone EH10	53	BE21
Highlea Circle, Bal. EH14	58	AK28
Highlea Gro, Bal. EH14	58	AK27
High Pk Ri, Pen. EH26	69	BB39
High Riggs EH3	6	BE12
High Sch Yards EH1	7	BG12
High St EH1	7	BF11
High St, Bonny. EH19	55	BR27
High St, Dalk. EH22	57	BW24
High St, K'lis. EH29	20	AD10
High St, Lass. EH18	55	BQ26
High St, Lnhd EH20	54	BL27
High St, Muss. EH21	31	BY13
High St, Pen. EH26	69	BB39
High St, Pres. EH32	18	CG10
High St (Cock.), Pres. EH32	19	CL7
High St, S Q'fry EH30	8	AD2
High St, Tran. EH33	35	CM13
Highway, The EH8	29	BN11
Hillcoat Ln EH15 4	29	BQ10
Hillcoat Pl EH15 5	29	BQ10
Hill Ct, S Q'fry EH30 2	8	AD2
HILLEND	52	BD25
Hillend EH10	53	BE25
Hillend Pl EH8 10	28	BL10
Hillhead, Bonny. EH19	55	BR27
Hillhead Ct, Bonny. EH19	55	BR27
Hillhouse Rd EH4	24	AV8
Hillpark Av EH4	24	AV8
Hillpark Brae EH4	24	AV10
Hillpark Ct EH4	24	AV8
Hillpark Cres EH4	24	AV9
Hillpark Dr EH4	24	AV8
Hillpark Gdns EH4	24	AV9
Hillpark Grn EH4	24	AV9
Hillpark Gro EH4	24	AV9
Hillpark Ln EH4	25	AW9
Hillpark Rd EH4	24	AV9
Hillpark Ter EH4	24	AV9
Hillpark Way EH4	25	AW9
Hillpark Wd EH4	25	AW9
Hill Pl EH8	7	BG12
Hill Pl (Mayf.), Dalk. EH22	71	CA30
HILLSIDE	27	BH9
Hillside Cres EH7	27	BG9
Hillside Cres N, Gore. EH23	70	BZ35
Hillside Cres S, Gore. EH23	70	BZ35
Hillside Rd (Craig.), S Q'fry EH30	22	AM7
Hillside St EH7	27	BH9
Hillside Ter (Craig.), S Q'fry EH30	10	AM6
Hill Sq EH8	7	BG12
Hill St EH2	6	BD10
Hill St La N EH2	6	BD10
Hill St La S EH2	6	BE11
Hilltown Ter (Wool.), Dalk. EH22	46	BS18
Hillview EH4	25	AX9
Hillview Cotts (Ratho), Newbr. EH28	37	AF17
Hillview Cres EH12	24	AT12
Hillview Dr EH12	24	AS12
Hillview Gdns, Lnhd EH20	61	BH28
Hillview Rd EH12	24	AS12
Hillview Ter EH12	24	AS12
Hillwood Av (Ratho Sta), Newbr. EH28	37	AE14
Hillwood Cres (Ratho Sta), Newbr. EH28	37	AE14
Hillwood Gdns (Ratho Sta), Newbr. EH28	37	AE13
Hillwood Pl, S Q'fry EH30 4	8	AD2
Hillwood Prim Sch EH28	37	AE14
Hillwood Ri (Ratho Sta), Newbr. EH28	37	AE14
Hillwood Rd (Ratho Sta), Newbr. EH28	37	AE14
Hillwood Ter (Ratho Sta), Newbr. EH28	37	AE14
Hilton Edinburgh Airport Hotel EH28	22	AJ12
Hilton Edinburgh Grosvenor EH12	6	BC12
HM Prison Edinburgh EH11	41	AW16
Hogarth Av, Gore. EH23	70	BX33
Holiday Inn Edinburgh EH12	24	AV13
Holiday Inn Edinburgh North EH4	25	AY10
Holiday Inn Express Edinburgh EH1	7	BG10
Holiday Inn Express Edinburgh - Waterfront EH6	15	BG5
Hollybank (Mayf.), Dalk. EH22	71	CA28
Hollybank Ter EH11	42	BA15
Holly Ter, Bonny. EH19	63	BR29
Holly Wk, Lnhd EH20	61	BG28
Holy Cross RC Prim Sch EH6	15	BE6
Holyrood Business Pk EH16	28	BM15
Holyrood Ct EH8	7	BH11
Holyrood Park EH8	7	BH11
Holyrood Pk EH8	28	BJ11
Holyrood Pk Rd EH16	43	BH14
Holyrood RC High Sch EH15	28	BM13
Holyrood Rd EH8	7	BG11
Home St EH3	6	BD13
HOPEFIELD	63	BR29
Hopefield Pk, Bonny. EH19	63	BQ29
Hopefield Pl, Bonny. EH19	63	BQ29
Hopefield Prim Sch EH19	63	BQ29
Hopefield Ter EH6	15	BG5
Hopefield Ter, Bonny. EH19	63	BQ29
Hope La EH15	29	BR12
Hope La N EH15	29	BR11
Hope Pk Cres EH8	7	BG13
Hope Pk Sq EH8 1	7	BG13
Hope Pk Ter EH8	7	BG13
Hope Pl, Muss. EH21	32	CB13
Hope Pl, Tran. EH33 3	35	CL12
Hope St EH2	6	BD11
Hope St, S Q'fry EH30	8	AD3
Hope St La EH2	6	BD11
Hope Ter EH9	43	BE15
Hopetoun Cres EH7	27	BG9
Hopetoun Rd, S Q'fry EH30	8	AD2
Hopetoun St EH7	27	BG9
Horne Ter EH11	6	BC13
Horsburgh Bk, Bal. EH14	48	AL24
Horsburgh Gdns, Bal. EH14	48	AL24
Horsburgh Gro, Bal. EH14	48	AL24
Horse Wynd EH8	7	BH11
Hoseason Gdns EH4	24	AT10
Hosie Rigg EH15	29	BR14
House o'Hill Av EH4	25	AW8
House o'Hill Brae EH4	25	AW8
House o'Hill Cres EH4	25	AW8
House o'Hill Gdns EH4	25	AX8
House o'Hill Grn EH4	25	AW8
House o'Hill Gro EH4	25	AW8
House o'Hill Pl EH4	25	AW8
House o'Hill Rd EH4	25	AW8
House o'Hill Row EH4	25	AX8
House o'Hill Ter EH4	25	AX9
Howard Pl EH3	27	BE8
Howard St EH3	27	BE8
Howden Hall Ct EH16	53	BH21
Howden Hall Cres EH16	53	BH22
Howden Hall Dr EH16	53	BH21
Howden Hall Gdns EH16	44	BJ21
Howden Hall Ln EH16	53	BH21
Howden Hall Pk EH16	53	BH21
Howden Hall Rd EH16	54	BJ22
Howden Hall Way EH16	54	BJ22
Howden St EH8	7	BG12
Howe Dean EH16	43	BG19
Howe Pk EH10	52	BB22
Howe St EH3	6	BE10
Hub, The EH1	6	BE12
Hughes Cres (Mayf.), Dalk. EH22	71	CB29
Hugh Miller Pl EH3	26	BD9
Hugh Russell Pl, S Q'fry EH30	8	AD3
Huly Hill Rd, Newbr. EH28	36	AC14

Humbie Rd, K'lis. EH29 20 AC9
Hungerage Sq, Tran. EH33 35 CM14
Hunt Cl, Dalk. EH22 57 BW23
Hunter Av, Lnhd EH20 54 BM27
Hunter Ct, Lnhd EH20 54 BM27
Hunterfield Ct, Gore. EH23 70 BY35
Hunterfield Pk, Gore. EH23 70 BY34
Hunterfield Rd, Gore. EH23 70 BY34
Hunterfield Ter, Gore. EH23 70 BX34
Hunter's Cl EH1 13 6 BE12
Hunter's Hill, Pen. EH26 68 AZ37
Hunter Sq EH1 7 BF11
Hunter Sq, Gore. EH23 70 BZ35
Hunter's Tryst Prim Sch EH13 52 BB20
Hunter Ter, Bonny. EH19 63 BR28
Hunter Ter, Lnhd EH20 54 BM27
Huntingdon Pl EH7 27 BG9
Huntly St EH3 27 BE8
Hursted Av (Easth.), Dalk. EH22 57 BZ28
Hutchison Av EH14 41 AY16
Hutchison Cotts EH14 41 AY16
Hutchison Crossway EH14 41 AY15
Hutchison Gdns EH14 41 AY16
Hutchison Gro EH14 41 AZ16
Hutchison Ho EH14 41 AZ15
Hutchison Ln EH14 41 AY16
Hutchison Medway EH14 41 AZ15
Hutchison Pk EH14 41 AY15
Hutchison Pl EH14 41 AY16
Hutchison Rd EH14 41 AZ15
Hutchison Ter EH14 41 AY16
Hutchison Vw EH14 41 AY15
Hutton Cl EH8 7 BH11
Hutton Rd EH8 7 BH11
Hyvot Av EH17 44 BM21
Hyvot Bk Av EH17 45 BN21
Hyvot Ct EH17 54 BM22
Hyvot Gdns EH17 44 BM21
Hyvot Grn EH17 54 BM22
Hyvot Gro EH17 44 BM21
Hyvot Ln EH17 44 BM21
Hyvot Pk EH17 44 BM21
HYVOTS BANK 44 BL20
Hyvot Ter EH17 44 BM21
Hyvot Vw EH17 54 BM22

I
Ibis Edinburgh Centre Hotel EH1 7 BF11
Imperial Dock EH6 16 BJ4
Imrie Pl, Pen. EH26 69 BB38
INCH 44 BJ18
Inchcolm Ct EH4 13 AY6
Inchcolm Ter, S Q'fry EH30 8 AD3
Inchgarvie Ct EH4 13 AZ7
Inchgarvie Pk, S Q'fry EH30 8 AC2
Inchkeith Av, S Q'fry EH30 9 AE3
Inchkeith Ct EH7 27 BG8
Inchkeith Gro, Tran. EH33 35 CL12
Inchmickery Ct EH4 13 AW6
Inchview, Pres. EH32 18 CG10
Inchview Cres (Wall.), Muss. EH21 33 CE14
Inchview N, Pres. EH32 18 CG10
Inchview Rd (Wall.), Muss. EH21 33 CD14
Inchview Ter EH7 29 BP10
India Bldgs EH1 3 7 BF12
India Pl EH3 6 BD10
India St EH3 6 BD10
Industrial Rd EH6 16 BJ7
Industry Home EH6 1 15 BG6
Industry La EH6 15 BG6
Infirmary St EH1 7 BG12
Inglewood Pl EH16 44 BK19
Inglis Av (Port S.), Pres. EH32 19 CL7
Inglis Ct EH1 2 6 BE12
Inglis Fm (Cock.), Pres. EH32 19 CL7
Inglis Grn Gait EH14 41 AX17
Inglis Grn Rigg EH14 41 AX17
Inglis Grn Rd EH14 41 AX17

INGLISTON 21 AG12
Ingliston Rd (Inglis.), Newbr. EH28 37 AH13
Inkerman Ct, Pen. EH26 66 BC35
International Language Acad EH3 6 BC11
Inveralmond Dr EH4 11 AQ6
Inveralmond Gdns EH4 11 AQ6
Inveralmond Gro EH4 11 AQ6
Inveravon Rd, Lnhd EH20 54 BK26
Inveresk Ter, Muss. EH21 31 BY14
INVERESK 31 BZ15
Inveresk Brae, Muss. EH21 31 BZ14
Inveresk Est, The (Inv.), Muss. EH21 31 BZ15
Inveresk Gate (Inv.), Muss. EH21 2 31 BZ14
Inveresk Lodge Garden (NTS) EH21 31 BZ15
Inveresk Mills Ind Pk, Muss. EH21 31 BX14
Inveresk Rd, Muss. EH21 31 BY14
Inveresk Village Rd, Muss. EH21 31 BY14
INVERLEITH 14 BB7
Inverleith Av EH3 14 BD7
Inverleith Av S EH3 14 BD7
Inverleith Gdns EH3 14 BC7
Inverleith Gro EH3 26 BB8
Inverleith Pl EH3 14 BC7
Inverleith Pl La EH3 14 BD7
Inverleith Row EH3 14 BD7
Inverleith Ter EH3 26 BD8
Inverleith Ter La EH3 26 BD8
Iona St EH6 27 BH8
Iona St La EH6 27 BH8
Ironmills Rd, Dalk. EH22 56 BV24
Ivanhoe Cres EH16 44 BK18
Ivy Ter EH11 42 BA14

J
Jackson's Entry EH8 7 7 BH11
Jackson St, Pen. EH26 68 BA38
Jacobite Way, Pres. EH32 19 CL10
Jacobs Way, Gore. EH23 70 BY35
Jamaica Ms EH3 6 BD10
Jamaica St EH3 6 BD10
Jamaica St N La EH3 6 BD10
Jamaica St S La EH3 6 BD10
Jamaica St W EH3 2 6 BD10
James' Ct EH1 4 7 BF11
James Craig Wk EH1 7 BF10
James Gillespie's High Sch EH9 43 BE14
James Gillespie's Prim Sch EH9 43 BE14
James Lean Av, Dalk. EH22 57 BX24
James Leary Way, Bonny. EH19 56 BS27
Jameson Pl EH6 27 BH8
James St EH15 30 BS11
James St, Muss. EH21 31 BZ13
James St La EH15 30 BS11
Janefield EH17 54 BJ23
Jane St EH6 15 BH7
Jane Ter EH7 2 28 BJ10
Jarnac Ct, Dalk. EH22 5 57 BW24
Jawbone Wk EH3 7 BF13
Jean Armour Av EH16 44 BJ18
Jean Armour Dr, Dalk. EH22 57 BZ25
Jeanette Stewart Dr, Dalk. EH22 64 BV31
Jeffrey Av EH4 25 AX10
Jeffrey St EH1 7 BF11
Jenks Ln (Newt.), Dalk. EH22 64 BV30
Jessfield Ter EH6 15 BF5
Jewel, The EH15 29 BR14
Jewel & Esk Valley Coll (Eskbank Campus) EH22 56 BV26
Jewel & Esk Valley Coll (Milton Rd Campus) EH15 30 BT13

JOCK'S LODGE 28 BL10
John Bernard Way, Gore. EH23 1 70 BY37
John Cotton Business Cen EH7 16 BJ9
John Cres, Tran. EH33 35 CL13
John Humble St (Mayf.), Dalk. EH22 71 CA30
John Knox House EH1 12 7 BG11
John Knox Pl, Pen. EH26 69 BB38
John Mason Ct, S Q'fry EH30 9 AE3
John Moat Pl, Pres. EH32 18 CH10
John Muir Way, Muss. EH21 31 BY12
Johnnie Cope's Rd, Pres. EH32 34 CJ11
Johnnie Cope's Rd, Tran. EH33 34 CJ12
Johnsburn Grn, Bal. EH14 58 AK26
Johnsburn Haugh, Bal. EH14 58 AK26
Johnsburn Pk, Bal. EH14 58 AK27
Johnsburn Rd, Bal. EH14 58 AK26
John's La EH6 16 BJ6
John's Pl EH6 16 BJ7
Johnston Pl, Pen. EH26 66 BB35
Johnston Ter EH1 6 BE12
Johnston Ter (Port S.), Pres. EH32 19 CM7
John St EH15 30 BS11
John St, Pen. EH26 69 BB38
John St La EH15 30 BS11
John St La, Pen. EH26 68 BA38
John St La E EH15 30 BS11
John St La W EH15 30 BS11
JOPPA 30 BT12
Joppa Gdns EH15 30 BS12
Joppa Gro EH15 30 BS12
Joppa Pans EH15 30 BU12
Joppa Pk EH15 30 BS11
Joppa Rd EH15 30 BS12
Joppa Sta Pl EH15 30 BS12
Joppa Ter EH15 30 BS12
Jordan La EH10 42 BD16
Jubilee Cres, Gore. EH23 70 BY34
Jubilee Rd EH12 21 AH12
Junction Pl EH6 15 BH7
Junction Two Ind Est, Newbr. EH28 36 AB16
Juner Pl, Gore. EH23 70 BY34
Juniper Av, Jun. Grn EH14 50 AS21
Juniper Gdns, Jun. Grn EH14 50 AS21
JUNIPER GREEN 50 AS21
Juniper Grn Prim Sch EH14 50 AT21
Juniper Gro, Jun. Grn EH14 50 AS21
Juniper La, Jun. Grn EH14 1 50 AT21
Juniperlee, Jun. Grn EH14 50 AT21
Juniper Pk Rd, Jun. Grn EH14 50 AT21
Juniper Pl, Jun. Grn EH14 50 AS22
Juniper Ter, Jun. Grn EH14 50 AS21
Jurys Inn Edinburgh Hotel EH1 7 BG11

K
Kaimes Rd EH12 24 AU12
Kaimes Sch EH16 44 BL21
Kaimes Vw (Dand.), Dalk. EH22 45 BR20
Katesmill Rd EH14 41 AX19
Kay Gdns (Cock.), Pres. EH32 19 CL7
Kedslie Pl EH16 53 BH20
Kedslie Rd EH16 53 BH20
Keir Hardie Dr (Mayf.), Dalk. EH22 71 CA30
Keir St EH3 6 BE12
Keith Cres EH4 25 AX10
Keith Row EH4 25 AY10
Keith Ter EH4 25 AY10

Kekewich Av EH7	17	BP9
Kemp Pl EH3	26	BD9
Kemp's End, Tran. EH33	35	CL15
Kempston Pl, S Q'fry EH30	9	AE3
Kenilworth Dr EH16	44	BJ19
Kenmure Av EH8	28	BL11
Kennedy Cres, Tran. EH33	35	CM12
Kennington Av, Lnhd EH20	62	BK28
Kennington Ter, Lnhd EH20	54	BK27
Kentigern Mall, Pen. EH26	69	BB38
Kerr Av, Dalk. EH22	56	BU25
Kerr-McNeill Service Rd, Tran. EH33 3	35	CL14
Kerr Rd, Tran. EH33	35	CL13
Kerr St EH3	26	BD9
Kerr's Wynd, Muss. EH21	31	BZ13
Kerr Way, Tran. EH33 5	35	CL14
Kevock Rd, Lass. EH18	55	BP27
Kevock Vale Caravan Pk, Lass.	55	BQ27
Kew Ter EH12	26	BA12
Kilchurn Ct EH12 3	23	AQ12
Kilgraston Ct EH9	43	BE15
Kilgraston Rd EH9	43	BF15
Kilmaurs Rd EH16	28	BJ15
Kilmaurs Ter EH16	28	BJ15
Kilncroftside EH14	41	AX17
Kilngate Brae EH17	54	BM22
Kilwinning Pl, Muss. EH21	31	BY13
Kilwinning St, Muss. EH21	31	BZ13
Kilwinning Ter, Muss. EH21	31	BZ13
Kincaid's Ct EH1	7	BF12
Kinellan Gdns EH12	25	AY12
Kinellan Rd EH12	25	AY11
King Edwards Way, K'lis. EH29	20	AC10
King George V Pk, Bonny. EH19	63	BQ28
Kinghorn Pl EH6	15	BF6
King Malcolm Cl EH10	53	BF22
Kings Acre Golf Course EH18	55	BQ24
King's Br EH3	6	BE12
King's Bldgs EH9	43	BH17
Kingsburgh Rd EH12	25	AY12
King's Cramond EH4	11	AR6
Kings Haugh EH16	28	BL15
Kingsinch Sch EH16	44	BJ17
KINGSKNOWE	40	AV18
Kingsknowe Av EH14	41	AW18
Kingsknowe Ct EH14	40	AV18
Kingsknowe Cres EH14	41	AW18
Kingsknowe Dr EH14	41	AW18
Kingsknowe Gdns EH14	41	AW19
Kingsknowe Golf Course EH14	40	AV19
Kingsknowe Gro EH14	41	AW19
Kingsknowe Pk EH14	41	AW19
Kingsknowe Pl EH14	40	AV18
Kingsknowe Rd N EH14	41	AW17
Kingsknowe Rd S EH14	41	AW18
Kingsknowe Sta EH14	41	AW18
Kingsknowe Ter EH14	41	AW18
Kingslaw Ct, Tran. EH33	35	CM12
King's Meadow EH16	28	BK15
King's Pk Prim Sch EH22	57	BW25
King's Pl EH15	17	BQ9
King's Rd EH15	29	BQ10
King's Rd, Tran. EH33	35	CL14
King's Stables La EH1	6	BE12
King's Stables Rd EH1	6	BE12
King's Ter EH15	29	BQ10
Kings Theatre EH3	6	BD13
Kingston Av EH16	44	BL18
King St EH6	15	BH6
King St, Muss. EH21	31	BZ14
Kinleith Ind Est, Currie EH14	49	AR23
Kinnear Rd EH3	14	BB7
Kippielaw Dr (Easth.), Dalk. EH22	57	BY25
Kippielaw Gdns (Easth.), Dalk. EH22	57	BY26
Kippielaw Medway (Easth.), Dalk. EH22	57	BY26
Kippielaw Pk (Mayf.), Dalk. EH22	57	BZ27
Kippielaw Rd (Easth.), Dalk. EH22	57	BY26
Kippielaw Steading, Dalk. EH22	57	BY26
Kippielaw Wk (Easth.), Dalk. EH22	57	BY25
Kirk Brae EH16	44	BJ18
Kirk Cramond EH4	12	AS5
Kirkgate EH6	16	BJ6
Kirkgate EH16	44	BJ20
Kirkgate, Currie EH14	49	AQ23
KIRKHILL	69	BC38
Kirkhill Ct, Gore. EH23	70	BY36
Kirkhill Dr EH16	28	BJ15
Kirkhill Gdns EH16	28	BJ14
Kirkhill Gdns, Pen. EH26	69	BB38
Kirkhill Rd EH16	28	BJ14
Kirkhill Rd, Pen. EH26	69	BB38
Kirkhill Ter EH16	28	BJ14
Kirkhill Ter, Gore. EH23	65	BW34
Kirkhill Way, Pen. EH26	69	BB38
Kirklands EH12	40	AT15
Kirklands, Pen. EH26	68	BA38
Kirklands Pk Cres, K'lis. EH29	20	AB9
Kirklands Pk Gdns, K'lis. EH29	20	AB9
Kirklands Pk Gro, K'lis. EH29	20	AB9
Kirklands Pk Rigg, K'lis. EH29	20	AC9
Kirklands Pk St, K'lis. EH29	20	AB9
KIRKLISTON	20	AD10
Kirkliston Prim Sch EH29	20	AC9
Kirkliston Rd, Newbr. EH28	20	AB12
Kirkliston Rd, S Q'fry EH30	8	AD3
Kirk Ln EH12	24	AU13
Kirk Pk EH16	44	BJ19
Kirk St EH6	15	BH7
Kirk St, Pres. EH32	18	CH10
Kirkstyle Gdns, K'lis. EH29	20	AD10
Kirkton Bk, Pen. EH26	68	AZ38
Kirk Vw, Pen. EH26	69	BB39
Kirkwood Pl EH7 3	28	BJ10
Kirk Wynd, Pres. EH32	18	CH9
Kisimul Ct EH12 1	23	AR12
Kittle Yards EH9	43	BG14
Klondyke St (Newcr.), Muss. EH21	30	BU15
Klondyke Way (Newcr.), Muss. EH21	30	BT15
Knightslaw Pl, Pen. EH26	68	AZ38
Knowetop Pl, Ros. EH25	67	BH32
Komarom Pl, Dalk. EH22	57	BZ24
Kyle Pl EH7	7	BH10

L		
Laburnum Arch Ct, Pres. EH32	18	CH10
Laburnum Av (Port S.), Pres. EH32	19	CM7
Laburnum Pl (Mayf.), Dalk. EH22	71	CA29
Lade, The, Bal. EH14	58	AM27
Ladehead EH6	15	BF7
Ladiemeadow EH12	40	AU14
Lady Brae, Gore. EH23	70	BZ36
Lady Brae Pl, Gore. EH23	70	CA35
Ladycroft, Bal. EH14	58	AL26
Lady Emily Way, Gore. EH23	70	BY35
Lady Lawson St EH3	6	BE12
Lady Menzies Pl EH7	28	BJ10
Lady Nairne Cres EH8	28	BM12
Lady Nairne Gro EH8	28	BM12
Lady Nairne Ln EH8	28	BM12
Lady Nairne Pl EH8	28	BM12
Lady Rd EH16	44	BJ16
Lady Rd Pl (Newt.), Dalk. EH22 1	65	BX29
Ladysmith Rd EH9	43	BF17

Lady Stair's Cl EH1 6	7	BF11
Lady Victoria Business Cen (Newt.), Dalk. EH22	65	BW32
Ladywell, Muss. EH21	31	BY13
Ladywell Av EH12	24	AT13
Ladywell Ct EH12	24	AT13
Ladywell Gdns EH12	24	AT13
Ladywell Ho EH12	24	AT13
Ladywell Rd EH12	24	AS13
Ladywell Way, Muss. EH21	31	BY13
LADYWOOD	69	BC37
Ladywood Prim Sch EH26	69	BC36
Lady Wynd EH1	6	BE12
Laichfield EH14	41	AX16
Laichpark Ln EH14 1	41	AX16
Laichpark Pl EH14	41	AX16
Laichpark Rd EH14	41	AX16
Laing Ter EH15	30	BS11
Laing Ter, Pen. EH26	69	BB36
Laird Ter, Bonny. EH19	64	BS29
Lamb's Cl EH8 2	7	BG13
Lamb's Ct EH6 1	15	BE4
Lamb's Pend, Pen. EH26	69	BB39
Lammermoor Gdns, Tran. EH33	34	CK13
Lammermoor Ter EH16	44	BL18
Lammermoor Ter, Tran. EH33	34	CK13
Lammerview, Tran. EH33	35	CL14
Lampacre Rd EH12	40	AU14
Lanark Rd EH13	50	AV20
Lanark Rd EH14	41	AW19
Lanark Rd, Jun. Grn EH14	50	AT22
Lanark Rd W, Bal. EH14	58	AJ25
Lanark Rd W, Currie EH14	49	AQ23
Langlaw Prim Sch EH22	57	BZ27
Langlaw Rd, Dalk. EH22	57	BZ27
Lang Linn Path EH10	43	BE18
Lang Ln EH17	54	BK25
Lang Ln, Lnhd EH20	54	BK25
Langton Rd EH9	43	BG16
Lansbury Ct, Dalk. EH22	57	BW24
Lansdowne Cres EH12	26	BB12
Lapicide Pl EH6	15	BG6
Larbourfield EH11	40	AT18
Larch Cres (Mayf.), Dalk. EH22	71	CB29
Larchfield, Bal. EH14	58	AL25
Larchfield Neuk, Bal. EH14	58	AL25
Largo Pl EH6	15	BG6
Larkfield Dr, Dalk. EH22	56	BT26
Larkfield Rd, Dalk. EH22	56	BU25
Laserquest EH11	26	BB12
Lasswade Bk EH17	54	BL22
Lasswade Gro EH17	54	BL22
Lasswade High Sch Cen EH19	63	BQ28
Lasswade Junct EH15	55	BN24
Lasswade Prim Sch EH19	56	BS27
Lasswade Rd EH16	44	BK20
Lasswade Rd EH17	44	BL21
Lasswade Rd, Dalk. EH22	56	BT25
Lasswade Rd, Lass. EH18	55	BP26
Lasswade Rd, Lnhd EH20	54	BM27
Latch Pk EH13	51	AZ20
Lauderdale St EH9	43	BE14
Lauder Ln EH9	43	BG15
Lauder Rd EH9	43	BF14
Lauder Rd, Dalk. EH22	57	BX25
Laurel Bk, Dalk. EH22	57	BY25
Laurelbank Pl (Mayf.), Dalk. EH22 1	71	CA29
Laurelbank Rd (Mayf.), Dalk. EH22	71	CA29
Laurel Ter EH11 1	42	BA14
Laurie St EH6	16	BJ7
Lauriston Castle EH4	12	AU6
Lauriston Fm Rd EH4	12	AU7
Lauriston Gdns EH3	6	BE12
Lauriston Pk EH3	6	BE12
Lauriston Pl EH3	6	BD13
Lauriston St EH3	6	BE12
Lauriston Ter EH3	6	BE12
Laverockbank Av EH5	15	BE5
Laverockbank Cres EH5	15	BE5
Laverockbank Gdns EH5	15	BE5

Laverockbank Gro EH5	15	BE5
Laverockbank Rd EH5	15	BE5
Laverockbank Ter EH5	15	BE5
Laverockdale Cres EH13	51	AX21
Laverockdale Ln EH13	51	AX22
Laverockdale Pk EH13	51	AX22
Laverock Dr, Pen. EH26	68	AZ36
Lawers Sq, Pen. EH26	69	BC36
Lawfield Rd (Mayf.), Dalk. EH22	57	BZ28
Lawhead Pl, Pen. EH26	68	AY38
Lawnmarket EH1	7	BF11
Law Pl EH15 10	29	BQ10
Lawrie Dr, Pen. EH26	68	BA36
Lawrie Ter, Lnhd EH20	62	BK28
Lawson Cres, S Q'fry EH30	9	AE3
Leadervale Rd EH16	43	BH19
Leadervale Ter EH16	43	BH19
Leamington La EH10	42	BD14
Leamington Pl EH10	6	BD13
Leamington Rd EH3	6	BC13
Leamington Ter EH10	6	BD13
Learmonth Av EH4	26	BB9
Learmonth Ct EH4	26	BB10
Learmonth Cres EH4	26	BB10
Learmonth Gdns EH4	26	BB10
Learmonth Gdns La EH4	26	BB10
Learmonth Gdns Ms EH4	26	BC9
Learmonth Gro EH4	26	BB9
Learmonth Hotel EH4	26	BB10
Learmonth Pk EH4	26	BB9
Learmonth Pl EH4	26	BB9
Learmonth Ter EH4	26	BB10
Learmonth Ter La EH4	26	BB10
Learmonth Vw EH4 1	6	BC10
Ledi Ter, Pen. EH26	69	BC36
Lee Cres EH15	29	BQ11
Leighton Cres (Easth.), Dalk. EH22	57	BY28
LEITH	16	BJ6
Leith Acad EH6	16	BJ8
Leith Docks EH6	15	BH4
Leith Links EH6	16	BJ7
Leith Prim Sch EH6	16	BJ7
Leith St EH1	7	BF10
Leith Wk EH6	27	BH8
Leith Wk EH7	27	BG9
Leith Wk Prim Sch EH7	27	BG9
Lennel Av EH12	25	AY11
Lennie Cotts EH12	22	AM11
Lennox Row EH5	14	BD5
Lennox St EH4	6	BC10
Lennox St La EH4	6	BC10
Lennymuir EH12	22	AK10
Leopold Pl EH7	27	BG9
Leslie Pl EH4	26	BC9
Leven Cl EH3 1	6	BD13
LEVENHALL	32	CC13
Leven St EH3	6	BD13
Leven Ter EH3	6	BE13
Lewis Ter EH11 12	6	BC12
Lewisvale Av, Muss. EH21	32	CA14
Lewisvale Ct, Muss. EH21	32	CA14
Leyden Pk, Bonny. EH19	55	BR27
Leyden Pl, Bonny. EH19 1	63	BR28
LIBERTON	44	BJ19
Liberton Brae EH16	44	BJ19
Liberton Dr EH16	43	BH19
Liberton Gdns EH16	44	BJ21
Liberton Golf Course EH16	44	BL18
Liberton High Sch EH17	44	BL19
Liberton Hosp EH16	44	BK20
Liberton Pl EH16	44	BJ20
Liberton Prim Sch EH16	44	BK17
Liberton Rd EH16	44	BJ18
Liberton Twr La EH16	43	BG19
Liddesdale Pl EH3	26	BD8
Lidgate Steps (Ratho), Newbr. EH28	37	AF17
Lilac Av (Mayf.), Dalk. EH22	71	CB29
Lilyhill Ter EH8	28	BL10
Lily Ter EH11 1	42	BA15
Limefield EH17	55	BN22
Lime Gro (Mayf.), Dalk. EH22	71	CA29
Lime Pl, Bonny. EH19	63	BR29
Limes, The EH10	42	BC15
Lindean Pl EH6	16	BK7
Linden Pl, Lnhd EH20 3	54	BM27
Lindores Dr, Tran. EH33	35	CM13
Lindsay Pl EH6	15	BG5
Lindsay Rd EH6	15	BG5
Lindsay St EH6	15	BG5
Lingerwood Cotts (Newt.), Dalk. EH22 1	65	BX31
Lingerwood Rd (Newt.), Dalk. EH22	65	BW31
Lingerwood Wk (Newt.), Dalk. EH22	65	BX31
Linkfield Ct, Muss. EH21 1	32	CA13
Linkfield Rd, Muss. EH21	31	BZ13
Links Av, Muss. EH21	31	BX12
Links Ct (Port S.), Pres. EH32	19	CM7
Links Gdns EH6	16	BK6
Links Gdns La EH6	16	BK6
Links La EH6 3	16	BJ6
Links Pl EH6	16	BJ6
Links Pl (Port S.), Pres. EH32	19	CN7
Links Rd (Port S.), Pres. EH32	19	CN7
Links St, Muss. EH21	31	BY13
Links Vw, Muss. EH21	31	BX12
Links Vw (Port S.), Pres. EH32	19	CN7
Linksview Ho EH6	16	BJ6
Links Wk (Port S.), Pres. EH32	19	CN7
Linn Mill, S Q'fry EH30	8	AA2
Linty La, Pen. EH26	68	AZ37
Lismore Av EH8	28	BL10
Lismore Cres EH8	28	BL10
Lismore Prim Sch EH15	29	BP14
Liston Dr, K'lis. EH29	20	AC9
Liston Pl, K'lis. EH29	20	AC9
Liston Rd, K'lis. EH29	20	AC10
Little Acre, Dalk. EH22	57	BZ27
Little France Cres EH16	44	BM18
Little France Dr EH16	45	BN18
Little France Ho EH17	44	BM19
Little France Mills EH16	44	BM18
Littlejohn Av EH10	42	BB19
Littlejohn Rd EH10	42	BA19
Littlejohn Wynd EH10	42	BB19
Little King St EH1	7	BF10
Little Rd EH16	44	BJ20
Livesey Ter, Pen. EH26	66	BC35
Livingstone Pl EH9	43	BF14
Lixmount Av EH5	15	BE5
Lixmount Gdns EH5	15	BE5
Loan, The, Lnhd EH20	62	BK28
Loan, The, S Q'fry EH30	8	AD2
LOANBURN	68	BA38
Loanburn, Pen. EH26	68	BA38
Loanburn Av, Pen. EH26	69	BB37
LOANHEAD	54	BM26
Loanhead Hosp EH20	54	BM27
Loanhead Prim Sch EH20	54	BL27
Loanhead Rd (Strait.), Lnhd EH20	54	BJ25
Loaning Cres EH7	16	BM9
Loaning Mills EH7	16	BL9
Loaning Rd EH7	16	BL9
LOANSTONE	69	BD38
Lochend (Ratho Sta), Newbr. EH28	36	AD13
Lochend Av EH7	16	BK9
Lochend Castle Barns EH7	16	BK9
Lochend Cl EH8	7	BH11
Lochend Cres EH7	16	BL9
Lochend Dr EH7	16	BK9
Lochend Gdns EH7	16	BK9
Lochend Gro EH7	16	BL9
Lochend Ind Est, Newbr. EH28	36	AD14
Lochend Pk EH7	16	BK9
Lochend Quad EH7	16	BL9
Lochend Rd EH6	16	BK8
Lochend Rd EH7	16	BK8
Lochend Rd, K'lis. EH29	20	AC11
Lochend Rd, Newbr. EH28	20	AC12
Lochend Rd N, Muss. EH21	31	BX13
Lochend Rd S EH7	16	BK9
Lochend Rd S, Muss. EH21	31	BX13
Lochend Sq EH7	16	BK9
Lochinvar Dr EH5	14	BB4
Loch Ness Discovery Centre EH1 8	7	BF11
Loch Pl, S Q'fry EH30	8	AD2
Lochrin Bldgs EH3	6	BD13
Lochrin Pl EH3	6	BD13
Lochrin Ter EH3 3	6	BD13
Loch Rd EH4	25	AW9
Loch Rd, S Q'fry EH30	8	AD2
Loch Rd, Tran. EH33	35	CM13
Lochside Av EH12	39	AP14
Lochside Ct EH12	39	AQ15
Lochside Cres EH12	39	AP14
Lochside Pl EH12	39	AP15
Lochside Vw EH12	39	AP14
Lochside Way EH12	39	AQ15
Loch Sq, Tran. EH33	35	CM13
Lochview Ct EH8	7	BH11
Lockerby Cotts EH16	44	BL21
Lockerby Cres EH16	44	BL21
Lockerby Gro EH16	44	BL21
Lockharton Av EH14	41	AZ17
Lockharton Cres EH14	41	AZ17
Lockharton Gdns EH14	42	BA16
Lockhart Ter, Ros. EH25	67	BH32
Loganlea Av EH7	16	BM9
Loganlea Dr EH7	28	BL10
Loganlea Gdns EH7	16	BL9
Loganlea La EH7	16	BM9
Loganlea Pl EH7	28	BM10
Loganlea Rd EH7	16	BM9
Loganlea Ter EH7	16	BM9
Logan St EH3	27	BE9
Logie Grn Gdns EH7	27	BE8
Logie Grn Ln EH7	27	BE8
Logie Grn Rd EH7	27	BE8
Logie Mill EH7	27	BE8
Lomond Rd EH5	14	BD5
Lomond Vale, Pen. EH26	69	BC36
Lomond Wk, Lnhd EH20	61	BH26
London Rd EH7	7	BG10
London Rd EH8	28	BL10
London Rd, Dalk. EH22	57	BW24
London St EH3	27	BF9
Long Craig Rigg EH5	13	AY4
Long Craig Rd EH5	13	AY4
Long Craigs (Port S.), Pres. EH32	19	CN8
Long Crook, S Q'fry EH30	8	AC3
Long Dalmahoy Rd, Bal. EH14	48	AL22
Longdykes Rd, Pres. EH32	18	CK9
Longformacus Rd EH16	44	BJ20
LONGSTONE	41	AW17
Longstone Av EH14	41	AW17
Longstone Cotts EH14 1	41	AW17
Longstone Cres EH14	41	AW17
Longstone Gdns EH14	40	AV16
Longstone Gro EH14	41	AW17
Longstone Pk EH14	41	AW17
Longstone Pl EH14	41	AW17
Longstone Prim Sch EH14	41	AW18
Longstone Rd EH14	41	AW17
Longstone St EH14	41	AW17
Longstone Ter EH14	40	AV16
Longstone Vw EH14	40	AV16
Lonsdale Ter EH3	6	BE13
Lord Russell Pl EH9 1	43	BG14
Loretto Ct, Muss. EH21	31	BX15
Loretto RC Prim Sch EH21	31	BY13
Loretto RC Prim Sch EH21	31	BZ13
Lorimer Vw, Jun. Grn EH14	50	AU21
Lorne Gro (Strait.), Lnhd EH20	54	BJ26
Lorne Pl EH6	27	BH8
Lorne Prim Sch EH6	27	BH8
Lorne Sq EH6	27	BH8
Lorne St EH6	27	BH8
Lothian Bk, Dalk. EH22	56	BV26

LOTHIANBURN	53	BE24
Lothianburn Golf Course		
EH10	*52*	*BC24*
Lothianburn Junct *EH10*	52	BD23
Lothian Dr (Easth.),		
Dalk. *EH22*	57	BY27
Lothian Rd *EH1*	6	BD11
Lothian Rd *EH3*	6	BD11
Lothian Rd, Dalk. *EH22*	57	BW24
Lothian St *EH1*	7	BF12
Lothian St, Bonny. *EH19*	63	BR28
Lothian St, Dalk. *EH22*	57	BW24
Lothian St, Rose. *EH24*	62	BM33
Lothian Ter (Newt.),		
Dalk. *EH22*	65	BX31
Louisa Sq, Rose. *EH24*	62	BM33
Lovedale Av, Bal. *EH14*	58	AK26
Lovedale Cres, Bal. *EH14*	58	AK26
Lovedale Gdns, Bal. *EH14*	58	AL26
Lovedale Gro, Bal. *EH14*	58	AK26
Lovedale Rd, Bal. *EH14*	58	AL26
Lovers La, S Q'fry *EH30*	9	AE3
Lovers' Ln *EH9*	43	BF14
Lower Broomieknowe,		
Lass. *EH18*	63	BQ28
Lower Gilmore Pl *EH3*	6	BC13
Lower Granton Rd *EH5*	14	BD5
Lower Joppa *EH15*	30	BS11
Lower London Rd *EH7*	28	BJ10
Lower Valleyfield Vw, Pen.		
EH26	69	BB39
Lowrie Av, Pen. *EH26*	68	AY38
Lufra Bk *EH5*	14	BC5
Lugton Brae, Dalk. *EH22*	56	BV23
Lumsden Ct (Ratho),		
Newbr. *EH28*	37	AF17
Lussielaw Rd *EH9*	43	BH17
Lutton Pl *EH8*	7	BG13
Lygon Rd *EH16*	43	BH17
Lyndene Sq, Lnhd *EH20*	61	BH26
Lynedoch Pl *EH3*	6	BC11
Lynedoch Pl La *EH3*	6	BC11
Lyne St *EH7*	28	BJ10
Lyne Ter, Pen. *EH26*	69	BC36

M

Maby's Way, Newbr.		
EH28	21	AF12
Macbeth Moir Rd, Muss.		
EH21	32	CC13
McCathie Dr (Newt.),		
Dalk. *EH22*	65	BX29
Mac Cormick Ter, Pen.		
EH26	66	BB35
McDiarmid Gro (Newt.),		
Dalk. *EH22*	65	BX31
Macdonald Holyrood Hotel		
EH8	*7*	*BH11*
McDonald Pl *EH7*	27	BF8
McDonald Rd *EH7*	27	BF8
McDonald St *EH7*	27	BG8
Macdowall Rd *EH9*	43	BG16
McGahey Ct (Newt.),		
Dalk. *EH22*	65	BX31
McKelvie Par *EH5*	14	BD4
Mackenzie Pl *EH3*	6	BD10
McKinlay Ter, Lnhd *EH20*	62	BJ28
McKinnon Dr (Mayf.),		
Dalk. *EH22*	71	CA31
McLaren Rd *EH9*	28	BJ15
McLaren Ter *EH11* 11	6	BC12
Maclean Pl, Gore. *EH23*	70	BZ34
Maclean Pl, Lass. *EH18*	63	BN29
McLean Wk (Newt.),		
Dalk. *EH22*	65	BX31
McLeod Cres, Pres. *EH32*	18	CH10
McLeod St *EH11*	26	BA13
McNeill Av, Lnhd *EH20*	54	BK27
McNeill Path, Tran. *EH33*	35	CL13
McNeill Pl, Lnhd *EH20*	54	BK27
McNeill St *EH11*	6	BC13
McNeill Ter, Lnhd *EH20*	54	BJ27
McNeill Wk, Tran. *EH33* 4	35	CL14
McNeill Way, Tran. *EH33*	35	CL14
Mcphail Sq, Tran. *EH33*	35	CM13

McQuade St, Bonny. *EH19*	56	BT27
Mactaggart Ln (Newt.),		
Dalk. *EH22*	65	BX31
Madeira Pl *EH6*	15	BG6
Madeira St *EH6*	15	BG5
Maesterton Pl (Newt.),		
Dalk. *EH22*	65	BX31
Magdala Cres *EH12*	26	BB12
Magdala Ms *EH12*	26	BB12
Magdalene Av *EH15*	29	BR13
Magdalene Ct *EH15*	29	BQ14
Magdalene Dr *EH15*	29	BR13
Magdalene Gdns *EH15*	29	BR13
Magdalene Ln *EH15*	29	BR13
Magdalene Medway *EH15*	29	BR13
Magdalene Pl *EH15*	29	BR13
Maidencraig Ct *EH4*	25	AY9
Maidencraig Cres *EH4*	25	AY9
Maidencraig Gro *EH4*	25	AY9
Maid of the Forth EH30	*9*	*AF2*
Main Pt *EH3*	6	BE12
Mains Gdns, Tran. *EH33*	35	CM12
Mains of Craigmillar *EH16*	44	BM17
Main St (David.M.) *EH4*	24	AV8
Main St, Bal. *EH14*	58	AL25
Main St (Newt.), Dalk.		
EH22	65	BW30
Main St, Gore. *EH23*	70	BY36
Main St, K'lis. *EH29*	20	AD9
Main St, Lnhd *EH20*	61	BH28
Main St (Ratho),		
Newbr. *EH28*	37	AF17
Main St, Ros. *EH25*	61	BH31
Main St (Dalm.),		
S Q'fry *EH30*	9	AG4
Maitland Av, Muss. *EH21*	31	BW13
Maitland Br, K'lis. *EH29*	20	AC11
Maitland Hog La, K'lis.		
EH29	20	AC10
Maitland Pk Rd, Muss.		
EH21	31	BW13
Maitland Rd, K'lis. *EH29*	20	AC9
Maitland St, Muss. *EH21*	31	BW13
Malbet Pk *EH16*	44	BK20
Malbet Wynd *EH16*	44	BK20
Malcolmstone Cotts,		
Currie *EH14*	48	AM21
Mall Av, Muss. *EH21*	31	BY13
Malleny Av, Bal. *EH14*	58	AL26
Malleny Garden (NTS)		
EH14	*58*	*AM25*
Malleny Millgate, Bal.		
EH14	58	AM28
Malmaison Edinburgh Hotel		
EH6	*16*	*BJ5*
Malta Grn *EH4* 2	26	BD9
Malta Ter *EH4*	26	BD9
Manderston St *EH6*	15	BH7
Mannering Pl *EH16*	44	BK19
Manor Pl *EH3*	6	BC11
Manse La, Muss. *EH21*	31	BZ13
Manse La (Port S.),		
Pres. *EH32*	19	CL7
Manse Rd *EH12*	24	AT13
Manse Rd, K'lis. *EH29*	20	AC10
Manse Rd, Ros. *EH25*	62	BJ32
Manse St *EH12*	24	AT13
Mansfield Av (Newt.),		
Dalk. *EH22*	65	BX29
Mansfield Av, Muss. *EH21*	31	BY14
Mansfield Ct, Muss. *EH21*	31	BZ14
Mansfield Pl *EH3*	27	BF9
Mansfield Pl (Newt.),		
Dalk. *EH22*	65	BX29
Mansfield Pl, Muss. *EH21*	31	BY14
Mansfield Rd, Bal. *EH14*	58	AL27
Mansfield Rd (Newt.),		
Dalk. *EH22*	65	BX29
Mansfield Rd, Muss. *EH21*	31	BY13
Mansionhouse Rd *EH9*	43	BF14
Marchbank Dr, Bal. *EH14*	58	AL27
Marchbank Gdns, Bal.		
EH14	58	AL27
Marchbank Gro, Bal. *EH14*	58	AL27
Marchbank Pl, Bal. *EH14*	58	AL27
Marchbank Way, Bal. *EH14*	58	AL26

Marchburn Dr, Pen. *EH26*	68	AY38
Marchfield Gro *EH4*	25	AW8
Marchfield Pk *EH4*	24	AV8
Marchfield Pk La *EH4*	24	AV8
Marchfield Ter *EH4*	25	AW9
March Gait *EH4*	24	AV9
March Gro *EH4*	24	AV9
Marchhall Cres *EH16*	28	BJ14
Marchhall Pl *EH16*	28	BJ14
Marchhall Rd *EH16*	28	BJ14
MARCHMONT	43	BE14
Marchmont Cres *EH9*	43	BE14
Marchmont Rd *EH9*	43	BE14
Marchmont St *EH9*	43	BE14
March Pines *EH4*	24	AV9
March Rd *EH4*	24	AV9
Mardale Cres *EH10*	42	BC15
Margaret Rose Av *EH10*	53	BE22
Margaret Rose Cres *EH10*	53	BE22
Margaret Rose Dr *EH10*	53	BE22
Margaret Rose Ln *EH10*	53	BE22
Margaret Rose Wk *EH10*	53	BE22
Margaret Rose Way *EH10*	53	BE22
Marine Dr *EH4*	13	AW5
Marine Dr *EH5*	12	AT5
Marine Esplanade *EH6*	16	BL6
Marionville Av *EH7*	16	BK9
Marionville Cres *EH7*	16	BL9
Marionville Dr *EH7*	16	BL9
Marionville Gro *EH7*	16	BL9
Marionville Medway *EH7* 1	16	BL9
Marionville Pk *EH7*	16	BK9
Marionville Rd *EH7*	28	BJ10
Marischal Pl *EH4* 1	25	AY10
Maritime La *EH6*	16	BJ6
Maritime St *EH6*	16	BJ6
Market Ln, Tran. *EH33*	35	CL12
Market St *EH1*	7	BF11
Market St, Muss. *EH21*	31	BX13
Market Vw, Tran. *EH33*	35	CL13
Market Way, Tran. *EH33*	35	CL12
Marlborough St *EH15*	29	BR11
Marmion Av, Ros. *EH25*	61	BH31
Marmion Cres *EH16*	44	BK18
Marshall Rd, K'lis. *EH29*	20	AC10
Marshall's Ct *EH1* 3	7	BG10
Marshall St *EH8* 2	7	BG12
Marshall St (Cock.),		
Pres. *EH32*	18	CK7
Martello Ct *EH4*	13	AW6
Martin Gro, Bonny. *EH19*	56	BT27
Martin Pl, Dalk. *EH22*	56	BU25
Maryburn Rd (Easth.),		
Dalk. *EH22*	57	BY27
Mary Erskine &		
Stewart's Melville		
Jun Sch EH4	*26*	*BA10*
Mary Erskine Sch EH4	*25*	*AX10*
Maryfield *EH7*	7	BH10
Maryfield *EH15*	29	BR10
Maryfield Pl *EH7*	28	BJ10
Maryfield Pl, Bonny. *EH19*	56	BS28
Mary's Pl *EH4* 1	26	BC9
Marytree Ho *EH17*	44	BM19
Masefield Way *EH12*	22	AK10
Mason Pl, Lass. *EH18*	63	BP29
Matthews Dr (Newt.),		
Dalk. *EH22*	64	BV31
Maulsford Av (Dand.),		
Dalk. *EH22*	45	BR20
Maurice Pl *EH9*	43	BF17
MAURICEWOOD	68	BA36
Mauricewood Av, Pen.		
EH26	69	BB36
Mauricewood Bk, Pen.		
EH26	69	BB36
Mauricewood Gro, Pen.		
EH26	69	BB36
Mauricewood Pk, Pen.		
EH26	69	BB36
Mauricewood Prim Sch		
EH26	*66*	*BB35*
Mauricewood Ri, Pen.		
EH26	69	BB36
Mauricewood Rd, Pen.		
EH26	66	BA34

Name	Page	Grid
Mavisbank, Lnhd EH20	62	BL28
Mavisbank Pl, Lass. EH18	63	BN29
Maxton Ct, Dalk. EH22 1	57	BW24
Maxwell St EH10	42	BC17
Maybank Vil EH12	24	AT12
Mayburn Av, Lnhd EH20	54	BK26
Mayburn Br, Lnhd EH20	54	BK26
Mayburn Ct, Lnhd EH20	54	BK27
Mayburn Cres, Lnhd EH20	54	BK26
Mayburn Dr, Lnhd EH20	54	BK26
Mayburn Gro, Lnhd EH20	54	BK26
Mayburn Hill, Lnhd EH20	54	BK27
Mayburn Ln, Lnhd EH20	54	BK26
Mayburn Ter, Lnhd EH20	54	BK26
Mayburn Vale, Lnhd EH20	54	BJ27
Mayburn Wk, Lnhd EH20	54	BK27
Maybury Dr EH12	23	AR10
Maybury Gdns, Lnhd EH20	54	BK26
Maybury Rd EH4	23	AQ11
Maybury Rd EH12	23	AQ12
May Ct EH4	13	AW6
MAYFIELD	71	CB28
Mayfield Av, Muss. EH21	31	BX15
Mayfield Ct, Lnhd EH20	52	BL28
Mayfield Cres, Lnhd EH20	54	BL27
Mayfield Cres, Muss. EH21	31	BW15
Mayfield Gdns EH9	43	BH15
Mayfield Gdns La EH9	43	BH15
Mayfield Ind Est, Dalk. EH22	65	BY30
Mayfield Pk, Muss. EH21	31	BX16
Mayfield Pl EH12	24	AT13
Mayfield Pl (Mayf.), Dalk. EH22	65	BZ29
Mayfield Pl, Muss. EH21	31	BX16
Mayfield Prim Sch EH22	71	CA30
Mayfield Rd EH9	43	BH15
Mayfield Rd (Easth.), Dalk. EH22	57	BZ27
Mayshade Rd, Lnhd EH20	54	BK26
Mayville Bk, Muss. EH21	32	CC13
Mayville Gdns EH5	15	BE5
Mayville Gdns E EH5	15	BE5
MEADOWBANK	28	BK10
Meadowbank Av EH8	28	BK10
Meadowbank Cres EH8	28	BK10
Meadowbank Ho EH7	28	BL10
Meadowbank Pl EH8 7	28	BL10
Meadowbank Shopping Park EH7	16	BJ9
Meadowbank Ter EH8	28	BK10
Meadowfield Av EH8	28	BM12
Meadowfield Ct EH8	28	BM12
Meadowfield Dr EH8	28	BM12
Meadowfield Gdns EH8	28	BM13
Meadowfield Rd EH12	23	AN11
Meadowfield Ter EH8	28	BM13
Meadowhouse Rd EH12	24	AU13
Meadow La EH8	7	BF13
Meadowmill Ln, Tran. EH33	35	CM12
Meadow Pl EH9	6	BE13
Meadow Pl (Bils.), Ros. EH25	61	BG29
Meadow Pl La EH9	43	BF14
Meadow Pl Rd EH12	24	AS13
Meadow Rd (Ricc.), Currie EH14	49	AP20
Meadowside, Tran. EH33	35	CN14
Meadowspot EH10	42	BA17
Mearenside EH12	23	AQ11
Medwin Ho EH11	40	AS18
Meeting Ho Dr, Tran. EH33	35	CL13
Meggat Pl, Pen. EH26	69	BC36
Meggetland Gate EH14	41	AY16
Meggetland Sq EH14	41	AZ16
Meggetland Ter EH14	42	BA16
Meggetland Vw EH14	41	AZ16
Meggetland Wynd EH14	41	AZ16
Melbourne Pl EH1 7	7	BF11
Melgund Ter EH7	27	BF9
Melville Cres EH3	6	BC11
Melville Dr EH9	6	BE13
Melville Dykes Rd, Lass. EH18	55	BR26
Melville Dykes Rd Rbt, Dalk. EH22	56	BT25
Melville Gate Rd, Dalk. EH22	56	BT24
Melville Golf Course EH18	56	BS25
Melville Golf Range EH18	56	BS25
Melville Pl EH3 6	6	BC11
Melville Rd, Dalk. EH22	56	BU25
Melville St EH3	6	BC11
Melville St La EH3	6	BC11
Melville Ter EH9	43	BF14
Melville Ter, Dalk. EH22	56	BU26
Melville Vw, Lass. EH18 1	55	BQ27
Mentone Av EH15	29	BR10
Mentone Gdns EH9	43	BH15
Mentone Ter EH9	43	BH16
Menzies Belford Hotel EH4	26	BB11
Merchants of Edinburgh Golf Course EH10	42	BB18
Merchant St EH1	7	BF12
MERCHISTON	42	BB15
Merchiston Av EH10	42	BC14
Merchiston Bk Av EH10	42	BC15
Merchiston Bk Gdns EH10	42	BC15
Merchiston Castle Coll EH13	51	AX20
Merchiston Cres EH10	42	BC15
Merchiston Gdns EH10	42	BB16
Merchiston Gro EH11	42	BA14
Merchiston Ms EH10	42	BC14
Merchiston Pk EH10	42	BC14
Merchiston Pl EH10	42	BC15
Merlyon Way, Pen. EH26	68	AZ36
Mertoun Pl EH11	42	BB14
Methven Ter, Lass. EH18	63	BP29
Meuse La EH2	7	BF11
Middleby St EH9	43	BH15
Middlefield EH7	27	BG8
Middleknowe EH14	40	AS19
Middle Meadow Wk EH3	7	BF13
Middlepark EH14 2	40	AS19
Middle Pier EH5	14	BB4
Middleshot EH14 3	40	AS19
Middleshot Sq, Pres. EH32	18	CK9
Mid Gillsland Rd EH10	42	BB15
Mid Gogarloch Syke EH12	39	AQ14
Mid Liberton EH16	44	BJ17
Midlothian Snowsports Centre EH10	52	BC25
Midmar Av EH10	43	BE17
Midmar Dr EH10	43	BE17
Midmar Gdns EH10	42	BD17
Mid New Cultins EH11	39	AQ17
Mid Rd, Pres. EH32	34	CH11
Mid Rd Ind Est, Pres. EH32	34	CH11
Mid Steil EH10	42	BA18
Mid Ter, S Q'fry EH30 2	9	AE2
Millar Cres EH10	42	BC16
Millar Pl EH10	42	BC16
Millar Pl La EH10	42	BC16
Millar Rd, Tran. EH33	35	CL14
Millbank, Bal. EH14	58	AL26
Millbank Gro, Gore. EH23	70	BY36
Millbrae, Currie EH14	50	AU21
Millbrae Wynd EH14	41	AX17
Miller Ct, Tran. EH33	34	CK14
Millerfield Pl EH9	43	BF14
MILLERHILL	46	BU20
Millerhill Rd, Dalk. EH22	45	BR17
Miller Row EH4	6	BC11
Millhill, Muss. EH21	31	BZ13
Millhill La, Muss. EH21	31	BZ13
Millhill Wynd, Muss. EH21	31	BZ13
Mill La EH6	15	BH6
Mill Wynd, Pres. EH32	18	CH9
Milnacre EH6	15	BF7
MILTON BRIDGE	66	BD33
Milton Br, Pen. EH26	67	BE33
Milton Cres EH15	29	BQ13
Milton Dr EH15	30	BT12
Milton Gdns N EH15	29	BQ13
Milton Gdns S EH15	29	BQ13
Milton Gro EH15	30	BU12
Milton Link EH15	30	BS13
Milton Rd EH15	29	BQ13
Milton Rd E EH15	30	BT13
Milton Rd W EH15	29	BN13
Milton St EH8	28	BJ10
Milton Ter EH15	30	BU12
Miner's Ter (Wall.), Muss. EH21	33	CD14
Minstrel St, Ros. EH25	62	BJ32
Minto St EH9	43	BH14
Mitchell St EH6	16	BJ6
Mitchell St, Dalk. EH22	56	BV24
Mitchell Way, Tran. EH33	35	CM12
Moat Dr EH14	41	AZ15
Moat Ho EH14	41	AZ15
Moat Pl EH14	41	AZ15
Moat St EH14	41	AZ15
Moat Ter EH14	41	AZ15
Moat Vw, Ros. EH25	67	BH32
Moffat Av, Bonny. EH19	63	BR29
Moira Pk EH7	29	BN10
Moira Ter EH7	29	BN10
Moira Ter La EH7	29	BN10
Moir Av, Muss. EH21	32	CC13
Moir Cres, Muss. EH21	32	CC13
Moir Dr, Muss. EH21	33	CD13
Moir Pl, Muss. EH21	32	CC13
Moir Ter, Muss. EH21	32	CC13
Moncreiffe Ho EH17	44	BM19
Moncrieff Ter EH9	43	BG14
Monkbarns Gdns EH16	44	BK19
Monksrig Rd, Pen. EH26	68	AY38
Monkswood Rd (Newt.), Dalk. EH22	65	BX31
Monktonhall Pl, Muss. EH21	31	BX16
Monktonhall Ter, Muss. EH21	31	BX15
Monkwood Ct EH9	43	BF15
Monmouth Ter EH3	14	BD6
Montague St EH8	7	BG13
Montagu Ter EH3	14	BD7
Montgomery St EH7	27	BG9
Montgomery St La EH7	27	BG9
Montpelier EH10	42	BC14
Montpelier Pk EH10	42	BC14
Montpelier Ter EH10	42	BC14
Montrose Ter EH7	7	BH10
Moorfield Cotts, Dalk. EH22	46	BS19
Moorfoot Ct, Bonny. EH19 4	63	BR28
Moorfoot Pl, Bonny. EH19	63	BR29
Moorfoot Pl, Pen. EH26	68	BA37
Moorfoot Vw, Bonny. EH19	63	BR29
Moorfoot Vw, Gore. EH23	70	BY36
Moorfoot Vw (Bils.), Ros. EH25	61	BG30
Moray Pk EH7	28	BJ10
Moray Pk Ter EH7	28	BJ10
Moray Pl EH3	6	BD10
MOREDUN	45	BN20
Moredun Dykes Rd EH17	44	BM21
Moredun Ho EH17	44	BM19
Moredun Pk Ct EH17	44	BM20
Moredun Pk Dr EH17	44	BM20
Moredun Pk Gdns EH17	44	BM19
Moredun Pk Grn EH17	45	BN20
Moredun Pk Gro EH17	45	BN20
Moredun Pk Ln EH17	44	BM20
Moredun Pk Rd EH17	44	BM20
Moredun Pk St EH17	44	BM20
Moredun Pk Vw EH17	44	BM20
Moredun Pk Wk EH17	45	BN20
Moredun Pk Way EH17	44	BM20
Moredunvale Bk EH17	44	BM19
Moredunvale Grn EH17	44	BM19
Moredunvale Gro EH17	44	BM19
Moredunvale Ln EH17	44	BM19
Moredunvale Pk EH17	44	BM19
Moredunvale Pl EH17	44	BM19
Moredunvale Rd EH17	44	BM19
Moredunvale Vw EH17	44	BM19
Moredunvale Way EH17	44	BM19
Morham Gait EH10 6	42	BA19
Morham Gdns EH10 3	42	BA19

Name		
Morham Lea EH10 1	42	BA19
Morham Pk EH10 5	42	BA19
Morison Gdns, S Q'fry EH30	8	AD2
Morison's Haven, Pres. EH32	33	CE11
MORNINGSIDE	42	BD17
Morningside Ct EH10	42	BC17
Morningside Dr EH10	42	BB17
Morningside Gdns EH10	42	BB17
Morningside Gro EH10	42	BB17
Morningside Pk EH10	42	BC16
Morningside Pl EH10	42	BC16
Morningside Rd EH10	42	BC15
Morningside Ter EH10	42	BC16
Morrison Av, Tran. EH33	35	CN14
Morrison Circ EH3	6	BC12
Morrison Cres EH3	6	BC12
Morrison Link EH3	6	BC12
Morrison St EH3	6	BC12
Morris Rd (Newt.), Dalk. EH22	65	BY29
MORTONHALL	53	BH22
Mortonhall Gate EH16	53	BG22
Mortonhall Golf Course EH10	53	BE20
Mortonhall Pk Av EH17	53	BH22
Mortonhall Pk Bk EH17	54	BJ22
Mortonhall Pk Cres EH17	54	BJ22
Mortonhall Pk Dr EH17	54	BJ22
Mortonhall Pk Gdns EH17	53	BH22
Mortonhall Pk Grn EH17	53	BH22
Mortonhall Pk Gro EH17	53	BH22
Mortonhall Pk Ln EH17	53	BH22
Mortonhall Pk Pl EH17	54	BJ22
Mortonhall Pk Ter EH17	54	BJ22
Mortonhall Pk Vw EH17	53	BH22
Mortonhall Pk Way EH17	53	BH22
Mortonhall Rd EH9	43	BE16
Morton St EH15	30	BS12
Morvenside EH14	40	AS19
Morvenside Cl EH14	40	AS19
Morven St EH4	24	AS10
Mossgiel Wk EH16	44	BJ18
Moston Ter EH9	43	BH15
Moubray Gro, S Q'fry EH30	9	AE3
Mound, The EH1	6	BE11
Mound, The EH2	6	BE11
Mound Pl EH1	6	BE11
Mount Alvernia EH16	44	BK20
Mountcastle Bk EH8	29	BP11
Mountcastle Cres EH8	29	BN11
Mountcastle Dr N EH8	29	BN11
Mountcastle Dr N EH15	29	BN11
Mountcastle Dr S EH15	29	BP12
Mountcastle Gdns EH8	29	BN11
Mountcastle Grn EH8	28	BM10
Mountcastle Gro EH8	29	BN11
Mountcastle Ln EH8	29	BN11
Mountcastle Pk EH8	29	BN10
Mountcastle Pl EH8	29	BN10
Mountcastle Ter EH8	29	BN11
Mount Gra EH9	43	BE15
Mounthooly Ln EH10	53	BE22
Mountjoy Ct, Muss. EH21	31	BY12
Mountjoy Ter, Muss. EH21	31	BY12
Mount Lo Pl EH15	29	BR11
Mount Vernon Rd EH16	44	BK19
Mucklets Av, Muss. EH21	31	BW15
Mucklets Ct, Muss. EH21	31	BW15
Mucklets Cres, Muss. EH21	31	BW15
Mucklets Dr, Muss. EH21	31	BW15
Mucklets Pl, Muss. EH21	31	BW15
Mucklets Rd, Muss. EH21	30	BV16
Muirdale Ter EH4 1	25	AX9
Muirend Av, Jun. Grn EH14	50	AU20
Muirfield Gdns, Lnhd EH20	62	BL28
Muirhead Pl, Pen. EH26	66	BB35
MUIRHOUSE	13	AX6
Muirhouse Av EH4	13	AX7
Muirhouse Av N EH4	13	AX6
Muirhouse Bk EH4	13	AX7
Muirhouse Cl EH4	13	AW7
Muirhouse Cres EH4	13	AX6
Muirhouse Dr EH4	13	AW6

Muirhouse Gdns EH4	13	AW6
Muirhouse Grn EH4	13	AX7
Muirhouse Gro EH4	13	AW6
Muirhouse Ln EH4	13	AX6
Muirhouse Medway EH4	13	AW6
Muirhouse Pk EH4	13	AW7
Muirhouse Parkway EH4	13	AX6
Muirhouse Pl E EH4	13	AX7
Muirhouse Pl W EH4	13	AX7
Muirhouse Ter EH4	13	AW7
Muirhouse Vw EH4	13	AW6
Muirhouse Way EH4	13	AX7
Muirpark, Dalk. EH22	56	BU26
Muirpark Ct, Tran. EH33	35	CN14
Muirpark Dr, Tran. EH33	35	CN14
Muirpark Gdns, Tran. EH33	35	CN14
Muirpark Gro, Tran. EH33	35	CN14
Muirpark Pl, Tran. EH33	35	CN14
Muirpark Rd, Tran. EH33	35	CN14
Muirpark Ter, Tran. EH33	35	CN14
Muirpark Wynd, Tran. EH33	35	CN14
Muirside EH13	52	BA22
Muirside Dr, Tran. EH33	35	CL14
Muir Wd Cres, Currie EH14	49	AR22
Muir Wd Dr, Currie EH14	49	AR22
Muir Wd Gro, Currie EH14	49	AR22
Muir Wd Pl, Currie EH14	49	AR21
Muir Wd Rd, Currie EH14	49	AR21
Mulberry Pl EH6 1	15	BF6
Multrees Wk EH1	7	BF10
Munro Dr EH13	51	AW22
Munro Pl EH3 1	27	BE8
Murano Pl EH7	27	BH9
Murderdean Rd (Newt.), Dalk. EH22	65	BW30
Murdoch Ter EH11	6	BC13
Murieston Cres EH11	26	BA13
Murieston Cres La EH11 2	26	BB13
Murieston La EH11	26	BA13
Murieston Pl EH11	26	BA13
Murieston Rd EH11	26	BA13
Murieston Ter EH11	26	BA13
Murrayburn App EH14	40	AT18
Murrayburn Dr EH14	40	AT18
Murrayburn Gdns EH14	40	AU18
Murrayburn Gate EH14	40	AT19
Murrayburn Grn EH14	40	AU18
Murrayburn Gro EH14	40	AU18
Murrayburn Pk EH14	40	AT18
Murrayburn Pl EH14	40	AT18
Murrayburn Prim Sch EH11	40	AT17
Murrayburn Rd EH14	40	AU17
Murray Cotts EH12	24	AS13
MURRAYFIELD	25	AY12
Murrayfield Av EH12	25	AZ12
Murrayfield Dr EH12	25	AY12
Murrayfield Gdns EH12	25	AZ11
Murrayfield Golf Course EH4	25	AX11
Murrayfield Pl EH12 1	25	AZ12
Murrayfield Rd EH12	25	AY11
Murrayfield Stadium EH12	25	AZ13
Murrays, The EH17	54	BL23
Murrays Brae, The EH17	54	BL23
Museum of Childhood EH1 11	7	BG11
Museum of Edinburgh EH8 15	7	BG11
Museum of Fire EH3	6	BE12
Museum of Scotland EH1	7	BF12
MUSSELBURGH	31	BX15
Musselburgh Burgh Prim Sch EH21	31	BY13
Musselburgh Dolls Museum EH21	31	BY13
Musselburgh Golf Course EH21	31	BX16
Musselburgh Gram Sch EH21	31	BY14
Musselburgh Links Golf Course (The Old Course) EH21	32	CA12
Musselburgh Racecourse EH21	31	BZ12

Musselburgh Rd EH15	30	BT12
Musselburgh Rd, Dalk. EH22	57	BX23
Musselburgh Sta EH21	31	BW15
Myre Dale, Bonny. EH19	64	BS29
Myreside, Bonny. EH19	64	BT30
Myreside Ct EH10	42	BB17
Myreside Rd EH10	42	BB16
Myreside Vw EH14	42	BA16
Myrtle Cres (Bils.), Ros. EH25	61	BG29
Myrtle Gro (Mayf.), Dalk. EH22	57	BZ28
Myrtle Ter EH11	42	BA14

N

Namur Rd, Pen. EH26	66	BB35
Nantwich Dr EH7	17	BN8
Napier Ln EH10	42	BB15
Napier Rd EH10	42	BB15
Napier Uni (Canaan La Campus) EH9	43	BE16
Napier Uni (Comely Bk Campus) EH4	26	BA9
Napier Uni (Craighouse Campus) EH10	42	BA17
Napier Uni (Craiglockhart Campus) EH9	41	AZ18
Napier Uni (Marchmount Campus) EH9	43	BE14
Napier Uni (Merchiston Campus) EH10	42	BC15
Napier Uni (Morningside Campus) EH10	42	BD15
Napier Uni (Redwood Campus) EH10	42	BB15
Napier Uni (Sighthill Campus) EH11	40	AT17
National Gallery of Scotland EH2	6	BE11
National Library of Scotland EH1	7	BF12
National Monument EH7	7	BG10
National War Museum of Scotland EH1	6	BE11
Neidpath Ct EH12 4	23	AQ12
Nellfield EH16	44	BK19
Nelson Monument EH7	7	BG10
Nelson Pl EH3 1	6	BE10
Nelson St EH3	6	BE10
Nether Bakehouse EH8 9	7	BH11
Netherbank EH16	53	BH21
Netherbank Vw EH16	53	BH21
Netherby Rd EH5	14	BC6
Nether Craigour EH17	44	BM18
Nether Craigwell EH8	7	BH10
Nether Currie Cres, Currie EH14	49	AR22
Nether Currie Pl, Currie EH14	49	AR22
Nether Currie Prim Sch EH14	49	AR22
Nether Currie Rd, Currie EH14	49	AR22
Nether Lennie EH12	22	AL8
Nether Liberton Ct EH16 1	44	BJ17
Nethersmith Rd, Pres. EH32	18	CJ9
Nevis Gdns, Pen. EH26	69	BC36
New Arthur Pl EH8	7	BG12
New Arthur St EH8 5	7	BG12
NEWBATTLE	57	BW27
Newbattle Abbey Coll EH22	57	BW26
Newbattle Abbey Cres, Dalk. EH22	56	BV27
Newbattle Gdns, Dalk. EH22	57	BW26

Newbattle Golf Course *EH22*	57	BW25
Newbattle High Sch *EH22*	57	BY28
Newbattle Ind Est, Dalk. *EH22*	65	BY29
Newbattle Rd, Dalk. *EH22*	56	BV25
Newbattle Ter *EH10*	42	BD15
New Belfield *EH8*	29	BN12
New Bells Ct *EH6* **4**	16	BJ6
Newbigging, Muss. *EH21*	31	BZ14
NEWBRIDGE	36	AC13
New Br, Newbr. *EH28*	36	AB13
Newbridge Ind Est, Newbr. *EH28*	36	AB14
Newbridge Rd, Newbr. *EH28*	36	AC14
New Broompark *EH5*	14	BA4
New Broughton *EH3*	27	BF9
Newbyres Av, Gore. *EH23*	70	BY34
Newbyres Cres, Gore. *EH23*	70	BY35
Newbyres Gdns, Gore. *EH23*	70	BY35
NEWCRAIGHALL	30	BT14
Newcraighall Dr (Newcr.), Muss. *EH21*	30	BT15
Newcraighall Prim Sch *EH21*	30	BU15
Newcraighall Rd *EH15*	29	BR15
Newcraighall Rd, Muss. *EH21*	30	BT15
Newcraighall Sta *EH21*	30	BT15
New Cut Rigg *EH6*	15	BF6
NEWHAILES	30	BV13
Newhailes Av, Muss. *EH21*	31	BW13
Newhailes Cres, Muss. *EH21*	30	BV13
Newhailes Ind Est, Muss. *EH21*	30	BV14
Newhailes (NTS) *EH21*	30	BV13
Newhailes Rd, Muss. *EH21*	30	BV14
New Halls Rd, S Q'fry *EH30*	9	AF2
NEWHAVEN	15	BF5
Newhaven Heritage Museum *EH6*	15	BF4
Newhaven Main St *EH6*	15	BE4
Newhaven Pl *EH6*	15	BF4
Newhaven Rd *EH6*	15	BG7
New Hunterfield, Gore. *EH23*	70	BX33
NEWINGTON	43	BH14
Newington Rd *EH9*	43	BG14
New John's Pl *EH8*	7	BG13
Newkirkgate *EH6* **2**	15	BH7
New Lairdship Pl *EH11*	40	AT16
New Lairdship Yards *EH11*	40	AT16
Newlands Pk *EH9*	43	BH15
New La *EH6*	15	BF5
New Liston Rd, K'lis. *EH29*	20	AC11
Newmains Fm La, K'lis. *EH29*	20	AC9
Newmains Rd, K'lis. *EH29*	20	AC9
New Mkt Rd *EH14*	41	AY16
New Mart Pl *EH14*	41	AX16
New Mart Rd *EH14*	41	AX16
New Mart Sq *EH14*	41	AX16
New Meadowspott, Dalk. *EH22* **1**	56	BV25
Newmills Av, Bal. *EH14*	48	AM23
Newmills Cres, Bal. *EH14*	48	AM23
Newmills Gro, Bal. *EH14*	48	AM24
Newmills Rd, Bal. *EH14*	48	AM24
Newmills Rd, Dalk. *EH22*	57	BW24
Newmills Ter, Dalk. *EH22* **1**	57	BX24
New Orchardfield *EH6*	15	BH7
NEW PENTLAND	61	BH27
New Poltonhall, Bonny. *EH19*	63	BP31
New Row, Tran. *EH33*	35	CL13
New Skinner's Cl *EH1*	7	BG11
News Steps *EH1*	7	BF11
New Star Bk (Newt.), Dalk. *EH22*	65	BW30
New St *EH8*	7	BG11
New St *EH17*	54	BM22
New St, Muss. *EH21*	31	BW13
New St, Pres. *EH32*	18	CH10
New St (Cock.), Pres. *EH32*	19	CL7
New St, Tran. *EH33*	35	CL12
New Swanston *EH10*	52	BB22
Newtoft St *EH17*	55	BN22
Newton Ch Rd (Dand.), Dalk. *EH22*	45	BR20
NEWTONGRANGE	64	BV29
Newtongrange Pl (Newt.), Dalk. *EH22*	65	BW30
Newtongrange Prim Sch *EH22*	65	BX30
NEWTONLOAN	65	BW32
Newtonloan Ct, Gore. *EH23*	70	BX33
Newton St *EH11*	42	BA14
Newton St (Easth.), Dalk. *EH22*	57	BY27
NEWTON VILLAGE	46	BT19
Newton Village, Dalk. *EH22*	46	BT19
New Twr Pl *EH15* **1**	29	BR10
Nichollfield *EH6*	15	BF5
Nicolson Sq *EH8*	7	BF12
Nicolson St *EH8*	7	BG12
NIDDRIE	29	BQ15
Niddrie Cotts *EH15* **1**	30	BS15
Niddrie Fm Gro *EH16*	29	BN15
Niddrie Ho Av *EH16*	45	BP16
Niddrie Ho Dr *EH16*	45	BQ16
Niddrie Ho Gdns *EH16*	45	BP16
Niddrie Ho Gro *EH16* **2**	45	BQ16
Niddrie Ho Pk *EH16*	45	BP16
Niddrie Ho Sq *EH16*	45	BP16
Niddrie Mains Dr *EH16*	29	BN15
Niddrie Mains Rd *EH15*	29	BN15
Niddrie Mains Rd *EH16*	29	BN15
Niddrie Mains Ter *EH16*	29	BN15
Niddrie Marischal Cres *EH16*	29	BP15
Niddrie Marischal Dr *EH16*	45	BP16
Niddrie Marischal Gdns *EH16*	29	BP15
Niddrie Marischal Grn *EH16*	45	BP16
Niddrie Marischal Gro *EH16*	29	BQ15
Niddrie Marischal Ln *EH16*	29	BP15
Niddrie Marischal Pl *EH16*	45	BP16
Niddrie Marischal Rd *EH16*	29	BQ15
Niddrie Marischal St *EH16*	29	BP15
Niddrie Mill Av *EH15*	29	BQ14
Niddrie Mill Cres *EH15*	29	BQ14
Niddrie Mill Dr *EH15*	29	BQ15
Niddrie Mill Gro *EH15*	29	BQ15
Niddrie Mill Pl *EH15*	29	BQ15
Niddrie Mill Prim Sch *EH15*	29	BQ15
Niddrie Mill Ter *EH15*	29	BQ15
Niddry St *EH1*	7	BF11
Niddry St S *EH1* **3**	7	BG12
Nigel Ln *EH16*	44	BK19
Nile Gro *EH10*	42	BD16
Nimmo Av, Pres. *EH32*	18	CJ10
Ninth St (Newt.), Dalk. *EH22*	65	BX29
Nisbet Ct *EH7*	16	BK8
Nivensknowe Caravan Pk, Lnhd *EH20*	61	BG28
Niven's Knowe Rd, Lnhd *EH20*	61	BH28
No. 28 Charlotte Square (NTS) *EH2*	6	BD11
Nobel Pl, Ros. *EH25*	67	BH32
Noble Pl *EH6*	16	BK7
North Bk Rd, Pres. *EH32*	18	CG10
North Bk St *EH1*	7	BF11
North Br *EH1*	7	BF11
North Br Arc *EH1* **10**	7	BF11
North Bughtlin Bk *EH12*	23	AR10
North Bughtlin Brae *EH12*	23	AR10
North Bughtlinfield *EH12*	23	AQ10
North Bughtlin Gate *EH12*	23	AR10
North Bughtlin Neuk *EH12* **3**	23	AR10
North Bughtlin Pl *EH12* **2**	23	AR10
North Bughtlinrig *EH12*	23	AQ10
North Bughtlin Rd *EH12*	23	AQ10
North Bughtlinside *EH12*	23	AQ10
North Cairntow *EH16*	28	BM14
North Castle St *EH2*	6	BD10
North Charlotte St *EH2*	6	BD10
North Clyde St La *EH1* **1**	7	BF10
Northcote St *EH11*	26	BB13
North Cres, Pres. *EH32*	18	CJ10
North E Circ Pl *EH3*	6	BD10
North Edinburgh Arts Centre *EH4*	13	AX6
NORTHFIELD	29	BN12
Northfield, Pres. *EH32*	34	CH11
Northfield, Tran. *EH33*	35	CN13
Northfield Av *EH8*	28	BM11
Northfield Bdy *EH8*	28	BM10
Northfield Circ *EH8*	28	BM11
Northfield Ct, Pres. *EH32*	34	CH11
Northfield Cres *EH8*	28	BM11
Northfield Dr *EH8*	29	BN12
Northfield E, Tran. *EH33*	35	CN13
Northfield Fm Av *EH8*	29	BN12
Northfield Fm Rd *EH8*	29	BN11
Northfield Gdns *EH8*	29	BN11
Northfield Gdns, Pres. *EH32*	34	CH11
Northfield Gro *EH8*	29	BN12
Northfield Hts *EH8* **1**	28	BM11
Northfield Pk *EH8*	29	BN11
Northfield Pk Gro *EH8*	29	BN11
Northfield Rd *EH8*	28	BM11
Northfield Sq *EH8*	29	BN11
Northfield Ter *EH8*	28	BM11
North Fort St *EH6*	15	BG5
North Gra Av, Pres. *EH32*	34	CG11
North Gra Gro, Pres. *EH32*	18	CH10
North Gra Rd, Pres. *EH32*	18	CH10
North Grns *EH15*	29	BR14
North Gyle Av *EH12*	39	AQ13
North Gyle Dr *EH12*	23	AQ12
North Gyle Fm Ct *EH12*	39	AQ13
North Gyle Fm La *EH12*	39	AQ13
North Gyle Gro *EH12*	39	AQ13
North Gyle Ln *EH12*	23	AQ12
North Gyle Pk *EH12*	23	AQ12
North Gyle Rd *EH12*	23	AR12
North Gyle Ter *EH12*	39	AQ13
North High St, Muss. *EH21*	31	BX13
North Hillhousefield *EH6*	15	BG5
North Junct St *EH6*	15	BG5
Northlawn Ct *EH4* **6**	12	AU7
Northlawn Ter *EH4*	12	AU7
NORTH LEITH	15	BG6
North Leith Mill *EH6* **4**	15	BG5
North Leith Sands *EH6*	15	BG5
North Lorimer Pl (Cock.), Pres. *EH32* **2**	18	CK7
North Meadow Wk *EH3*	6	BE13
North Meadow Wk *EH8*	6	BE13
North Meggetland *EH14*	41	AZ16
North Pk Ter *EH4*	26	BC9
North Peffer Pl *EH16*	28	BM15
North Richmond St *EH8* **1**	7	BG12
North St. Andrew La *EH2*	7	BF10
North St. Andrew St *EH2*	7	BF10
North St. David St *EH2*	7	BF10
North Seton Pk (Port S.), Pres. *EH32* **2**	19	CL7
North St (Ratho), Newbr. *EH28*	37	AF17
Northumberland Pl *EH3* **3**	6	BE10
Northumberland Pl La *EH3*	6	BE10
Northumberland St *EH3*	6	BE10
Northumberland St N E La *EH3*	6	BE10
Northumberland St N W La *EH3*	6	BE10
Northumberland St S E La *EH3*	6	BE10
Northumberland St S W La *EH3*	6	BE10
Northview Ct *EH4*	13	AX6
North Wk, The *EH10*	42	BC17

Name		
North Way, The EH8	28	BM11
North Werber Pk EH4	26	BA8
North Werber Pl EH4	14	BA7
North Werber Rd EH4	26	BA8
North W Circ Pl EH3	6	BD10
North Wynd, Dalk. EH22	57	BW24
Norton House Hotel EH28	37	AF15
Norton Pk EH7	16	BJ9
Novotel Edinburgh Centre EH3	6	BE12

O

Name		
Oak Av, Lnhd EH20	61	BH28
Oak Cres (Mayf.), Dalk. EH22	71	CA29
Oakfield Pl EH8	7	BG12
Oaklands Sch EH11	40	AU16
Oak La EH12	24	AU10
Oak Pl (Mayf.), Dalk. EH22	71	CA29
Oakville Ter EH6	16	BK7
Observatory Grn EH9	43	BG17
Observatory Rd EH9	43	BG17
Ocean Dr EH6	15	BG5
Ocean Terminal Shopping Centre EH6	15	BG4
Ochil Ct, S Q'fry EH30	9	AE3
Ochiltree Gdns EH16	44	BL18
Odeon Cinema (Lothian Road) EH3	6	BD12
Odeon Cinema (Wester Hailes) EH14	40	AT19
Ogilvie Ter EH11	42	BA15
Old Assembly Cl EH1 9	7	BF11
Old Broughton EH3 2	27	BF9
Old Burdiehouse Rd EH17	54	BJ24
Old Ch La EH15	28	BL13
OLD CRAIGHALL	47	BW17
Old Craighall Junct, Muss. EH21	47	BX17
Old Craighall Rd, Dalk. EH22	46	BU20
Old Dalkeith Rd EH16	44	BK16
Old Dalkeith Rd EH17	45	BP20
Old Dalkeith Rd (Dand.), Dalk. EH22	46	BS21
Old Edinburgh Rd, Dalk. EH22	56	BV24
Old Fm Av EH13	51	AY20
Old Fm Pl EH13	51	AX20
Old Fishmarket Cl EH1	7	BF11
Old Kirk Rd EH12	24	AU12
Old Liston Rd, Newbr. EH28	36	AC13
Old Mill La EH16	44	BJ17
Old Newmills Rd, Bal. EH14	48	AM24
OLD PENTLAND	61	BH26
Old Pentland Rd EH10	53	BE25
Old Pentland Rd, Lnhd EH20	61	BG26
Old Star Rd (Newt.), Dalk. EH22	65	BW30
Old Tolbooth Wynd EH8	7	BG11
Old Waverley Hotel EH2	7	BF11
Oliphant Gdns (Wall.), Muss. EH21	33	CD14
Olivebank Retail Pk, Muss. EH21	31	BW13
Olive Bk Rd, Muss. EH21	31	BW13
Omni EH1	7	BG10
Orchard, The, Tran. EH33	35	CL12
Orchard Bk EH4	26	BA10
ORCHARD BRAE	26	BA10
Orchard Brae EH4	26	BB9
Orchard Brae Av EH4	26	BA10
Orchard Brae Gdns EH4	26	BA10
Orchard Brae Gdns W EH4	26	BA10
Orchard Brae W EH4	26	BB9
Orchard Cres EH4	25	AZ10
Orchard Cres, Pres. EH32	18	CH10
Orchard Dr EH4	25	AZ10
Orchardfield Av EH12	24	AT13
Orchardfield La EH6	27	BH8
Orchard Gro EH4	26	BB9
Orchardhead Ln EH16	44	BJ19
Orchardhead Rd EH16	44	BJ18
Orchard Pk, Tran. EH33	35	CL12
Orchard Pl EH4	26	BA9
Orchard Rd EH4	26	BA10
Orchard Rd S EH4	25	AZ10
Orchard Ter EH4	26	BA10
Orchard Toll EH4	26	BA10
Orchard Vw, Dalk. EH22	56	BU25
Ormelie Ter EH15	30	BS11
Ormidale Ter EH12	25	AY12
Ormiston Av, Tran. EH33	35	CN13
Ormiston Cres E, Tran. EH33	35	CN13
Ormiston Cres W, Tran. EH33	35	CN13
Ormiston Pl, Pres. EH32	18	CG10
Ormiston Rd, Tran. EH33	35	CM13
Ormiston Ter EH12	24	AT13
Orrok Pk EH16	44	BJ17
Orwell Pl EH11	26	BB13
Orwell Prim Sch EH11	26	BB13
Orwell Ter EH11	26	BB13
Osborne Ct (Cock.), Pres. EH32	19	CL7
Osborne Ter EH12	26	BB12
Osborne Ter (Cock.), Pres. EH32	19	CL7
Oswald Ct EH9	43	BF16
Oswald Rd EH9	43	BF16
Oswald Ter EH12 1	24	AT13
Oswald Ter, Pres. EH32	18	CJ10
Otterburn Pk EH14	41	AX18
Our Dynamic Earth EH8	7	BH11
Oxcars Ct EH4	13	AW6
Oxcraig St EH5	14	BB4
Oxford St EH8	7	BH13
Oxford Ter EH4	6	BC10
OXGANGS	52	BA21
Oxgangs Av EH13	52	BA21
Oxgangs Bk EH13	52	BB21
Oxgangs Brae EH13	52	BB21
Oxgangs Bdy EH13 2	52	BB21
Oxgangs Cres EH13	52	BB20
Oxgangs Dr EH13	52	BB20
Oxgangs Fm Av EH13	52	BA21
Oxgangs Fm Dr EH13	52	BA21
Oxgangs Fm Gdns EH13	52	BA21
Oxgangs Fm Gro EH13	52	BA21
Oxgangs Fm Ln EH13	52	BA21
Oxgangs Fm Ter EH13	52	BA21
Oxgangs Gdns EH13	52	BA20
Oxgangs Grn EH13	52	BB20
Oxgangs Gro EH13	52	BB20
Oxgangs Hill EH13	52	BB20
Oxgangs Ln EH13	52	BB20
Oxgangs Medway EH13	52	BB21
Oxgangs Pk EH13	52	BB21
Oxgangs Path EH13	52	BB21
Oxgangs Path E EH13 1	52	BB21
Oxgangs Pl EH13	52	BB20
Oxgangs Prim Sch EH13	41	AZ19
Oxgangs Ri EH13	52	BB20
Oxgangs Rd EH10	52	BB22
Oxgangs Rd EH13	52	BB21
Oxgangs Rd N EH13	41	AZ19
Oxgangs Rd N EH14	41	AZ19
Oxgangs Row EH13	52	BB21
Oxgangs St EH13	52	BB21
Oxgangs Ter EH13	52	BA21
Oxgangs Vw EH13	52	BB21

P

Name		
Paddock, The, Muss. EH21 1	31	BZ12
Paddockholm, The EH12	24	AU13
Paisley Av EH8	28	BM11
Paisley Cres EH8	28	BL11
Paisley Dr EH8	28	BM12
Paisley Gdns EH8	28	BL11
Paisley Gro EH8	28	BM12
Paisley Ter EH8	28	BL11
Palace of Holyroodhouse EH8	7	BH11
Palmer Pl, Currie EH14	49	AP23
Palmer Rd, Currie EH14	49	AP22
Palmerston Pl EH12	6	BC11
Palmerston Pl La EH12	6	BC12
Palmerston Rd EH9	43	BF14
Pankhurst Ln, Dalk. EH22	57	BZ24
Panmure Pl EH3	6	BE13
Papermill Wynd EH7	27	BG8
Pape's Cotts EH12	25	AZ12
Paradykes Av, Lnhd EH20	54	BJ27
Paradykes Prim Sch EH20	54	BK27
Park Av EH15	29	BQ12
Park Av, Gore. EH23	70	BY34
Park Av, Lnhd EH20	62	BJ28
Park Av, Muss. EH21	32	CA14
Park Av (Bils.), Ros. EH25	61	BF29
Park Ct, Muss. EH21	32	CA14
Park Cres EH16	44	BK19
Park Cres, Bonny. EH19	63	BR28
Park Cres (Easth.), Dalk. EH22	57	BY27
Park Cres, Lnhd EH20	62	BK28
Parker Av EH7	29	BN10
Parker Rd EH7	29	BN10
Parker Ter EH7	29	BP10
Park Gdns EH16	44	BK19
Park Gdns, Muss. EH21	32	CA14
Park Gro EH16	44	BK20
Parkgrove Av EH4	24	AS9
Parkgrove Bk EH4	24	AS9
Parkgrove Cres EH4	24	AS9
Parkgrove Dr EH4	23	AR9
Parkgrove Gdns EH4	24	AS9
Parkgrove Grn EH4	24	AS9
Parkgrove Ln EH4	24	AS9
Parkgrove Neuk EH4	24	AS9
Parkgrove Path EH4	24	AT9
Parkgrove Pl EH4	24	AS9
Park Gro Pl, Muss. EH21	32	CA14
Parkgrove Rd EH4	24	AS9
Parkgrove Row EH4	24	AS9
Parkgrove St EH4	24	AT9
Parkgrove Ter EH4	24	AS9
Park Gro Ter, Muss. EH21	32	CA14
Parkgrove Vw EH4	24	AS9
PARKHEAD	40	AV17
Parkhead Av EH11	40	AU17
Parkhead Cres EH11	40	AU17
Parkhead Dr EH11	40	AV17
Parkhead Gdns EH11	40	AU17
Parkhead Gro EH11	40	AU17
Parkhead Ln EH11	40	AU17
Parkhead Pk (Easth.), Dalk. EH22 1	57	BY27
Parkhead Pl EH11	40	AU17
Parkhead Pl (Easth.), Dalk. EH22	57	BY27
Parkhead St EH11	40	AU17
Parkhead Ter EH11	40	AV16
Parkhead Vw EH11	40	AU17
Park Hill, Gore. EH23	70	BX34
Park La EH15	29	BQ12
Park La, Dalk. EH22	56	BV25
Park La, Muss. EH21	32	CA14
Park Pl EH6	15	BE5
Park Rd EH6	15	BE5
Park Rd, Bonny. EH19	63	BR28
Park Rd, Dalk. EH22	56	BV25
Park Rd (Newt.), Dalk. EH22	65	BX29
Park Rd, Gore. EH23	70	BY34
Park Rd (Port S.), Pres. EH32	19	CM7
Parkside, Newbr. EH28	36	AC13
Parkside Ct, Dalk. EH22 6	57	BW24
Parkside Pl, Dalk. EH22	57	BW24
Parkside St EH8	7	BH13
Parkside Ter EH8	7	BH13
Park Ter (Newcr.), Muss. EH21	30	BU15
Parkvale Pl EH6	16	BK7
Park Vw, Lnhd EH20	62	BK28
Park Vw, Muss. EH21	32	CA14
Park Vw (Newcr.), Muss. EH21	30	BT15
Park Vw, Pres. EH32	18	CJ10

Name		
Park Vw E (Port S.), Pres. EH32	19	CM7
Park Vw W (Port S.), Pres. EH32	19	CM7
Parliament House Hotel EH1	7	BG10
Parliament Sq EH1	7	BF11
Parliament St EH6	15	BH6
Parrot La, Gore. EH23	70	BY35
Parrotshot EH15	29	BQ14
Parsonage, Muss. EH21	31	BZ13
Parson's Grn Prim Sch EH8	28	BM12
Parsons Grn Ter EH8 2	28	BL10
Parsonspool, Bonny. EH19	64	BS30
Path Brae, K'lis. EH29	20	AC10
Patie's Rd EH14	41	AY19
Patrick Geddes Steps EH1 14	6	BE12
Patriothall EH3 3	26	BD9
Pattison St EH6	16	BJ6
Peacock Av, Bonny. EH19	64	BU29
Peacock Ct EH6	15	BF4
Peacock Parkway, Bonny. EH19	64	BU29
Peacock Pl, Bonny. EH19	64	BT29
Peacocktail Cl EH15	29	BR15
Pearce Av EH12	24	AS12
Pearce Gro EH12	24	AS12
Pearce Rd EH12	24	AS12
Peatville Gdns EH14	41	AW18
Peatville Ter EH14	41	AW18
Peebles Rd, Pen. EH26	69	BB39
Peel Ter EH9	43	BH15
Peffer Bk EH16	28	BM15
Peffermill Ct EH16 1	44	BM16
Peffermill Ind Est EH16	28	BL15
Peffermill Rd EH16	44	BK16
Peffer Pl EH16	28	BM15
Peffer St EH16	28	BM15
Peggy's Mill Rd EH4	23	AQ7
Pembroke Pl EH12	26	BA12
Pendreich Av, Bonny. EH19	56	BS27
Pendreich Dr, Bonny. EH19	56	BS27
Pendreich Gro, Bonny. EH19	56	BS27
Pendreich Ter, Bonny. EH19	56	BS27
Pendreich Vw, Bonny. EH19	56	BS27
PENICUIK	69	BB39
Penicuik High Sch EH26	68	BA38
Penicuik Rd, Ros. EH25	67	BF32
Pennywell Cotts EH4	13	AX5
Pennywell Ct EH4	13	AX6
Pennywell Gdns EH4	13	AW6
Pennywell Gro EH4	13	AX6
Pennywell Medway EH4	13	AW6
Pennywell Pl EH4	13	AX6
Pennywell Rd EH4	13	AX6
Pennywell Vil EH4	13	AY5
Pentad Business Pk EH12	39	AR16
Pentland Av EH13	50	AV21
Pentland Av, Currie EH14	49	AP23
Pentland Av (Gowks.), Gore. EH23	65	BX32
Pentland Av, Pen. EH26	68	BA37
Pentland Br EH10	61	BG26
Pentland Caravan Pk, Lnhd EH20	61	BG27
Pentland Ct (Bils.), Ros. EH25	61	BG29
Pentland Cres EH10	52	BC20
Pentland Cres, Rose. EH24	62	BM32
Pentland Dr EH10	52	BB21
Pentland Gait EH11	39	AR18
Pentland Gdns EH10	52	BC20
Pentland Gro EH10	52	BC20
Pentland Ind Est, Lnhd EH20	54	BJ27
Pentland Pl, Currie EH14	49	AP23
Pentland Rd EH13	51	AW20
Pentland Rd, Bonny. EH19	63	BP29
Pentlands Science Pk, Pen. EH26	67	BE32
Pentland Ter EH10	42	BC19
Pentland Ter, Pen. EH26	68	BA37
Pentland Vw EH10	52	BC21
Pentland Vw, Currie EH14	49	AP23
Pentland Vw, Dalk. EH22	57	BY25
Pentland Vw Ct, Currie EH14 1	49	AQ23
Pentland Vw Cres, Ros. EH25	67	BH32
Pentland Vw Pl, Ros. EH25	67	BH32
Pentland Vw Rd, K'lis. EH29	20	AC10
Pentland Vw Rd, Ros. EH25	67	BH32
Pentland Vw Ter, Ros. EH25	67	BH32
Pentland Vil, Jun. Grn EH14 1	50	AT22
People's Story EH8 14	7	BG11
Perdrixknowe EH14	41	AZ16
Persevere Ct EH6	15	BH5
Perth's Gro, Pres. EH32	18	CJ9
Perth St EH3	26	BD9
Pettigrew's Cl, Dalk. EH22 3	57	BW24
Peveril Ter EH16	44	BJ19
Philip Pl, Pen. EH26	68	BA36
Picardy Pl EH1	7	BG10
Pier Pl EH6	15	BE4
Piersfield Gro EH8	28	BM10
Piersfield Pl EH8	28	BM10
Piersfield Ter EH8	28	BM10
PIERSHILL	28	BM11
Piershill La EH8 3	28	BL10
Piershill Pl EH8 4	28	BL10
Piershill Sq E EH8	28	BM10
Piershill Sq W EH8	28	BL10
Piershill Ter EH8	28	BM11
Pillars, The EH17	44	BM20
PILRIG	15	BG7
Pilrig Cotts EH6	27	BH8
Pilrig Gdns EH6	15	BG7
Pilrig Glebe EH6	27	BH8
Pilrig Hts EH6	15	BF7
Pilrig Ho Cl EH6	15	BG7
Pilrig Ind Est EH6	15	BG7
Pilrig Pk Sch EH6	15	BG7
Pilrig Pl EH6	27	BH8
Pilrig St EH6	15	BG7
PILTON	13	AZ6
Pilton Av EH5	13	AZ6
Pilton Cres EH5	14	BB6
Pilton Dr EH5	14	BA6
Pilton Dr N EH5	14	BA5
Pilton Gdns EH5	14	BA6
Pilton Ln EH5	14	BA6
Pilton Pk EH5	14	BA6
Pilton Pl EH5	14	BA6
Pinegrove Gdns EH4	23	AR9
Pinewood Pl (Mayf.), Dalk. EH22	71	CA29
Pinewood Rd (Mayf.), Dalk. EH22	71	CA29
Pinewood Vw (Mayf.), Dalk. EH22	71	CA29
Pinkhill EH12	24	AV13
PINKIE	32	CB14
Pinkie Av, Muss. EH21	32	CA14
Pinkie Dr, Muss. EH21	32	CA14
Pinkie Hill Cres, Muss. EH21	32	CA14
Pinkie Pl, Muss. EH21	32	CA14
Pinkie Rd, Muss. EH21	32	CA14
Pinkie St. Peter's Prim Sch EH21	32	CA13
Pinkie Ter, Muss. EH21	32	CA14
Pinkie Wk, Tran. EH33 7	35	CL14
Pipe La EH15	29	BQ10
Pipe St EH15	29	BQ10
Pirniefield Bk EH6	16	BL7
Pirniefield Gdns EH6	16	BL7
Pirniefield Gro EH6	16	BL7
Pirniefield Pl EH6	16	BL7
Pirniefield Ter EH6	16	BL7
Pirniehall Prim Sch EH4	13	AY6
Pirrie St EH6	15	BH7
Pitlochry Pl EH7	16	BJ9
Pitsligo Rd EH10	42	BD15
Pittencrieff Ct, Muss. EH21 1	32	CB13
Pitt St EH6	15	BF6
Pittville St EH15	29	BR11
Pittville St La EH15	29	BR11
Place Charente, Dalk. EH22 1	57	BY24
Playfair Steps EH2 1	6	BE11
Playhouse Theatre EH1	7	BG10
Pleasance EH8	7	BG12
Plewlandcroft, S Q'fry EH30	8	AD2
Plewlands Av EH10	42	BB17
Plewlands Gdns EH10	42	BB17
Plewlands Pl, S Q'fry EH30	8	AD3
Plewlands Ter EH10	42	BB17
Pleydell Pl EH16	44	BK19
Plough La, Tran. EH33 2	35	CM13
Plummer Ct, Dalk. EH22 2	57	BW24
Point Hotel EH3	6	BD12
Pollard Glebe EH11	41	AW15
Polson Gdns, Tran. EH33	34	CK13
POLTON	62	BM29
Polton Av Rd, Bonny. EH19	63	BP29
Polton Bk, Lass. EH18	63	BN29
Polton Bk Ter, Lass. EH18	63	BN29
Polton Cotts, Lass. EH18	62	BM29
Polton Ct, Bonny. EH19	63	BR29
Polton Dr, Lass. EH18	63	BP29
Polton Gdns, Lass. EH18	63	BQ28
POLTONHALL	63	BP29
Poltonhall, Bonny. EH19 2	63	BQ30
Polton Pl, Bonny. EH19	63	BR28
Polton Rd, Lass. EH18	63	BQ28
Polton Rd (Polt.), Lass. EH18	62	BM29
Polton Rd, Lnhd EH20	62	BL28
Polton Rd W, Lass. EH18	63	BN29
Polton St, Bonny. EH19	63	BR29
Polton Ter, Lass. EH18 1	63	BQ28
Polton Vale, Lnhd EH20	62	BL28
POLWARTH	42	BA14
Polwarth Cres EH11	42	BC14
Polwarth Cres, Pres. EH32	18	CJ10
Polwarth Gdns EH11	42	BB14
Polwarth Gro EH11	42	BB15
Polwarth Pk EH11	42	BB14
Polwarth Pl EH11	42	BB14
Polwarth Ter EH11	42	BB15
Polwarth Ter, Pres. EH32	18	CJ10
Pomathorn Bk, Pen. EH26	69	BB39
Pomathorn Rd, Pen. EH26	69	BB39
Ponton St EH3	6	BD13
Poplar La EH6	16	BJ6
Poplar Pk (Port S.), Pres. EH32	19	CM8
Poplar Path, Lnhd EH20	61	BH28
Poplar St (Mayf.), Dalk. EH22	71	CA29
Poplar Ter, Bonny. EH19	63	BR29
PORT EDGAR	8	AB1
Port Edgar Marina & Sailing School EH30	8	AC1
Porterfield Rd EH4	26	BA8
Portgower Pl EH4	26	BC9
Port Hamilton EH3	6	BD12
Portland Gdns EH6	15	BG5
Portland Row EH6	15	BG5
Portland St EH6	15	BG5
Portland Ter EH6 3	15	BG5
PORTOBELLO	29	BR10
Portobello High Sch EH15	29	BP12
Portobello High St EH15	29	BQ10
Portobello Pubic Golf Course EH15	29	BQ12
Portobello Rd EH8	28	BM10
Port Royal Golf Range EH28	21	AH12
Portsburgh Sq EH1 5	6	BE12
Port Seton Harbour (Port S.), Pres. EH32	19	CL7
Post Rd, Tran. EH33	34	CJ13
POST SETON	19	CL6
Potterrow EH8	7	BF12
Potter's Path, Tran. EH33 4	35	CL13
Pottery, The EH15 14	29	BQ10
Pottery, The, Pres. EH32	18	CG10
Povert Rd, Bonny. EH19	64	BV33
Povert Rd, Gore. EH23	64	BV34

Powderhall Brae EH7 15 BF7
Powderhall Rigg EH7 15 BF7
Powderhall Rd EH7 27 BF8
Powdermill Brae, Gore.
  EH23 70 BY37
Premier Travel Inn City Centre
  (Lauriston Place) EH3 6 BE12
Premier Travel Inn City Centre
  (Morrison Street) EH3 6 BC12
Premier Travel Inn
  Edinburgh East EH8 29 BN12
Premier Travel Inn
  (Newcraighall) EH21 30 BT15
Premier Travel Inn Edinburgh
  (South Queensferry)
  EH30 8 AC3
Premier Travel Inn Leith
  EH6 15 BE4
PRESTON 34 CJ11
Preston Av, Pres. EH32 18 CK10
Preston Ct, Pres. EH32 34 CH11
Preston Cres, Pres. EH32 18 CK9
Preston Cross Cotts,
  Pres. EH32 3 18 CJ10
PRESTONFIELD 28 BK15
Prestonfield Av EH16 28 BJ15
Prestonfield Bk EH16 28 BJ15
Prestonfield Cres EH16 28 BJ15
Prestonfield Gdns EH16 28 BJ15
Prestonfield Golf Course
  EH16 28 BL14
Prestonfield Hotel EH16 28 BK14
Prestonfield Prim Sch
  EH16 44 BK16
Prestonfield Rd EH16 28 BJ15
Prestonfield Ter EH16 28 BJ15
Prestongrange, Pres. EH32 33 CF11
Prestongrange Industrial
  Heritage Museum EH32 33 CE11
Prestongrange Ter, Pres.
  EH32 34 CG11
Prestonhall Cres, Rose.
  EH24 62 BM32
Prestonhall Rd, Rose.
  EH24 62 BM33
Preston Lo High Sch EH32 18 CJ10
PRESTONPANS 18 CG9
Prestonpans Ind Est, Pres.
  EH32 34 CJ11
Prestonpans Inf Sch EH32 18 CH10
Prestonpans Prim Sch
  EH32 34 CJ11
Prestonpans Sta EH32 34 CJ11
Preston Rd, Pres. EH32 34 CH11
Preston St, Rose. EH24 62 BM33
Preston St Prim Sch EH16 43 BH14
Preston Ter, Pres. EH32 18 CK10
Priestfield Av EH16 28 BK15
Priestfield Cres EH16 28 BK15
Priestfield Gdns EH16 28 BK15
Priestfield Gro EH16 28 BJ14
Priestfield Rd EH16 28 BJ15
Priestfield Rd N EH16 28 BJ14
Priesthill Bk Rd EH5 14 BD5
Priesthill Pl EH16 44 BK21
Priesthill St EH16 44 BK21
Primrose Cres, Dalk.
  EH22 57 BY25
Primrose Dr (Craig.),
  S Q'fry EH30 22 AM8
Primrose Gdns, S Q'fry
  EH30 9 AE3
Primrose St EH6 16 BJ7
Primrose Ter EH11 42 BA14
Primrose Ter, Dalk. EH22 1 57 BY25
Prince of Wales Dock EH6 15 BH4
Prince Regent St EH6 15 BG5
Princes Golf Course EH16 43 BF19
Princes Mall EH2 7 BF11
Princess Alexandra Eye
  Pav EH3 6 BE13
Princes St EH1 6 BE11
Princes St EH2 6 BE11
Priory Gro, S Q'fry EH30 8 AD3
Private Rd, Gore. EH23 70 BZ36
Promenade EH15 17 BP8

Promenade, Muss. EH21 31 BX12
Promenade, The (Port S.),
  Pres. EH32 19 CM7
Promenade Ter EH15 29 BQ10
Prospect Bk Cres EH6 16 BK7
Prospect Bk Gdns EH6 16 BK8
Prospect Bk Gro EH6 16 BL7
Prospect Bk Pl EH6 16 BL7
Prospect Bk Rd EH6 16 BK7
Prospect Bk Sch EH6 16 BK7
Prospect Bk Ter EH6 16 BL7
Provost Haugh, Currie
  EH14 49 AR22
Provost Milne Gro, S Q'fry
  EH30 9 AF4
Pryde Av, Bonny. EH19 63 BQ28
Pryde Ter, Bonny. EH19 63 BQ28
Pypers Wynd, Pres. EH32 18 CH9

Q

Quadrant, The, Pen. EH26 69 BB37
Quality Hotel Edinburgh
  Airport EH28 21 AG12
Quality St EH4 24 AV8
Quality St La EH4 24 AV8
Quarrybank EH14 40 AS19
Quarrybank Cl EH14 40 AS19
Quarrybank Ct EH14 40 AS19
Quarrybank End EH14 40 AS19
Quarry Cl EH8 7 BG13
Quarry Cotts EH15 29 BR15
Quarryfoot Gdns, Bonny.
  EH19 63 BR28
Quarryfoot Grn, Bonny.
  EH19 56 BS28
Quarryfoot Pl, Bonny.
  EH19 63 BR28
QUARRYHEAD 55 BR27
Quarry Howe, Bal. EH14 1 58 AL26
Quarryview EH14 1 40 AS19
Quayside Mills EH6 3 15 BH6
Quayside St EH6 15 BH6
Queen Anne Dr, Newbr.
  EH28 36 AD13
Queen Charlotte La EH6 16 BJ6
Queen Charlotte St EH6 16 BJ6
Queen Margaret Cl EH10 53 BE22
Queen Margaret Dr, S Q'fry
  EH30 9 AE2
Queen Margaret Uni Coll
  (Corstorphine Campus)
  EH12 24 AT11
Queen's Av EH4 25 AX9
Queen's Av S EH4 25 AY9
Queen's Bay Cres EH15 30 BT12
Queen's Cres EH9 43 BH15
Queen's Dr EH8 7 BH12
Queensferry High Sch
  EH30 9 AF3
Queensferry Museum
  EH30 9 AE2
Queensferry Prim Sch
  EH30 9 AE2
Queensferry Rd EH4 26 BB10
Queensferry Rd (Cram.)
  EH4 24 AS9
Queensferry Rd, K'lis.
  EH29 20 AC9
Queensferry St EH2 6 BC11
Queensferry St La EH2 6 BC11
Queensferry Ter EH4 26 BA10
Queen's Gallery
  (Palace of Holyroodhouse)
  EH8 7 BH11
Queen's Gdns EH8 25 AY9
Queen's Pk Av EH8 28 BK10
Queen's Pk Ct EH8 28 BL11
Queen's Rd EH4 25 AY9
Queens's Hall Theatre EH8 7 BG13
Queen St EH2 6 BD10
Queen St Gdns E EH3 6 BE10
Queen St Gdns W EH3 6 BE10
Queen's Wk EH16 29 BN15
Queensway, Pen. EH26 68 BA36
Quilts, The EH6 15 BG6

Quilts Wynd EH6 15 BG6

R

Radisson SAS Hotel EH1 7 BG11
Raeburn Ms EH4 26 BC9
Raeburn Pl EH4 26 BC9
Raeburn St EH4 26 BC9
Rae's Ct EH16 54 BJ22
Raes Gdns, Bonny. EH19 63 BR28
Ramada Jarvis Edinburgh
  Murrayfield EH12 25 AY12
Ramada Mount Royal Hotel
  EH2 7 BF11
Ramillies Ct, Pen. EH26 66 BC35
Ramsay Cres (Mayf.),
  Dalk. EH22 71 CA30
Ramsay Gdn EH1 6 BE11
Ramsay La EH1 6 BE11
Ramsay Pl EH15 9 29 BQ10
Ramsay Pl, Pen. EH26 68 AY37
Ramsay Ter, Lass. EH18 63 BP29
Ramsay Wk (Mayf.),
  Dalk. EH22 4 71 CA30
Randolph Cliff EH3 6 BC11
Randolph Cres EH3 6 BC11
Randolph La EH3 6 BD11
Randolph Pl EH3 6 BD11
Rankeillor St EH8 7 BG13
Rankin Av EH9 43 BH17
Rankin Dr EH9 43 BG17
Rankin Rd EH9 43 BH16
Rannoch Gro EH4 24 AT10
Rannoch Pl EH4 24 AT10
Rannoch Rd EH4 24 AU10
Rannoch Ter EH4 24 AT10
Ransome Gdns EH4 24 AT10
Ratcliffe Ter EH9 43 BG14
Rathbone Pl EH15 29 BR10
RATHO 37 AG17
Ratho Pk (Ratho Sta),
  Newbr. EH28 37 AE13
Ratho Park Golf Course
  EH28 38 AJ17
Ratho Pk Rd (Ratho),
  Newbr. EH28 37 AG17
Ratho Prim Sch EH28 37 AF17
RATHO STATION 37 AF14
Rattray Cres EH10 42 BA19
Rattray Dr EH10 42 BA19
Rattray Gro EH10 42 BA19
Rattray Ln EH10 42 BA19
Rattray Way EH10 42 BB19
Ravelrig Dr EH14 58 AK25
Ravelrig Gait, Bal. EH14 58 AK25
Ravelrig Hill, Bal. EH14 58 AK25
Ravelrig Pk, Bal. EH14 58 AK25
Ravelrig Rd, Bal. EH14 48 AK22
Ravelrig Wynd EH14 58 AK25
RAVELSTON 25 AY10
Ravelston Ct EH12 25 AZ11
Ravelston Dykes EH4 25 AZ11
Ravelston Dykes EH12 25 AY11
Ravelston Dykes La EH4 25 AW11
Ravelston Dykes Rd EH4 25 AX10
Ravelston Gdn EH4 25 AY11
Ravelston Golf Course
  EH4 25 AW10
Ravelston Hts EH4 25 AY10
Ravelston Ho Gro EH4 25 AY10
Ravelston Ho Ln EH4 25 AY10
Ravelston Ho Pk EH4 25 AY10
Ravelston Ho Rd EH4 25 AY10
Ravelston Pk EH4 26 BA11
Ravelston Pl EH4 4 26 BB11
Ravelston Ri EH4 25 AY11
Ravelston Ter EH4 26 BB10
Ravelsykes Rd, Pen.
  EH26 68 AY38
Ravendean Gdns, Pen.
  EH26 68 AY38
Ravenscroft Gdns EH17 55 BN22
Ravenscroft Pl EH17 55 BN22
Ravenscroft St EH17 55 BN22
Ravensheugh Cres,
  Muss. EH21 32 CC13

Ravensheugh Rd, Muss. *EH21* 32 CC13
Ravenswood Av *EH16* 44 BK18
Real Mary King's Close *EH1* **7** 7 BF11
Redbraes Gro *EH7* 15 BF7
Redbraes Pl *EH7* 15 BF7
Redburn Rd, Pres. *EH32* 18 CG10
Redburn Rd N, Pres. *EH32* 18 CG10
Redcroft St, Dalk. *EH22* 45 BQ19
Redford Av *EH13* 51 AX21
Redford Barracks *EH13* 51 AY20
Redford Cres *EH13* 51 AY21
Redford Dr *EH13* 51 AX21
Redford Gdns *EH13* 51 AY21
Redford Gro *EH13* 51 AZ20
Redford Loan *EH13* 51 AX21
Redford Neuk *EH13* 51 AZ21
Redford Pl *EH13* 51 AZ20
Redford Rd *EH13* 52 BA21
Redford Ter *EH13* 51 AY21
Redford Wk *EH13* 51 AY21
Red Fox Cres, Pen. *EH26* 66 BC34
Redgauntlet Ter *EH16* 44 BK18
Redhall Av *EH14* 41 AW17
Redhall Bk Rd *EH14* 41 AX18
Redhall Cres *EH14* 41 AW17
Redhall Dr *EH14* 41 AW17
Redhall Gdns *EH14* 41 AW17
Redhall Gro *EH14* 41 AW17
Redhall Ho Dr *EH14* 41 AY18
Redhall Pl *EH14* 41 AW17
Redhall Rd *EH14* 41 AW17
Redhall Vw *EH14* 41 AX18
Redheughs Ln, Gore. *EH23* **2** 70 BY34
Redheughs Av *EH12* 39 AQ15
Redheughs Rigg *EH12* 39 AQ14
Redwood Gro (Newt.), Dalk. *EH22* 64 BV30
Redwood Wk (Newt.), Dalk. *EH22* 65 BW30
Reed Dr (Newt.), Dalk. *EH22* 65 BX29
Reekie's Ct *EH8* 7 BG12
Regent Br *EH1* **2** 7 BF10
Regent Pl *EH7* 28 BJ10
Regent Rd *EH1* 7 BG10
Regent Rd *EH7* 7 BG10
Regent's Ct *EH11* **1** 26 BB13
Regent St *EH15* 29 BR11
Regent St La *EH15* 29 BR11
Regent Ter *EH7* 7 BG10
Regent Ter Ms *EH7* 7 BH10
Regis Ct *EH4* 23 AR7
Register Pl *EH2* 7 BF10
Reid's Cl *EH8* 7 BH11
Reid's Ct *EH8* **1** 7 BH11
Reid Ter *EH3* 26 BC9
Relugas Gdns *EH9* 43 BG16
Relugas Pl *EH9* 43 BG16
Relugas Rd *EH9* 43 BG16
Rennie's Isle *EH6* 15 BH5
Research Av N (Ricc.), Currie *EH14* 49 AN19
Research Av S (Ricc.), Currie *EH14* 49 AP20
RESTALRIG 16 BL10
Restalrig Av *EH7* 28 BL10
Restalrig Circ *EH7* 16 BL8
Restalrig Cres *EH7* 16 BL8
Restalrig Dr *EH7* 16 BL9
Restalrig Gdns *EH7* 16 BL9
Restalrig Pk *EH7* 16 BK8
Restalrig Rd *EH6* 16 BK7
Restalrig Rd *EH7* 16 BK8
Restalrig Rd S *EH7* 28 BL10
Restalrig Sq *EH7* 16 BL8
Restalrig Ter *EH6* 16 BJ7
RICCARTON 49 AN20
Riccarton Av, Currie *EH14* 49 AP22
Riccarton Cres, Currie *EH14* 49 AQ22
Riccarton Dr, Currie *EH14* 49 AP22
Riccarton Gro, Currie *EH14* 49 AQ22

Riccarton Mains Rd, Currie *EH14* 39 AP18
Riccarton Prim Sch *EH14* 49 AQ23
Richmond La *EH8* 7 BG12
Richmond Pl *EH8* 7 BG12
Richmond Ter *EH11* 6 BC12
Riding Pk *EH4* 23 AR7
Riego St *EH3* 6 BD12
Riggonhead Ct, Tran. *EH33* 35 CM12
Riggonhead Gdns, Tran. *EH33* 35 CM12
Rigley Ter, Pres. *EH32* 34 CG11
Rillbank Cres *EH9* 43 BF14
Rillbank Ter *EH9* 43 BF14
Ringwood Pl *EH16* 44 BK19
Rintoul Pl *EH3* 26 BD9
Riselaw Cres *EH10* 52 BC20
Riselaw Pl *EH10* 42 BC19
Riselaw Rd *EH10* 42 BC19
Riselaw Ter *EH10* 42 BC19
Ritchie Pl *EH11* 42 BB14
River Gore Gro, Gore. *EH23* 70 BY35
River Gore Rd, Gore. *EH23* 70 BY35
River Gore Vw, Gore. *EH23* 70 BY35
Riversdale Cres *EH12* 25 AY13
Riversdale Gro *EH12* 25 AY12
Riversdale Rd *EH12* 25 AX12
Riverside *EH4* **1** 11 AR4
Riverside, Newbr. *EH28* 36 AB13
Riverside Gdns, Muss. *EH21* 31 BX14
Riverside Rd (Craig.), S Q'fry *EH30* 23 AN8
Roanshead Rd (Easth.), Dalk. *EH22* 57 BY27
Robb's Ln *EH14* 41 AY15
Robb's Ln Gro *EH14* 41 AY15
Robert Burns Dr *EH16* 44 BJ18
Robert Burns Ms, Dalk. *EH22* **1** 57 BZ24
Robert De Quincy Pl, Pres. *EH32* **2** 34 CH11
Robert Smillie Av (Mayf.), Dalk. *EH22* 71 CA30
Robertson Av *EH11* 41 AZ14
Robertson Av, Pres. *EH32* 18 CJ9
Robertson Av, Tran. *EH33* 35 CM13
Robertson Bk, Gore. *EH23* 70 BZ36
Robertson Dr, Tran. *EH33* 35 CM12
Robertson Gait *EH11* 41 AZ15
Robertson's Cl *EH1* 7 BG12
Robertson's Cl, Dalk. *EH22* 57 BW24
Robertson's Ct *EH8* **2** 7 BH11
Rocheid Pk *EH4* 14 BB7
Rocheid Path *EH3* 26 BD8
Rochester Ter *EH10* 42 BC15
Rockville Ter, Bonny. *EH19* 55 BR27
Roddinglaw Rd *EH12* 38 AK15
Rodney Pl *EH7* 27 BE9
Rodney St *EH7* 27 BE8
Romero Pl *EH16* 43 BH14
Ronaldson's Wf *EH6* 15 BH6
Rope Wk, Pres. *EH32* 18 CG10
Rosabelle Rd, Ros. *EH25* 67 BH32
Rose Av, Bonny. *EH19* 64 BT29
Rosebank Cotts *EH3* 6 BC12
Rosebank Gdns *EH5* 14 BC6
Rosebank Gro *EH5* 14 BC6
Rosebank Rd *EH5* 14 BC6
Rosebery Av, S Q'fry *EH30* 9 AE3
Rosebery Ct, S Q'fry *EH30* 9 AE3
Rosebery Cres *EH12* 26 BB12
Rosebery Cres, Gore. *EH23* 70 BY37
Rosebery Cres La *EH12* 26 BB12
ROSEBURN 25 AZ12
Roseburn Av *EH12* 25 AZ12
Roseburn Cliff *EH12* 25 AZ12
Roseburn Cres *EH12* 25 AZ13
Roseburn Dr *EH12* 25 AZ12
Roseburn Gdns *EH12* **2** 25 AZ12
Roseburn Maltings *EH12* 26 BA12
Roseburn Pl *EH12* 25 AZ12
Roseburn Prim Sch *EH12* 25 AZ13
Roseburn St *EH12* 25 AZ13
Roseburn Ter *EH12* 25 AZ12
Rose Cotts, Bonny. *EH19* 64 BT29

Rose Ct *EH4* **7** 12 AU7
Rosefield Av *EH15* 29 BQ11
Rosefield Av La *EH15* 29 BQ11
Rosefield La *EH15* 29 BQ11
Rosefield Pl *EH15* 29 BQ11
Rosefield St *EH15* 29 BQ11
Rose Gdns, Bonny. *EH19* 64 BT29
Rose Gro, Bonny. *EH19* 64 BT29
Rose La, S Q'fry *EH30* 8 AD2
Rosemount Bldgs *EH3* 6 BC12
Rosemount Ms, Pres. *EH32* **4** 18 CH9
Roseneath Pl *EH9* 43 BE14
Roseneath St *EH9* 43 BF14
Roseneath Ter *EH9* 43 BF14
Rose Neuk, Bonny. *EH19* 64 BT29
Rose Pk *EH5* 14 BD6
Rose Pk, Bonny. *EH19* 64 BT29
Rose Path, Bonny. *EH19* 64 BT29
Rose Pl, Bonny. *EH19* 64 BT29
Rose St *EH2* 6 BD11
Rose St N La *EH2* 6 BD11
Rose St S La *EH2* 6 BD11
Rose Ter, Bonny. *EH19* 64 BT29
Rosevale Pl *EH6* **1** 16 BK7
Rosevale Ter *EH6* 16 BJ7
Roseville Gdns *EH5* 15 BE5
Rose Way, Bonny. *EH19* 64 BT29
ROSEWELL 62 BL33
Rosewell Prim Sch *EH24* 63 BN33
Rosewell Rd, Bonny. *EH19* 63 BP31
ROSLIN 67 BH32
Roslin Prim Sch *EH25* 67 BH32
Ross Cres, Tran. *EH33* 35 CM14
Ross Gdns *EH9* 43 BG16
Rossglen Ct, Ros. *EH25* 62 BJ32
Ross High Sch *EH33* 35 CL13
Rosshill Ter (Dalm.), S Q'fry *EH30* 9 AF3
Rossie Pl *EH7* 27 BH9
Rosslyn Chapel *EH25* 62 BJ32
Rosslyn Cres *EH6* 27 BG8
Rosslyn Ter *EH6* 27 BG8
Ross Open Air Theatre *EH2* 6 BE11
Ross Pl *EH9* 43 BH16
Ross Pl (Newt.), Dalk. *EH22* 65 BX29
Ross Rd *EH16* 43 BH17
Rothesay Ms *EH3* 26 BB11
Rothesay Pl *EH3* 26 BB11
Rothesay Pl, Muss. *EH21* 31 BZ14
Rothesay Ter *EH3* 26 BB11
Roull Gro *EH12* 40 AT14
Roull Pl *EH12* 40 AU14
Roull Rd *EH12* 40 AT14
Rowallan Ct *EH12* **2** 23 AQ12
Rowanfield Prim Sch *EH4* 25 AY8
Rowan Gdns, Bonny. *EH19* 63 BR29
Rowanhill Cl (Port S.), Pres. *EH32* 19 CM8
Rowanhill Dr (Port S.), Pres. *EH32* 19 CM8
Rowanhill Pk (Port S.), Pres. *EH32* 19 CL8
Rowanhill Way (Port S.), Pres. *EH32* 19 CM8
Rowan Tree Av, Currie *EH14* 49 AN23
Rowan Tree Gro, Currie *EH14* 49 AN24
Rowantree Rd (Mayf.), Dalk. *EH22* 71 CA28
Roxburghe Hotel *EH2* 6 BD11
Roxburgh Pl *EH8* 7 BG12
Roxburgh St *EH8* 7 BG12
Royal Blind Sch (Canaan Lane) *EH10* 42 BD16
Royal Blind Sch (Craigmillar Park) *EH16* 43 BH16
Royal Botanic Garden Edinburgh *EH3* 26 BD8
Royal British Hotel *EH2* 7 BF10
Royal Burgess Golf Course *EH4* 23 AR7
Royal Circ *EH3* 6 BD10

Royal Coll of Nursing *EH9* 43 BE16
Royal Commonwealth Pool
  EH16 43 BH14
Royal Ct, Pen. *EH26* 68 AZ36
Royal Cres *EH3* 27 BE9
Royal (Dick) Sch of Vet Studies
  (Easter Bush) *EH25* 61 BE30
Royal (Dick) Sch of Vet Studies
  (Summerhall) *EH9* 7 BG13
Royal Edinburgh Hosp
  EH10 42 BC16
Royal Elizabeth Yd, K'lis.
  EH29 9 AG6
Royal High Prim Sch *EH8* 28 BM11
Royal High Sch, The *EH4* 24 AT8
Royal Hosp for Sick Children
  EH9 43 BF14
Royal Infirmary of Edinburgh
  (Little France) *EH16* 45 BN17
Royal Lyceum Theatre *EH1* 6 BD12
Royal Mile *EH1* 6 BE11
Royal Mile Prim Sch *EH8* 7 BH11
Royal Museum *EH1* 7 BF12
Royal Pk Pl *EH8* 28 BK10
Royal Pk Ter *EH8* 28 BK10
Royal Scots Dragoon Guards
  Regimental Museum *EH1* 6 BE12
Royal Scots Regimental
  Museum *EH1* 6 BE12
Royal Scottish Academy
  EH2 6 BE11
Royal Ter *EH7* 7 BG10
Royal Terrace Hotel *EH7* 7 BG10
Royal Ter Ms *EH7* 7 BH10
Royal Victoria Hosp *EH4* 26 BA9
Royal Yacht Britannia *EH6* 15 BH4
Royston Mains Av *EH5* 13 AZ5
Royston Mains Cl *EH5* 14 BA5
Royston Mains Cres *EH5* 13 AZ5
Royston Mains Gdns *EH5* 14 BA5
Royston Mains Grn *EH5* 14 BA5
Royston Mains Pl *EH5* 13 AZ5
Royston Mains Rd *EH5* 14 BA5
Royston Mains St *EH5* 13 AZ5
Royston Prim Sch *EH5* 14 BA5
Royston Ter *EH3* 14 BD7
Rudolf Steiner Sch *EH10* 42 BB15
Rullion Grn Av, Pen. *EH26* 68 AZ36
Rullion Grn Cres, Pen.
  EH26 68 AZ36
Rullion Grn Gro, Pen.
  EH26 68 AZ36
Rullion Rd, Pen. *EH26* 68 AZ36
Ruskin Pl (Mayf.),
  Dalk. *EH22* 71 CA30
Russell Gdns *EH12* 26 BA12
Russell Pl *EH5* 14 BD5
Russell Rd *EH11* 26 BA13
Russell Rd *EH12* 26 BA12
Rustic Cotts *EH13 1* 51 AX20
Rutherford Dr *EH16* 44 BK18
Ruthven Pl *EH16* 44 BK18
Rutland Ct *EH3 2* 6 BD12
Rutland Ct La *EH3* 6 BD12
Rutland Pl *EH1 1* 6 BD11
Rutland Sq *EH1* 6 BD11
Rutland St *EH1* 6 BD11
Ryehill Av *EH6* 16 BK7
Ryehill Gdns *EH6* 16 BK7
Ryehill Gro *EH6* 16 BK8
Ryehill Pl *EH6* 16 BK7
Ryehill Ter *EH6* 16 BK7

S

Sacred Heart RC Prim Sch
  EH26 68 AZ38
Saddletree Ln *EH16 1* 44 BL17
St. Alban's Rd *EH9* 43 BG16
St. Andrew Pl *EH6* 16 BJ7
St. Andrew Sq *EH1* 7 BF10
St. Andrew Sq *EH2* 7 BF10
St. Andrew's RC Prim Sch
  EH23 65 BW32
St. Andrew St, Dalk. *EH22* 57 BW24
St. Annes Ct, Dalk. *EH22* 65 BW30

St. Annes Path, Lass. *EH18* 63 BN29
St. Ann's Av, Lass. *EH18* 63 BN29
St. Anthony La *EH6* 15 BH6
St. Anthony Pl *EH6 5* 15 BH6
St. Anthony St *EH6 6* 15 BH6
St. Augustine's RC
  High Sch *EH12* 40 AS15
St. Bernard's Cres *EH4* 6 BC10
St. Bernard's Row *EH4* 26 BD9
St. Catherine's Gdns *EH12* 25 AW13
St. Catherine's Pl *EH9* 43 BG14
St. Catherine's
  Prim Sch *EH16* 54 BK22
St. Clair Av *EH6* 16 BJ8
St. Clair Cres, Ros. *EH25* 62 BJ32
St. Clair Pl *EH6* 16 BJ8
St. Clair Rd *EH6* 16 BJ8
St. Clair St *EH6* 16 BJ8
St. Clair Ter *EH10* 42 BB17
St. Clements Cres (Wall.),
  Muss. *EH21* 33 CD15
St. Clements Gdns N (Wall.),
  Muss. *EH21* 33 CD15
St. Clements Gdns S (Wall.),
  Muss. *EH21* 33 CD15
St. Clements Ter (Wall.),
  Muss. *EH21* 33 CD15
St. Colme St *EH3* 6 BD11
St. Crispin's Sch *EH9* 43 BG16
St. Cuthbert's RC
  Prim Sch *EH14* 41 AZ15
St. Davids (Newt.),
  Dalk. *EH22* 65 BW30
St. David's Pl *EH3 9* 6 BC12
St. David's RC
  High Sch *EH22* 57 BZ23
St. David's RC
  Prim Sch *EH4* 13 AY6
St. David's RC
  Prim Sch *EH22* 57 BY25
St. David's Ter *EH3 10* 6 BC12
St. Fillan's Ter *EH10* 42 BC17
St. Francis' RC
  Prim Sch *EH16* 29 BN15
St. Gabriel's RC
  Prim Sch *EH32* 18 CH10
St. George's Sch *EH12* 26 BA11
St. Germains Cor, Tran.
  EH33 35 CM12
St. Giles' Cathedral *EH1* 7 BF11
St. Giles' St *EH1* 7 BF11
St. James' Pl *EH1* 7 BF10
St. James's Gdns, Pen.
  EH26 68 BA39
St. James
  Shopping Centre *EH1* 7 BF10
St. James Sq *EH1* 7 BF10
St. James's Vw, Pen. *EH26* 68 BA39
St. John's Av *EH12* 24 AU13
St. John's Cres *EH12* 24 AV13
St. John's Gdns *EH12* 24 AU13
St. John's Hill *EH8 9* 7 BG12
St. John's RC
  Prim Sch *EH15* 29 BQ12
St. John's Rd *EH12* 24 AT13
St. John's Ter *EH12* 24 AU13
St. John St *EH8* 7 BG11
St. John Vianney RC
  Prim Sch *EH16* 44 BK18
St. Jospeh's RC
  Prim Sch *EH11* 40 AV16
St. Katharine's Brae *EH16* 44 BJ21
St. Katharine's Cres *EH16* 44 BJ21
St. Katharine's Ln *EH16* 54 BK22
St. Kentigern Rd, Pen.
  EH26 68 AZ37
St. Leonard's Bk *EH8* 7 BH13
St. Leonard's Crag *EH8 1* 7 BH13
St. Leonard's Hill *EH8* 7 BG13
St. Leonard's La *EH8* 7 BH13
St. Leonard's St *EH8* 7 BG13
St. Luke's RC
  Prim Sch *EH22* 65 BZ30
St. Margaret's Pl *EH9* 43 BE15
St. Margaret's RC
  Prim Sch *EH20* 54 BL27

St. Margaret's RC
  Prim Sch *EH30* 9 AE2
St. Margaret's Rd *EH9* 42 BD15
St. Margaret's Sch *EH16* 44 BJ16
St. Mark's La *EH15* 29 BR11
St. Mark's Pl *EH15* 29 BR11
St. Mark's RC
  Prim Sch *EH7* 52 BA20
St. Martins La, Tran. *EH33* 35 CN13
St. Martin's RC
  Prim Sch *EH33* 35 CM13
St. Mary's
  Episcopal Cathedral *EH12* 6 BC12
St. Mary's Music Sch *EH12* 26 BB12
St. Mary's Pl *EH15* 30 BS12
St. Mary's Pl La *EH15* 30 BS11
St. Mary's RC
  Prim Sch *EH6* 16 BK6
St. Mary's RC
  Prim Sch *EH7* 27 BF9
St. Mary's RC
  Prim Sch *EH19* 63 BR29
St. Mary's St *EH1* 7 BG11
St. Matthew's RC
  Prim Sch *EH24* 63 BN33
St. Michael's Av, Muss.
  EH21 31 BY14
St. Mungo's Vw, Pen.
  EH26 69 BB39
St. Ninian's Dr *EH12* 24 AT12
St. Ninian's RC
  Prim Sch *EH7* 16 BL9
St. Ninian's Rd *EH12* 24 AT12
St. Ninian's Row *EH8 3* 7 BF10
St. Ninian's Ter *EH10* 42 BB17
St. Ninians Way, Muss.
  EH21 32 CC13
St. Patrick Sq *EH8* 7 BG13
St. Patrick St *EH8 3* 7 BG13
St. Peter's Bldgs *EH3* 6 BC13
St. Peter's Pl *EH3* 6 BC13
St. Peter's RC
  Prim Sch *EH10* 42 BD16
St. Ronan's Ter *EH10* 42 BC17
St. Serf's Sch *EH12* 26 BA12
St. Stephen Pl *EH3* 26 BD9
St. Stephen St *EH3* 26 BD9
St. Teresa Pl *EH10* 42 BB15
St. Thomas of Acquin's RC
  High Sch *EH3* 6 BE13
St. Thomas Rd *EH9* 43 BF15
St. Triduana's Rest *EH7* 16 BL9
St. Vincent Pl *EH3* 26 BD9
St. Vincent St *EH3* 27 BE9
Salamanca Cres, Pen.
  EH26 66 BC35
Salamander Ct *EH6* 16 BK6
Salamander Pl *EH6* 16 BK6
Salamander St *EH6* 16 BJ6
Salamander Yards *EH6* 16 BL7
Salisbury Crags *EH8* 7 BH12
Salisbury Ms *EH9* 43 BH14
Salisbury Pl *EH9* 43 BG14
Salisbury Rd *EH16* 43 BH14
Salisbury Vw (Mayf.),
  Dalk. *EH22* 65 BZ29
Salmond Pl *EH7* 16 BJ9
Saltersgate Spec Sch
  EH22 47 BZ22
Salter's Gro, Dalk. *EH22* 57 BY23
Salter's Rd, Dalk. *EH22* 47 BZ20
Salter's Rd (Wall.),
  Muss. *EH21* 32 CC16
Salter's Ter, Dalk. *EH22* 57 BY24
Salt Preston Pl, Pres.
  EH32 1 18 CH10
Salvesen Cres *EH4* 13 AW5
Salvesen Gdns *EH4* 13 AX5
Salvesen Gro *EH4* 13 AX5
Salvesen Ter *EH4* 13 AX5
Samoa Ter, Pen. *EH26* 66 BC35
Sanderson's Gro, Tran.
  EH33 35 CM12
Sanderson's Wynd, Tran.
  EH33 35 CM12
Sandford Gdns *EH15* 29 BQ11

Sand Port *EH6* 16 BJ5
Sandport Pl *EH6* 15 BH5
Sandport St *EH6* 15 BH5
Sandport Way *EH6* 15 BH6
Sauchiebank *EH11* 26 BA13
Saugh Cotts (Newt.),
  Dalk. *EH22* 65 BW31
SAUGHTON 41 AX14
Saughton Av *EH11* 41 AY14
Saughton Cres *EH12* 25 AX13
Saughton Gdns *EH12* 25 AX13
Saughton Gro *EH12* 25 AX13
SAUGHTONHALL 25 AX13
Saughtonhall Av *EH12* 25 AX13
Saughtonhall Av W *EH12* 25 AX13
Saughtonhall Circ *EH12* 25 AY13
Saughtonhall Cres *EH12* 25 AX13
Saughtonhall Dr *EH12* 25 AX12
Saughtonhall Gdns *EH12* 25 AY13
Saughtonhall Gro *EH12* 25 AY13
Saughtonhall Pl *EH12* 25 AY13
Saughtonhall Ter *EH12* 25 AY13
Saughton Ln *EH12* 25 AX13
Saughton Mains Av *EH11* 40 AV15
Saughton Mains Bk *EH11* 40 AV15
Saughton Mains Dr *EH11* 40 AV16
Saughton Mains Gdns
  EH11 40 AV16
Saughton Mains Gro *EH11* 41 AW16
Saughton Mains Ln *EH11* 40 AV16
Saughton Mains Pk *EH11* 40 AV15
Saughton Mains Pl *EH11* 40 AV16
Saughton Mains St *EH11* 40 AV15
Saughton Mains Ter *EH11* 40 AV15
Saughton Pk *EH12* 25 AX13
Saughton Rd *EH11* 40 AV15
Saughton Rd N *EH12* 40 AU14
Saunders St *EH3* 6 BD10
Savile Pl *EH9* 43 BH16
Savile Ter *EH9* 43 BH16
Saxe-Coburg Pl *EH3* 26 BD9
Saxe Coburg St *EH3* 26 BD9
Saxe-Coburg Ter *EH3* 4 26 BD9
Scarlett Pk (Wall.),
  Muss. *EH21* 32 CC14
Schaw Rd, Pres. *EH32* 18 CK10
School Brae *EH4* 11 AR5
School Brae, Lass. *EH18* 55 BQ26
School Grn, Lass. *EH18* 55 BQ26
School La (Cock.),
  Pres. *EH32* 19 CL7
School Wynd (Ratho),
  Newbr. *EH28* 37 AF17
Schoolyard Ct, Ros.
  EH25 62 BJ32
Sciennes *EH9* 43 BG14
Sciennes Gdns *EH9* 43 BG14
Sciennes Hill Pl *EH9* 43 BG14
Sciennes Ho Pl *EH9* 43 BG14
Sciennes Pl *EH9* 2 43 BG14
Sciennes Prim Sch EH9 43 BF14
Sciennes Rd *EH9* 43 BF14
Scollon Av, Bonny. *EH19* 56 BS27
Scone Gdns *EH8* 28 BL10
*Scotch Whisky
  Heritage Centre EH1* 3 6 BE12
Scotland St *EH3* 27 BE9
Scotsman Hotel, The EH1 7 BF11
Scotstoun Av, S Q'fry *EH30* 9 AE3
Scotstoun Grn, S Q'fry
  EH30 8 AD3
Scotstoun Gro, S Q'fry
  EH30 2 9 AE3
Scotstoun Pk, S Q'fry *EH30* 9 AE4
*Scottish Agricultural Coll
  (Bush Estate) EH26* 60 BD31
*Scottish Agricultural Coll
  (King's) EH9* 43 BH18
*Scottish Mining Museum
  EH22* 65 BW31
*Scottish National Gallery
  of Modern Art EH4* 26 BA11
*Scottish National
  Portrait Gallery EH2* 7 BF10
Scottish Parliament EH8 7 BH11
Scottish Poetry Library EH8 7 BH11

*Scottish Storytelling Centre
  (Netherbow Arts Centre)
  EH1* 13 7 BG11
Scott Monument EH2 7 BF11
Scott Rd, Pen. *EH26* 68 BA36
Scotway Cen, The,
  Dalk. *EH22* 46 BU19
Seacot *EH6* 1 16 BL7
SEAFIELD, Leith 16 BM7
SEAFIELD, Roslin 61 BF29
Seafield Av *EH6* 16 BL7
Seafield Cres (Bils.),
  Ros. *EH25* 61 BG29
Seafield Ind Est *EH15* 17 BP9
Seafield Moor Rd *EH10* 61 BE26
Seafield Pl *EH6* 16 BL7
Seafield Rd *EH6* 16 BL7
Seafield Rd (Bils.),
  Ros. *EH25* 61 BF29
Seafield Rd E *EH15* 17 BN8
Seafield St *EH6* 16 BM7
Seafield Way *EH15* 17 BN8
Seaforth Dr *EH4* 25 AY9
Seaforth Ter *EH4* 25 AY9
Seaforth Ter, Bonny. *EH19* 63 BP29
Sealcarr St *EH5* 14 BA4
Seaport St *EH6* 5 16 BJ6
Seaview Cres *EH15* 30 BT12
Seaview Ter *EH15* 30 BT12
Second Gait (Ricc.),
  Currie *EH14* 49 AN19
Second St (Newt.),
  Dalk. *EH22* 65 BX30
Semple St *EH3* 6 BD12
SETON 19 CN9
*Seton Collegiate Church
  EH32* 19 CP8
Seton Ct (Port S.),
  Pres. *EH32* 19 CN7
Seton Ct, Tran. *EH33* 8 35 CL14
Seton Pl *EH9* 43 BG14
Seton Pl (Port S.),
  Pres. *EH32* 19 CM7
Seton Vw (Port S.),
  Pres. *EH32* 19 CN8
Seton Wynd (Port S.),
  Pres. *EH32* 19 CN7
Seventh St (Newt.),
  Dalk. *EH22* 65 BX30
Shadepark Cres, Dalk.
  EH22 57 BX23
Shadepark Dr, Dalk. *EH22* 57 BX23
Shadepark Gdns, Dalk.
  EH22 57 BX23
Shaftesbury Pk *EH11* 42 BA15
Shandon Cres *EH11* 42 BA15
Shandon Pl *EH11* 42 BA15
Shandon Rd *EH11* 42 BA15
Shandon St *EH11* 42 BA15
Shandon Ter *EH11* 42 BA15
Shandwick Pl *EH2* 6 BC12
Shanter Way *EH16* 44 BK18
Sharpdale Ln *EH16* 44 BJ17
Shaw Pl (Mayf.),
  Dalk. *EH22* 57 BZ27
Shaws Ct (Milt.Br),
  Pen. *EH26* 66 BC34
Shaw's Cres (Milt.Br),
  Pen. *EH26* 66 BC34
Shaw's Pl *EH7* 27 BG8
Shaw's Sq *EH7* 2 27 BG9
Shaw's St *EH7* 27 BG8
Shaw's Ter *EH7* 27 BG8
*Sheraton Grand Hotel
  EH3* 6 BD12
Sheriff Bk *EH6* 15 BH6
Sheriff Brae *EH6* 15 BH6
Sheriffhall Rbt, Dalk. *EH22* 56 BT23
Sheriff Pk *EH6* 15 BH6
Sherwood Av, Bonny. *EH19* 64 BS29
Sherwood Ct, Bonny. *EH19* 64 BS29
Sherwood Cres, Bonny.
  EH19 64 BS29
Sherwood Dr, Bonny. *EH19* 64 BS29
Sherwood Gro, Bonny.
  EH19 64 BS29

Sherwood Ind Est, Bonny.
  EH19 56 BS28
Sherwood Ln, Bonny. *EH19* 64 BS29
Sherwood Pk, Bonny. *EH19* 64 BS29
Sherwood Pl, Bonny. *EH19* 64 BS29
Sherwood Ter, Bonny. *EH19* 64 BS29
Sherwood Vw, Bonny. *EH19* 64 BS29
Sherwood Wk, Bonny.
  EH19 1 64 BT29
Sherwood Way, Bonny.
  EH19 64 BS29
Shore *EH6* 16 BJ6
Shore Pl *EH6* 16 BJ6
Shore Rd, S Q'fry *EH30* 8 AD1
Shorthope St, Muss. *EH21* 31 BY13
Shrub Mt *EH15* 29 BQ10
Shrub Pl *EH7* 27 BG8
Shrub Pl La *EH7* 27 BG8
Sienna Gdns *EH9* 43 BG14
SIGHTHILL 40 AS17
Sighthill Av *EH11* 40 AU17
Sighthill Bk *EH11* 40 AT17
Sighthill Ct *EH11* 40 AT17
Sighthill Cres *EH11* 40 AT18
Sighthill Dr *EH11* 40 AT18
Sighthill Gdns *EH11* 40 AT17
Sighthill Grn *EH11* 40 AT17
Sighthill Gro *EH11* 40 AU17
Sighthill Ind Est *EH11* 40 AS17
Sighthill Ln *EH11* 40 AT17
Sighthill Neuk *EH11* 40 AT18
Sighthill Pk *EH11* 40 AT17
Sighthill Pl *EH11* 40 AT17
Sighthill Prim Sch EH11 40 AS18
Sighthill Ri *EH11* 40 AT18
Sighthill Rd *EH11* 40 AT18
Sighthill Shop Cen *EH11* 40 AT17
Sighthill St *EH11* 40 AT18
Sighthill Ter *EH11* 40 AT18
Sighthill Vw *EH11* 40 AT17
Sighthill Wynd *EH11* 40 AT17
Silverburn Dr, Pen. *EH26* 68 AY37
SILVERKNOWES 12 AV7
Silverknowes Av *EH4* 12 AU7
Silverknowes Bk *EH4* 12 AV7
Silverknowes Brae *EH4* 12 AV7
Silverknowes Ct *EH4* 12 AV7
Silverknowes Cres *EH4* 12 AV6
Silverknowes Dell *EH4* 13 AW7
Silverknowes Dr *EH4* 12 AV7
Silverknowes Eastway *EH4* 12 AV7
Silverknowes Gdns *EH4* 12 AV6
*Silverknowes Golf Course
  EH4* 12 AV5
Silverknowes Grn *EH4* 13 AW7
Silverknowes Gro *EH4* 12 AV7
Silverknowes Hill *EH4* 12 AV7
Silverknowes Ln *EH4* 12 AU7
Silverknowes Midway *EH4* 13 AW7
Silverknowes Neuk *EH4* 25 AW8
Silverknowes Parkway
  EH4 12 AV6
Silverknowes Pl *EH4* 12 AV6
Silverknowes Rd *EH4* 12 AV6
Silverknowes Rd E *EH4* 12 AV7
Silverknowes Rd S *EH4* 24 AV8
Silverknowes Southway
  EH4 13 AW7
Silverknowes Ter *EH4* 12 AU7
Silverknowes Vw *EH4* 13 AW7
Silvermills *EH3* 26 BD9
Simon Sq *EH8* 4 7 BG12
Sinclair Cl *EH11* 2 42 BA15
Sinclair Gdns *EH11* 42 BA14
Sinclair Pl *EH11* 41 AZ14
Sir Harry Lauder Rd *EH15* 29 BP10
Sir Walter Scott Pend, Pres.
  EH32 1 18 CH9
Sir William Fraser Homes
  EH13 51 AW20
Sixth St (Newt.),
  Dalk. *EH22* 65 BW30
Skeltiemuir Av, Bonny.
  EH19 63 BQ30
Skeltiemuir Ct, Bonny.
  EH19 63 BQ30

Skeltiemuir Gro, Bonny. EH19 63 BR30
Slaeside, Bal. EH14 58 AL26
SLATEFORD 41 AX17
Slateford Gait EH11 41 AZ15
Slateford Grn EH14 41 AZ14
Slateford Grn (Slateford Junc) EH14 41 AZ16
Slateford Rd EH11 41 AZ15
Slateford Rd EH14 41 AY17
Slateford Rd Br EH11 42 BA15
Slateford Sta EH14 41 AY16
Slater's Steps EH8 6 7 BH11
Sleigh Dr EH7 16 BK9
Sleigh Gdns EH7 16 BL9
Sloan St EH6 27 BH8
Smeaton Gro (Inv.), Muss. EH21 31 BZ15
Smithfield St EH11 41 AZ14
Smith's Land, S Q'fry EH30 5 9 AE2
Smith's Pl EH6 15 BH7
Smithy Grn Av (Dand.), Dalk. EH22 45 BQ20
Society Rd, S Q'fry EH30 8 AB1
Solicitor's Bldgs EH1 4 7 BF12
Somerset Pl EH6 16 BJ7
Somers Pk, Tran. EH33 35 CL14
Sommerville Gdns, S Q'fry EH30 9 AF4
Sour Howe EH13 52 BB22
Southbank EH4 1 12 AU7
Southbank Ct EH4 2 12 AU7
South Barnton Av EH4 24 AU8
South Beechwood EH12 25 AW13
South Br EH1 7 BF11
South Br EH8 7 BF11
South Charlotte St EH2 6 BD11
South Clerk St EH8 7 BG13
South Coll St EH8 7 BF12
South Cres, Pres. EH32 18 CJ10
South Doors (Cock.), Pres. EH32 19 CL7
South E Circ Pl EH3 1 6 BD10
South Elixa Pl EH8 28 BM11
South Ettrick Rd EH10 42 BB15
Southfield Fm Gro EH15 29 BN12
Southfield Gdns E EH15 29 BP12
Southfield Gdns W EH15 29 BP13
Southfield Ln EH15 29 BP13
Southfield Pl EH15 29 BQ11
Southfield Rd E EH15 29 BP13
Southfield Rd W EH15 29 BN13
Southfield Sq EH15 29 BP13
Southfield Ter EH15 29 BP13
Southfield Vil EH15 1 29 BQ12
South Fort St EH6 15 BG6
South Gayfield La EH1 27 BG9
South Gillsland Rd EH10 42 BB15
South Gra Av, Pres. EH32 34 CG11
South Gray's Cl EH1 7 BE11
South Gray St EH9 43 BH15
South Groathill Av EH4 25 AY9
SOUTH GYLE 39 AR15
South Gyle Access EH12 40 AS15
South Gyle Bdy EH12 39 AR14
South Gyle Cres EH12 40 AS16
South Gyle Cres La EH12 39 AR15
South Gyle Gdns EH12 39 AR14
South Gyle Ind Est EH12 39 AR15
South Gyle Ln EH12 39 AR14
South Gyle Mains EH12 40 AS14
South Gyle Pk EH12 39 AR14
South Gyle Pk Business Est EH12 39 AR15
South Gyle Rd EH12 39 AR14
South Gyle Sta EH12 39 AR14
South Gyle Wynd EH12 40 AS15
SOUTHHOUSE 54 BK23
Southhouse Av EH17 54 BK22
Southhouse Boundary EH17 54 BK22
Southhouse Brae EH17 54 BK22
Southhouse Bdy EH17 54 BK22
Southhouse Cl EH17 54 BK23

Southhouse Cres EH17 54 BK23
Southhouse Crossway EH17 54 BK23
Southhouse Dr EH17 54 BK22
Southhouse Gdns EH17 54 BK23
Southhouse Gro EH17 54 BK23
Southhouse Ln EH17 54 BK22
Southhouse Pl EH17 54 BK22
Southhouse Rd EH17 54 BJ22
Southhouse Sq EH17 1 54 BK23
Southhouse Ter EH17 54 BK22
Southhouse Wk EH17 54 BK22
South Lauder Rd EH9 43 BG15
South Laverockbank Av EH5 15 BE5
Southlawn Ct EH4 3 12 AU7
South Learmonth Av EH4 26 BB10
South Learmonth Gdns EH4 26 BB10
SOUTH LEITH 16 BJ8
South Lorimer Pl (Cock.), Pres. EH32 19 CL8
South Lorne Pl EH6 27 BH8
South Maybury EH12 39 AQ13
South Meadow Wk EH9 6 BE13
South Mellis Pk EH8 29 BN11
South Morningside Prim Sch EH10 42 BC18
South Morton St EH15 30 BS12
South Oswald Rd EH9 43 BE16
South Oxford St EH8 43 BH14
South Pk EH6 15 BF5
South Parrotshot EH15 29 BQ14
SOUTH QUEENSFERRY 9 AE1
South St. Andrew St EH2 7 BF10
South St. David St EH2 7 BF10
South Scotstoun, S Q'fry EH30 9 AE4
South Seton Pk (Port S.), Pres. EH32 19 CL8
South Sloan St EH6 27 BH8
South Steil EH10 42 BA19
South St, Dalk. EH22 57 BW24
South St, Muss. EH21 31 BX13
South Trinity Rd EH5 14 BD6
South Vw, Pres. EH32 1 18 CJ10
Soutra Ct EH16 44 BK21
Spalding Cres, Dalk. EH22 57 BX24
Spa Pl EH15 7 29 BQ10
Speedwell Av, Dalk. EH22 45 BQ19
Spencer Pl EH5 14 BD5
Spence St EH16 43 BH14
Spey St EH7 27 BG8
Spey St La EH7 27 BG8
Spey Ter EH7 27 BG8
Spier's Pl EH6 7 15 BH6
Spinney, The EH17 44 BM21
Spirit of the Tattoo Visitor Centre EH1 2 6 BE11
Spittalfield Cres EH8 7 BG13
Spittal St EH3 6 BD12
Spittal St La EH3 3 6 BE12
Spottiswoode Rd EH9 43 BE14
Spottiswoode St EH9 43 BE14
Springfield EH6 15 BG7
Springfield Bldgs EH6 3 15 BH7
Springfield Cres, S Q'fry EH30 8 AB2
Springfield La EH6 15 BH7
Springfield Lea, S Q'fry EH30 8 AB2
Springfield Pl, Gore. EH23 70 BZ36
Springfield Pl, Ros. EH25 62 BJ31
Springfield Pl, S Q'fry EH30 8 AB2
Springfield Rd, S Q'fry EH30 8 AB2
Springfield St EH6 15 BH7
Springfield Ter, S Q'fry EH30 8 AB2
Springfield Vw, S Q'fry EH30 8 AB2
Spring Gdns EH8 28 BJ10
Springvalley Gdns EH10 42 BC16

Springvalley Ter EH10 42 BC16
Springwell Pl EH11 26 BB13
Springwell Ter, S Q'fry EH30 8 AD2
Springwood Pk EH16 44 BK19
Spruce Wk, Lnhd EH20 61 BG28
Spylaw Av EH13 50 AV20
Spylaw Bk Rd EH13 50 AV20
Spylaw Ho EH13 51 AW21
Spylaw Pk EH13 50 AV20
Spylaw Rd EH10 42 BB15
Spylaw St EH13 51 AW21
Square, The (Dand.), Dalk. EH22 45 BR19
Square, The (Newt.), Dalk. EH22 65 BX30
Square, The, K'lis. EH29 1 20 AD10
Square, The, Pen. EH26 69 BB39
Stable Cor, Pres. EH32 18 CH9
Stable La EH10 42 BC16
Stafford St EH3 6 BC11
Stair Pk EH12 25 AY12
Stair Pk, Tran. EH33 34 CK12
Standingstane Rd (Dalm.), S Q'fry EH30 9 AG4
Stanedykehead EH16 53 BH21
Stanhope Pl EH12 26 BA12
Stanhope St EH12 26 BA12
Stanley Av (Bils.), Ros. EH25 61 BG29
Stanley Pl EH7 28 BJ10
Stanley Rd EH6 15 BE5
Stanley St EH15 29 BQ12
Stanwell St EH6 15 BH7
Stapeley Av EH7 17 BN9
Starbank Rd EH5 15 BE5
Stark's Cotts EH13 1 52 BA20
Station Brae EH15 29 BQ11
Station Ln, Bal. EH14 48 AL24
Station Rd EH12 24 AU13
Station Rd, Dalk. EH22 56 BU25
Station Rd (Newt.), Dalk. EH22 65 BW29
Station Rd, Gore. EH23 70 BY36
Station Rd, K'lis. EH29 20 AD9
Station Rd, Lnhd EH20 54 BL27
Station Rd, Muss. EH21 31 BX14
Station Rd (Ratho Sta), Newbr. EH28 37 AE13
Station Rd, Pres. EH32 34 CJ11
Station Rd, Ros. EH25 62 BJ31
Station Rd, S Q'fry EH30 9 AF3
Station Ter, K'lis. EH29 20 AD10
Station Vw, S Q'fry EH30 9 AF3
Stead's Pl EH6 15 BH7
Steele Av (Mayf.), Dalk. EH22 71 CB29
Steel's Pl EH10 42 BD16
Steil Gro, Tran. EH33 35 CM14
Steils, The EH10 42 BA18
STENHOUSE 41 AX15
Stenhouse Av EH11 41 AW14
Stenhouse Av W EH11 41 AW15
Stenhouse Cotts EH11 41 AW15
Stenhouse Cres EH11 41 AW15
Stenhouse Cross EH11 41 AW15
Stenhouse Dr EH11 41 AW15
Stenhouse Gdns EH11 41 AW15
Stenhouse Gdns N EH11 41 AW15
Stenhouse Gro EH11 41 AW15
Stenhouse Mill Cres EH11 41 AX16
Stenhouse Mill La EH11 41 AX16
Stenhouse Mill Wynd EH11 41 AX16
Stenhouse Pl E EH11 41 AW15
Stenhouse Pl W EH11 41 AW15
Stenhouse Prim Sch EH11 41 AW15
Stenhouse Rd EH11 41 AW16
Stenhouse St E EH11 41 AW15
Stenhouse St W EH11 40 AV15
Stenhouse Ter EH11 41 AX15
Stennis Gdns EH17 1 44 BL20
Stevenlaw's Cl EH1 7 BF11
Stevenson Av EH11 41 AY14
Stevenson Coll (Duncan Place) EH6 16 BJ7
Stevenson Dr EH11 41 AW15

Stevenson Gro EH11	41	AY14
Stevenson La (Newt.), Dalk. EH22	65	BX31
Stevenson Pl, Lass. EH18	62	BM29
Stevenson Rd EH11	41	AY14
Stevenson Rd, Pen. EH26	66	BC35
Stevenson Ter EH11	41	AY14
Stewart Av, Currie EH14	49	AN24
Stewart Clark Av, S Q'fry EH30	9	AE3
Stewart Cres, Currie EH14	49	AN23
Stewartfield EH6	15	BF7
Stewart Gdns, Currie EH14	49	AN23
Stewart Gro, Dalk. EH22	45	BQ19
Stewart Pl, Currie EH14	49	AN24
Stewart Pl, K'lis. EH29	20	AD9
Stewart Rd, Currie EH14	49	AN24
Stewart's Melville Coll EH4	26	BA10
Stewart Ter EH11	41	AZ14
Stewart Ter, S Q'fry EH30	8	AD2
Stills Gallery EH1	7	BF11
Stirling Rd EH5	14	BD5
Stirling Rd, K'lis. EH29	20	AB9
Stobhill Prim Sch EH23	70	BZ35
Stobhill Rd (Newt.), Dalk. EH22	65	BX31
STOCKBRIDGE	26	BD9
Stockbridge Prim Sch EH3	26	BD9
Stone Av (Mayf.), Dalk. EH22	65	BZ29
Stone Cres (Mayf.), Dalk. EH22	65	BZ29
Stone Pl (Mayf.), Dalk. EH22	65	BZ30
STONEYBANK	31	BW15
Stoneybank Av, Muss. EH21	31	BW15
Stoneybank Ct, Muss. EH21	31	BW14
Stoneybank Cres, Muss. EH21	31	BW14
Stoneybank Dr, Muss. EH21	31	BW14
Stoneybank Gdns, Muss. EH21	31	BW14
Stoneybank Gdns N, Muss. EH21	31	BW14
Stoneybank Gdns S, Muss. EH21	31	BX15
Stoneybank Gro, Muss. EH21	31	BX15
Stoneybank Pl, Muss. EH21	31	BX15
Stoneybank Rd, Muss. EH21	31	BX15
Stoneybank Ter, Muss. EH21	31	BX15
Stoneycroft Rd, S Q'fry EH30	9	AE2
Stoneyflatts, S Q'fry EH30	8	AC2
Stoneyflatts Cres, S Q'fry EH30	8	AC2
Stoneyflatts Pk, S Q'fry EH30	8	AC3
STONEYHILL	31	BW15
Stoneyhill Av, Muss. EH21	31	BW14
Stoneyhill Ct, Muss. EH21	31	BW14
Stoneyhill Cres, Muss. EH21	31	BW14
Stoneyhill Dr, Muss. EH21	31	BW14
Stoneyhill Fm Rd, Muss. EH21	31	BW14
Stoneyhill Gdns, Muss. EH21 1	31	BW14
Stoneyhill Gro, Muss. EH21	31	BW14
Stoneyhill Pl, Muss. EH21	31	BW14
Stoneyhill Prim Sch EH21	31	BW14
Stoneyhill Ri, Muss. EH21	31	BW14
Stoneyhill Rd, Muss. EH21	31	BW14
Stoneyhill Steading, Muss. EH21	31	BW14
Stoneyhill Ter, Muss. EH21	31	BW14
Stoneyhill Wynd, Muss. EH21	31	BW14
Strachan Gdns EH4	25	AW9

Strachan Rd EH4	25	AX10
STRAITON	53	BH25
Straiton Junct, Lnhd EH20	54	BJ25
Straiton Mains (Strait.), Lnhd EH20	54	BJ26
Straiton Pk (Strait.), Lnhd EH20	54	BJ26
Straiton Pk Caravan Site (Strait.), Lnhd EH20	61	BH26
Straiton Pk Way (Strait.), Lnhd EH20	54	BJ26
Straiton Pl EH15	29	BR10
Straiton Retail Park EH20	54	BJ26
Straiton Rd (Strait.), Lnhd EH20	54	BJ25
Straiton Vw, Lnhd EH20	54	BJ26
Strathalmond Ct EH4	23	AP8
Strathalmond Grn EH4	23	AP8
Strathalmond Pk EH4	23	AP9
Strathalmond Rd EH4	23	AP8
Strathearn Pl EH9	42	BD15
Strathearn Rd EH9	43	BE15
Strathesk Gro, Pen. EH26	69	BC37
Strathesk Pl, Pen. EH26	69	BC37
Strathesk Rd, Pen. EH26	69	BC37
Strawberry Bk, Dalk. EH22	56	BU26
Stuart Cres EH12	23	AR11
Stuart Grn EH12	23	AR11
Stuart Pk EH12	23	AR11
Stuart Sq EH12	23	AR11
Stuart Wynd EH12	23	AR11
Succoth Av EH12	25	AZ11
Succoth Ct EH12	25	AZ11
Succoth Gdns EH12	25	AZ11
Succoth Pk EH12	25	AY11
Succoth Pl EH12	25	AZ11
Suffolk Rd EH16	43	BH16
Suffolk Rd La EH16	43	BH16
Summerbank EH3	27	BE9
Summerfield Gdns EH6	16	BK7
Summerfield Pl EH6	16	BK7
Summerhall EH9 4	43	BG14
Summerhall Cres EH9 4	7	BG13
Summerhall Pl EH9 5	43	BG14
Summerhall Sq EH9	43	BG14
Summerlee, Pres. EH32	18	CG10
Summer Pl EH3	27	BE8
Summerside Pl EH6	15	BF6
Summerside St EH6	15	BF6
Summertrees Ct EH16	44	BK18
Sunbury Ms EH4	26	BB11
Sunbury Pl EH4	26	BB11
Sunbury St EH4	26	BB11
Sunnybank EH7	28	BK10
Sunnybank Pl EH7	28	BK10
Sunnybank Ter EH7 4	28	BJ10
Sunnyside EH7	16	BJ9
Suntrap Garden EH12	39	AN17
Surgeons' Hall Museum EH8	7	BG12
Surrey Pl EH12 2	26	BA12
Sutherland St EH12	26	BA12
Suttieslea Cres (Newt.), Dalk. EH22	65	BY29
Suttieslea Dr (Newt.), Dalk. EH22	65	BY29
Suttieslea Pl (Newt.), Dalk. EH22	65	BY29
Suttieslea Rd (Newt.), Dalk. EH22	65	BY29
Suttieslea Wk (Newt.), Dalk. EH22	65	BY29
Swan Cres, Gore. EH23	70	BY34
Swanfield EH6	15	BH6
Swan Rd, Tran. EH33	35	CL14
Swan Spring Av EH10	52	BC20
Swanston Av EH10	52	BC22
Swanston Cres EH10	52	BC22
Swanston Dr EH10	52	BD23
Swanston Gdns EH10	52	BC22
Swanston Golf Course EH10	52	BB24
Swanston Grn EH10	52	BC22
Swanston Gro EH10	52	BD22
Swanston Ln EH10	52	BC22
Swanston Muir EH10	52	BA22

Swanston Pk EH10	52	BC22
Swanston Pl EH10	52	BC22
Swanston Rd EH10	52	BB22
Swanston Row EH10	52	BC22
Swanston Ter EH10	52	BD22
Swanston Vw EH10	52	BC22
SWANSTON VILLAGE	52	BC24
Swanston Way EH10	52	BC22
Sycamore Av (Port S.), Pres. EH32	19	CM8
Sycamore Gdns EH12	24	AT13
Sycamore Path, Lnhd EH20 1	61	BG28
Sycamore Rd (Mayf.), Dalk. EH22	71	CA29
Sycamore Ter EH12	24	AU13
Sydney Pk EH7	17	BN9
Sydney Pl EH7	17	BN9
Sydney Ter EH7	17	BN9
Sylvan Pl EH9	43	BF14
Syme Cres EH10	42	BA19
Syme Pl EH10 2	42	BA19
Syme Rigg EH10 4	42	BA19

T

Tait Dr, Pen. EH26	69	BB38
Tait St, Dalk. EH22	57	BW24
Talbot Rice Gallery EH1	7	BF12
Talisman Pl EH16	44	BK18
Tanfield EH3	27	BE8
Tantallon Pl EH9	43	BG14
Tartan Weaving Mill & Exhibition EH1 1	6	BE11
Tarvit St EH3	6	BD13
Tattoo Office EH1	7	BF11
Taylor Gdns EH6	15	BH6
Taylor Pl EH7	28	BJ10
Taylor Pl, Dalk. EH22	57	BY25
Tay St EH11	42	BB14
Telfer Sub EH11	26	BB13
Telferton EH7	29	BP10
Telford Coll EH5	13	AY5
Telford Coll (West Campus) EH4	25	AZ8
Telford Cotts, Pen. EH26	69	BB39
Telford Dr EH4	25	AZ8
Telford Gdns EH4	25	AZ8
Telford Gro EH4	13	AZ7
Telford March EH4	25	AZ8
Telford Pl EH4	25	AZ8
Telford Rd EH4	25	AZ8
Templar's Cramond EH4	23	AQ7
Templeland Gro EH12	24	AT12
Templeland Rd EH12	24	AS12
Temple Pk Cres EH11	42	BB14
Tennant St EH6	15	BH7
Tenth St (Newt.), Dalk. EH22	65	BX29
Terrars Cft EH8	7	BH13
Terregles, Pen. EH26	68	AZ37
Teviotdale Pl EH3	26	BD9
Teviot Gro, Pen. EH26	69	BB36
Teviot Pl EH1	7	BF12
Teviot Pl EH8	7	BF12
Third Gait (Ricc.), Currie EH14	49	AN19
Third St (Newt.), Dalk. EH22	65	BW31
Thirlestane La EH9	43	BE15
Thirlestane Rd EH9	43	BE14
Thistle Ct EH2 3	6	BE10
Thistle Hotel EH1	7	BF10
Thistle Pl EH11	6	BC13
Thistle St EH2	6	BE10
Thistle St N E La EH2	6	BE10
Thistle St N W La EH2	6	BE10
Thistle St S E La EH2	6	BE10
Thistle St S W La EH2	6	BE10
Thomson Cres, Currie EH14	49	AR22
Thomson Cres (Port S.), Pres. EH32	19	CM7
Thomson Dr, Currie EH14	49	AR22
Thomson Gro, Currie EH14	49	AR22
Thomson Rd, Currie EH14	49	AR22

Thomson's Ct EH1 **8** 6 BE12
Thorburn Gro EH13 51 AY21
Thorburn Rd EH13 51 AX20
Thorburn Ter, Pen. EH26 68 BA39
Thorntree Cres, Pres.
EH32 18 CK10
Thorntreeside EH6 16 BJ7
Thorntree St EH6 15 BH7
Thornville Ter EH6 16 BJ8
Thornybank, Dalk. EH22 57 BY23
Thornybank Ind Est,
Dalk. EH22 57 BY23
Thornybauk EH3 6 BD12
Thornyhall, Dalk. EH22 57 BY23
Threipmuir Av, Bal. EH14 58 AL27
Threipmuir Gdns, Bal.
EH14 58 AL27
Threipmuir Pl, Bal. EH14 58 AL27
Timber Bush EH6 16 BJ5
Timmins Ct (Ratho),
Newbr. EH28 37 AF17
Tinto Pl EH6 15 BG7
Tipperlinn Rd EH10 42 BC15
Toddshill Rd, K'lis. EH29 20 AC10
Tolbooth Wynd EH6 15 BH6
Tollcross Prim Sch EH3 6 BD13
Torduff Rd EH13 51 AW23
Torphichen Pl EH3 6 BC12
Torphichen St EH3 6 BC12
Torphin Bk EH13 50 AV22
Torphin Hill Golf Course
EH13 50 AU23
Torphin Rd EH13 50 AV22
Torrance Pk EH4 24 AS10
Torsonce Rd, Dalk. EH22 56 BV25
Toscana Ct, Dalk. EH22 45 BQ19
Toward Ct EH12 **1** 23 AQ12
Towerbank Prim Sch EH15 29 BR10
Tower Pl EH6 16 BJ5
Tower St EH6 16 BJ5
Tower St La EH6 16 BJ5
Tower Wynd EH6 16 BJ5
Townswomen's Guild Wk
EH3 7 BF13
Trafalgar La EH6 15 BF6
Trafalgar St EH6 15 BG6
TRANENT 35 CL14
Tranent Inf Sch EH33 35 CM13
Tranent Prim Sch EH33 35 CM12
Traprain Ter, Lnhd EH20 62 BL28
Traquair Pk E EH12 24 AV13
Traquair Pk W EH12 24 AU13
Travelodge Edinburgh
Central EH1 7 BG11
Travelodge Edinburgh
Dreghorn EH13 51 AZ22
Travelodge Edinburgh
Musselburgh EH21 47 BX17
Traverse Theatre EH1 6 BD12
Trelawney Ter, Pen. EH26 66 BC35
Trench Knowe EH10 52 BC22
Tressilian Gdns EH16 44 BK18
TRINITY 14 BD5
Trinity Acad EH6 15 BE5
Trinity Ct EH5 14 BD6
Trinity Cres EH5 14 BD4
Trinity Gro EH5 14 BD5
Trinity Mains EH5 14 BD6
Trinity Prim Sch EH6 15 BF5
Trinity Rd EH5 14 BD5
Trinity Way EH5 14 BD6
Tron Old Town Information
Centre, The EH1 **9** 7 BF11
Tron Sq EH1 **12** 7 BF11
Trotter Haugh EH9 43 BF16
Tryst Pk EH10 52 BB22
Turner Av, Bal. EH14 48 AK24
Turner Pk, Bal. EH14 48 AL24
TURNHOUSE 22 AL10
Turnhouse Fm Rd EH12 22 AL10
Turnhouse Golf Course
EH12 22 AM11
Turnhouse Rd EH12 22 AM11
Turret Gdns, Pres. EH32 34 CH11
Tyler's Acre Av EH12 40 AU14
Tyler's Acre Gdns EH12 40 AU14

Tyler's Acre Rd EH12 40 AU14
Tynecastle High Sch EH11 26 BA13
Tynecastle La EH11 42 BA14
Tynecastle Park
(Hearts FC) EH11 42 BA14
Tynecastle Ter EH11 42 BA14
Tytler Ct EH8 28 BJ10
Tytler Gdns EH8 7 BH10

U

UCI Cinema
(Fort Kinnaird) EH15 30 BS15
Ulster Cres EH8 28 BL11
Ulster Dr EH8 28 BL11
Ulster Gdns EH8 28 BM11
Ulster Gro EH8 28 BM12
Ulster Ter EH8 28 BM12
Union Pk, Bonny. EH19 63 BR29
Union Pl EH1 **2** 7 BG10
Union St EH1 27 BF9
University of Edinburgh
(Central Campus) EH8 7 BF13
University of Edinburgh
(King's Buildings) EH9 43 BH17
University of Edinburgh
Med Sch EH16 45 BN18
Upper Bow EH1 **8** 7 BF11
Upper Broomieknowe,
Lass. EH18 55 BQ27
Upper Coltbridge Ter EH12 25 AZ11
Upper Craigour EH17 45 BN18
Upper Craigour Way EH17 44 BM18
Upper Cramond Ct EH4 23 AR7
UPPER DALHOUSIE 64 BS32
Upper Damside EH4 26 BB11
Upper Dean Ter EH4 6 BC10
Upper Gilmore Pl EH3 6 BD13
Upper Gilmore Ter EH3 6 BD13
Upper Gray St EH9 43 BG14
Upper Greenside La EH1 **7** 7 BG10
Upper Gro Pl EH3 6 BC13
Upper Hermitage EH6 16 BJ7
Usher Hall EH1 6 BD12

V

VALLEYFIELD 69 BB39
Valleyfield Rd, Pen. EH26 69 BB39
Valleyfield St EH3 6 BD13
Valleyfield Vw, Pen. EH26 69 BB39
Vanburgh Pl EH6 16 BJ7
Vandeleur Av EH7 29 BN10
Vandeleur Gro EH7 29 BP10
Vandeleur Pl EH7 17 BN9
Vaucluse Pl, Pen. EH26 68 BA39
Veitch's Sq EH4 26 BD9
Vennel EH1 6 BE12
Vennel, S Q'fry EH30 **3** 9 AE2
Ventnor Pl EH9 28 BJ15
Ventnor Ter EH9 43 BH15
Vernon Cotts EH15 **1** 29 BR11
Vexhim Pk EH15 29 BR14
Victoria Dock EH6 15 BH5
Victoria Gdns (Newt.),
Dalk. EH22 64 BV29
Victoria Prim Sch EH6 15 BF4
Victoria Quay EH6 15 BH5
Victoria Rd (Newt.),
Dalk. EH22 64 BV29
Victoria St EH1 7 BF12
Victoria St, Rose. EH24 62 BM33
Victoria Ter EH1 **9** 6 BE12
Victoria Ter, Muss. EH21 32 CA13
Victor Pk Ter EH12 24 AT12
Viewbank Av, Bonny.
EH19 56 BT27
Viewbank Cres, Bonny.
EH19 **1** 56 BS27
Viewbank Dr, Bonny.
EH19 56 BS27
Viewbank Rd, Bonny.
EH19 55 BR27
Viewbank Vw, Bonny.
EH19 56 BS27
Viewcraig Gdns EH8 7 BG11
Viewcraig St EH8 7 BG11

Viewfield, Bonny. EH19 56 BT27
Viewfield Rd, Jun. Grn
EH14 50 AU20
Viewforth EH10 42 BC14
Viewforth EH11 6 BC13
Viewforth (Port S.),
Pres. EH32 19 CM7
Viewforth Bk,
S Q'fry EH30 8 AD2
Viewforth Gdns EH10 42 BD14
Viewforth Gdns, Tran.
EH33 **6** 35 CL13
Viewforth Pl, S Q'fry EH30 8 AD3
Viewforth Rd, S Q'fry EH30 8 AD2
Viewforth Sq EH10 42 BC14
Viewforth Ter EH10 42 BC14
Viewforth Ter, Tran.
EH33 **5** 35 CL13
Viewpark Gdns, Bonny.
EH19 55 BR27
Villa Rd, S Q'fry EH30 8 AD2
Violet Ter EH11 42 BA14
Vivian Ter EH4 24 AV8
Vogrie Cres S, Gore. EH23 70 BZ36
Vogrie Pl, Gore. EH23 70 BZ35
Vogrie Rd, Gore. EH23 70 BZ35
Vorlich Cres, Pen. EH26 69 BC36
Vue Cinema
(Ocean Terminal) EH6 15 BH4
Vue Cinema
(Omni Centre) EH1 7 BG10

W

Wadingburn La, Lass.
EH18 55 BP26
Wadingburn Rd, Lass.
EH18 55 BN27
Wakefield Av EH7 17 BP9
Walker Cres, Dalk. EH22 56 BT26
Walker Dr, S Q'fry EH30 8 AC2
Walker Pl, Lass. EH18 63 BN29
Walkers Ct EH14 **1** 40 AU18
Walkers Rigg EH14 40 AU18
Walker St EH3 6 BC11
Walkers Wynd EH14 40 AU18
Walker Ter EH11 **6** 6 BC12
Wallace Cres, Ros. EH25 62 BJ31
Wallace Pl, Tran. EH33 **1** 35 CL12
WALLYFORD 33 CE15
Wallyford Ind Est (Wall.),
Muss. EH21 33 CD15
Wallyford Ln Rd (Wall.),
Muss. EH21 33 CD13
Wallyford Prim Sch EH21 33 CD14
Wallyford Sta EH21 33 CD14
Wallyford Toll (Wall.),
Muss. EH21 33 CD13
Walter Scott Av EH16 44 BK18
Wanless Ct, Muss. EH21 31 BZ13
Warden's Cl EH1 7 BF12
WARDIE 14 BC5
Wardie Av EH5 14 BC6
Wardieburn Dr EH5 14 BB5
Wardieburn Pl E EH5 14 BB5
Wardieburn Pl N EH5 14 BB5
Wardieburn Pl S EH5 14 BB5
Wardieburn Pl W EH5 14 BA5
Wardieburn Rd EH5 14 BA5
Wardieburn St E EH5 14 BB5
Wardieburn St W EH5 14 BA5
Wardieburn Ter EH5 14 BA5
Wardie Cres EH5 14 BB5
Wardie Dell EH5 14 BC5
Wardiefield EH5 14 BB5
Wardie Gro EH5 14 BB5
Wardie Ho La EH5 14 BC4
Wardie Pk EH5 14 BC6
Wardie Prim Sch EH5 14 BC6
Wardie Rd EH5 14 BC6
Wardie Sq EH5 14 BC5
Wardie Steps EH5 14 BC5
Wardlaw Pl EH11 42 BA14
Wardlaw St EH11 42 BA14
Wardlaw Ter EH11 42 BA14
Warrender Pk Cres EH9 42 BD14

Name	Page	Grid
Warrender Pk Rd EH9	43	BE14
Warrender Pk Ter EH9	43	BE14
WARRISTON	15	BE7
Warriston Av EH3	15	BE7
Warriston Cres EH3	27	BE8
Warriston Dr EH3	14	BD7
Warriston Fm Rd, Currie EH14	48	AL21
Warriston Gdns EH3	14	BD7
Warriston Gro EH3	14	BD7
Warriston Pl EH3	27	BE8
Warriston Rd EH3	27	BE8
Warriston Rd EH7	15	BE6
Warriston's Cl EH1 15	7	BF11
Warriston Ter EH3	14	BD7
Washington La EH11	26	BB13
Washington St EH11	26	BB13
Waterfall Wk, Dalk. EH22	57	BX25
Waterfront Av EH5	13	AZ4
Waterfront Bdy EH5	13	AZ4
Waterfront Gate EH4	13	AX5
Waterloo Bk, Pen. EH26	69	BB39
Waterloo Pl EH1	7	BF10
Water of Leith Visitor Centre EH14	41	AY17
Water of Leith Walkway EH13	41	AW19
Water of Leith Walkway EH14	41	AW19
Water's Cl EH6 6	16	BJ6
Water St EH6	16	BJ6
Watertoun Rd EH9	43	BG16
Watson Cres EH11	42	BB14
Watson St, Pen. EH26	68	BA38
Watt Gro (Mayf.), Dalk. EH22	71	CA30
Watt Pk (Newt.), Dalk. EH22	65	BX31
Watt's Cl, Muss. EH21	31	BX13
Wauchope Av EH16	29	BN15
Wauchope Cres EH16	29	BN15
Wauchope Ho EH16	45	BP16
Wauchope Pl EH16	29	BN15
Wauchope Rd EH16	29	BP15
Wauchope Sq EH16	29	BP15
Wauchope Ter EH16	29	BP15
Waugh Path, Bonny. EH19	56	BT27
Waulkmill Dr, Pen. EH26	69	BB39
Waulkmill Ln, Currie EH14	49	AN24
Waulkmill Rd, Pen. EH26	69	BC38
Waulkmill Vw, Pen. EH26	69	BB39
Waverley Br EH1	7	BF11
Waverley Ct, Bonny. EH19	56	BS28
Waverley Cres, Bonny. EH19	56	BS28
Waverley Dr, Bonny. EH19	56	BS28
Waverley Pk EH8	28	BJ10
Waverley Pk, Bonny. EH19	56	BS28
Waverley Pk (Mayf.), Dalk. EH22	65	BZ29
Waverley Pk Ter EH8	28	BJ10
Waverley Pl EH7	28	BJ10
Waverley Rd, Bonny. EH19	56	BS28
Waverley Rd, Dalk. EH22	56	BV25
Waverley Sta EH1	7	BF11
Waverley St EH2	7	BF11
Waverley St (Mayf.), Dalk. EH22	65	BZ30
Waverley Ter, Bonny. EH19	56	BS28
Waverley Ter (Mayf.), Dalk. EH22	65	BZ29
Weaver's Knowe Cres, Currie EH14	49	AP22
Websters Land EH1 10	6	BE12
Wedderburn Ct (Inv.), Muss. EH21	31	BZ16
Wedderburn Ter (Inv.), Muss. EH21	31	BZ16
Wee Brae, Lass. EH18	55	BQ26
Weir Ct EH11	40	AT17
Weir Ct, Dalk. EH22 1	56	BU25
Weir Cres, Dalk. EH22	56	BU25
Well Ct EH4 4	6	BC11
Wellflats Rd, K'lis. EH29	20	AD10
Wellhead Cl, S Q'fry EH30	9	AF3
Wellington Pl EH6	16	BJ6
Wellington St EH7	27	BH9
Well Wynd, Tran. EH33	35	CM13
Wemyss Gdns (Wall.), Muss. EH21	33	CE14
Wemyss Pl EH3	6	BD10
Wemyss Pl (Port S.), Pres. EH32	19	CL7
Wemyss Pl Ms EH3	6	BD10
Werberside Ms EH4	14	BA7
Wesley Cres, Bonny. EH19	56	BT28
West Adam St EH8	7	BG12
West Annandale St EH7	27	BF8
West App Rd EH3	6	BD12
West App Rd EH11	26	BB13
Westbank Ln EH15 1	29	BQ10
Westbank Pl EH15	29	BQ10
Westbank St EH15	29	BQ10
West Bow EH1	7	BF12
West Bowl Grn St EH6	15	BG6
West Brighton Cres EH15	29	BQ11
West Bryson Rd EH11	42	BB14
Westburn Av EH14	40	AS19
Westburn Gro EH14	40	AS19
Westburn Middlefield EH14	40	AS19
Westburn Pk EH14	40	AT19
Westburn Prim Sch EH11	40	AT18
West Cairn Cres, Pen. EH26	68	BA37
West Caiystane Rd EH10	52	BC22
West Camus Rd EH10	52	BC21
West Carnethy Av EH13	51	AW22
West Castle Rd EH10	42	BC14
West Catherine Pl EH12	26	BA12
West Cherrybank EH6	15	BE5
West Coates EH12	26	BA12
West Coll St EH8	7	BF12
West Ct EH4	25	AY10
West Ct EH16	45	BN16
WEST CRAIGS	23	AP12
West Craigs Av EH12	39	AP13
West Craigs Cres EH12	39	AP13
West Craigs Ind Est EH12	23	AP12
West Cft (Ratho), Newbr. EH28	37	AG17
West Cromwell St EH6 1	15	BH5
West Crosscauseway EH8	7	BG13
WEST END	6	BC11
West End EH2	6	BD11
West End Pl EH11	26	BB13
Wester Auchendinny Br, Pen. EH26	67	BE35
Wester Broom Av EH12	40	AS14
Wester Broom Dr EH12	40	AS14
Wester Broom Gdns EH12	40	AS14
Wester Broom Gro EH12	40	AS14
Wester Broom Pl EH12	40	AS14
Wester Broom Ter EH12	40	AS14
Wester Cl EH6 3	15	BF4
Wester Coates Av EH12	26	BA12
Wester Coates Gdns EH12	26	BA12
Wester Coates Pl EH12	26	BA11
Wester Coates Rd EH12	26	BA12
Wester Coates Ter EH12	26	BA12
Wester Drylaw Av EH4	25	AX8
Wester Drylaw Dr EH4	25	AX8
Wester Drylaw Pk EH4	25	AY8
Wester Drylaw Pl EH4	25	AX8
Wester Drylaw Row EH4	25	AY9
WESTER HAILES	40	AT19
Wester Hailes Ed Cen EH14	40	AT19
Wester Hailes Pk EH14	40	AU19
Wester Hailes Rd EH11	40	AS17
Wester Hailes Rd EH14	40	AS17
Wester Hailes Rd, Jun. Grn EH14	50	AU20
Wester Hailes Sta EH14	40	AT19
Wester Hill EH10	42	BA19
Westerlea Sch EH12	25	AY12
Wester Millerhill, Dalk. EH22	46	BU20
Western Cor EH12 1	25	AX12
Western Gdns EH12	25	AY12
Western Gen Hosp EH4	25	AZ8
Western Harbour EH6	15	BG4
Western Harbour Breakwater EH6	15	BF3
Western Harbour Dr EH6	15	BF4
Western Harbour Midway EH6	15	BF3
Western Harbour Pl EH6	15	BF3
Western Harbour Ter EH6	15	BF3
Western Harbour Vw EH6	15	BF3
Western Harbour Way EH6	15	BF3
Western Pl EH12	25	AY12
Western Ter EH12	25	AY12
Wester Row, Currie EH14	39	AN18
Wester Steil EH10	42	BA18
West Fairbrae Cres EH11	40	AU16
West Fairbrae Dr EH11	40	AU16
West Ferryfield EH5	14	BB6
Westfield Av EH11	41	AY14
Westfield Bk, Dalk. EH22	56	BU26
Westfield Ct EH11	41	AY14
Westfield Ct, Dalk. EH22 2	56	BU26
Westfield Dr, Dalk. EH22 3	56	BU26
Westfield Gro, Dalk. EH22	56	BU26
Westfield Pk, Dalk. EH22	56	BU26
Westfield Rd EH11	41	AZ14
Westfield St EH11	41	AZ14
West Fountain Pl EH11	26	BB13
Westgarth Av EH13	51	AX21
West Gorgie Pk EH14	41	AY15
West Gorgie Pl EH14	41	AY16
West Gra Gdns EH9	43	BF15
West Granton Access EH5	13	AZ5
West Granton Rd EH5	14	BA5
Westhall Gdns EH10	42	BD14
West Harbour (Cock.), Pres. EH32	18	CK7
West Harbour Rd EH5	14	BA4
West Harbour Rd (Cock.), Pres. EH32	18	CK7
West Holmes Gdns, Muss. EH21	31	BX13
Westhouses Av (Mayf.), Dalk. EH22	71	CA30
Westhouses Dr (Mayf.), Dalk. EH22 3	71	CA30
Westhouses Rd (Mayf.), Dalk. EH22	71	CA30
Westhouses St (Mayf.), Dalk. EH22 2	71	CA30
Westland Cotts EH17	55	BN22
West Ln, Pres. EH32	18	CH10
West Ln Ct, Pres. EH32 1	34	CH11
West Lorimer Pl (Cock.), Pres. EH32	18	CK7
WEST MAINS	43	BH18
West Mains Rd EH9	43	BG17
West Maitland St EH12	6	BC12
West Mayfield EH9	43	BH15
West Mill Bk EH13	51	AW21
West Mill Ct, Lass. EH18 1	55	BQ26
West Mill La EH4	6	BC11
West Mill Rd EH13	50	AV21
Westmill Rd, Lass. EH18	55	BQ27
Westmill Wynd, Lass. EH18	55	BQ27
West Montgomery Pl EH7	27	BG9
West Newington Pl EH9	43	BG14
West Nicolson St EH8	7	BG12
West Norton Pl EH7	7	BH10
West One Business Pk EH11	39	AR17
WESTPANS	32	CC12
Westpark Gdns EH12	39	AQ13
West Pk Pl EH11	26	BB13
West Pier EH5	14	BA4
WEST PILTON	13	AZ6
West Pilton Av EH4	13	AY7
West Pilton Bk EH4	13	AX6
West Pilton Brae EH4	13	AX6
West Pilton Cres EH4	13	AX6
West Pilton Crossway EH4	13	AY6
West Pilton Dr EH4	13	AY6
West Pilton Gdns EH4	13	AY6

West Pilton Grn *EH4* 13 AY6
West Pilton Gro *EH4* 13 AY7
West Pilton Lea *EH4* 13 AY6
West Pilton Ln *EH4* 13 AY6
West Pilton March *EH4* 13 AZ5
West Pilton Pk *EH4* 13 AY6
West Pilton Pl *EH4* 13 AZ6
West Pilton Ri *EH4* 13 AY6
West Pilton Rd *EH4* 13 AZ6
West Pilton St *EH4* 13 AY6
West Pilton Ter *EH4* 13 AY6
West Pilton Vw *EH4* 13 AY7
West Pilton Way *EH4* 13 AZ6
West Port *EH1* 6 BE12
West Port *EH3* 6 BE12
West Powburn *EH9* 43 BG16
West Preston St *EH8* 43 BG14
West Register St *EH2* 7 BF10
West Register St La *EH2* **4** 7 BF10
West Relugas Rd *EH9* 43 BF16
West Richmond St *EH8* 7 BG12
West Savile Gdns *EH9* 43 BG16
West Savile Rd *EH16* 43 BH16
West Savile Ter *EH9* 43 BG16
West Scotland St La *EH3* 27 BE9
West Seaside, Pres. *EH32* 18 CG10
West Shore Business Cen
  EH5 13 AY4
West Shore Rd *EH5* 13 AX5
West Shore Rd Trd Est *EH5* 13 AY4
Westside Plaza Shop Cen
  EH14 40 AT19
West Silvermills La *EH3* 26 BD9
West Stanhope Pl *EH12* **1** 26 BA12
West St, Pen. *EH26* 68 BA39
West Telferton *EH7* 29 BP10
West Ter, S Q'fry *EH30* **3** 8 AD2
West Tollcross *EH3* 6 BD13
West Werberside *EH4* 14 BA7
West Windygoul Gdns, Tran.
  EH33 34 CK15
West Winnelstrae *EH5* 14 BB7
West Wds *EH26* 26 BA8
Wheatfield Gro, Lnhd
  EH20 54 BJ27
Wheatfield Ln, Lnhd
  EH20 54 BK26
Wheatfield Pl *EH11* 41 AZ14
Wheatfield Rd *EH11* 41 AZ14
Wheatfield St *EH11* 42 BA14
Wheatfield Ter *EH11* **1** 41 AZ14
Wheatfield Wk, Lnhd
  EH20 54 BJ27
Wheatsheaf La, Dalk.
  EH22 57 BW23
Whin Pk (Cock.),
  Pres. *EH32* 18 CK8
Whin Pk Ind Est,
  Pres. *EH32* 18 CK8
Whins Pl *EH15* **2** 29 BQ11
White Dales *EH10* 53 BE22
Whitehall Ct *EH4* 25 AX9
White Hart St, Dalk.
  EH22 **7** 57 BW24
Whitehead Gro, S Q'fry
  EH30 9 AE3
WHITEHILL 31 BW15
Whitehill Av, Muss. *EH21* 31 BW14
Whitehill Dr, Dalk. *EH22* 57 BZ25
Whitehill Fm Rd, Muss.
  EH21 31 BW15
Whitehill Gdns, Muss.
  EH21 31 BW15
Whitehill Gro, Dalk. *EH22* 57 BZ25
Whitehill Rd *EH15* 30 BS15
Whitehill Rd, Dalk. *EH22* 30 BS16
Whitehill Rd (Newcr.),
  Muss. *EH21* 30 BT16
Whitehill St (Newcr.),
  Muss. *EH21* 30 BT15
White Horse Cl *EH8* 7 BH11
Whitehouse Ln *EH9* 42 BD14
Whitehouse Rd *EH4* 23 AQ8
Whitehouse Ter *EH9* 43 BE15
Whitelea Cres, Bal. *EH14* 58 AL27
Whitelea Rd, Bal. *EH14* 58 AL27

White Pk *EH11* 42 BA14
White's Cl, Dalk. *EH22* 57 BW24
Whitingford *EH6* 15 BF6
Whitson Cres *EH11* 41 AX14
Whitson Gro *EH11* 41 AX14
Whitson Pl E *EH11* 41 AX14
Whitson Pl W *EH11* 41 AX14
Whitson Rd *EH11* 41 AX14
Whitson Ter *EH11* 41 AX14
Whitson Wk *EH11* 41 AW14
Whitson Way *EH11* 41 AX14
Whyte Pl *EH7* 28 BJ10
Wilfrid Ter *EH8* **5** 28 BL10
Wilkieston Rd (Ratho),
  Newbr. *EH28* 37 AE17
William Black Pl, S Q'fry
  EH30 9 AE3
Williamfield Sq *EH15* **1** 29 BQ11
William Jameson Pl
  EH15 **8** 29 BQ10
William St *EH3* 6 BC11
William St La N E *EH3* 6 BC11
William St La N W *EH3* 6 BC11
William St La S E *EH3* 6 BC11
William St La S W *EH3* 6 BC12
Willow Av, Bonny. *EH19* 63 BR29
Willowbank Row *EH6* 15 BF5
WILLOWBRAE 28 BL12
Willowbrae Av *EH8* 28 BL11
Willowbrae Gdns *EH8* 28 BM11
Willowbrae Rd *EH8* 28 BL11
Willow Path, Lnhd
  EH20 **2** 61 BH28
Willow Rd (Mayf.),
  Dalk. *EH22* 71 CA29
Willow Tree Pl, Bal. *EH14* 48 AM24
Wilson Av, Dalk. *EH22* 57 BY24
Wilson Av, Pres. *EH32* 18 CH10
Wilson Rd, Gore. *EH23* 70 BZ34
Wilson's Ct *EH8* **3** 7 BG11
Wilson's Pk *EH15* 29 BR10
Wilson St, Pen. *EH26* 68 BA38
Wilson Wk, Tran. *EH33* **2** 35 CL14
Wilton Rd *EH16* 43 BH17
Windmill Cl *EH8* 7 BG13
Windmill La *EH8* 7 BF13
Windmill Pl *EH8* **6** 7 BG13
Windmill St *EH8* 7 BF13
Windsor Cres, Pen. *EH26* 69 BC37
Windsor Dr, Pen. *EH26* 69 BC38
Windsor Gdns, Muss.
  EH21 32 CA13
Windsor Pk, Muss. *EH21* 32 CB13
Windsor Pk Dr, Muss.
  EH21 32 CB13
Windsor Pk Pl, Muss.
  EH21 32 CB13
Windsor Pk Ter, Muss.
  EH21 32 CA13
Windsor Pl *EH15* 29 BR11
Windsor Rd, Pen. *EH26* 69 BC37
Windsor Sq, Pen. *EH26* 69 BC37
Windsor St *EH7* 27 BG9
Windsor St La *EH7* 27 BG9
Windsor Ter, Pen. *EH26* 69 BC37
Windygoul Cres, Tran.
  EH33 35 CM14
Windy Wynd, Muss. *EH21* 31 BZ15
Winton Cl, Tran. *EH33* 35 CM15
Winton Ct (Cock.),
  Pres. *EH32* **1** 19 CL7
Winton Ct, Tran. *EH33* 35 CN15
Winton Dr *EH10* 52 BD23
Winton Gdns *EH10* 53 BE23
Winton Gro *EH10* 52 BD22
Winton Gro, Tran. *EH33* 35 CN15
Winton Ln *EH10* 53 BE23
Winton Pk *EH10* 52 BD23
Winton Pk (Cock.),
  Pres. *EH32* 19 CL8
Winton Pl, Tran. *EH33* 35 CM13
Winton Ter *EH10* 52 BD23
Winton Way, Tran. *EH33* 35 CM15
Wishart Av, Bonny. *EH19* 56 BT27
Wishart Pl, Dalk. *EH22* 56 BU25
Wishaw Ter *EH7* 28 BK10

Wisp, The *EH16* 45 BR16
Wisp Grn *EH15* 29 BR15
Witholm (Whitehill),
  Dalk. *EH22* 71 CA26
Wolrige Rd *EH16* 44 BJ19
Wolseley Cres *EH8* 28 BL10
Wolseley Gdns *EH8* **8** 28 BL10
Wolseley Pl *EH8* **9** 28 BL10
Wolseley Ter *EH8* **6** 28 BL10
Wolsey Av, Bonny. *EH19* 64 BS29
Woodbine Gdns, Pres.
  EH32 **2** 18 CH10
Woodbine Ter *EH6* 16 BJ8
WOODBURN 57 BY24
Woodburn Av, Dalk. *EH22* 57 BY24
Woodburn Bk, Dalk. *EH22* 57 BY24
Woodburn Dr, Dalk. *EH22* 57 BX24
Woodburn Gdns, Dalk.
  EH22 57 BY24
Woodburn Gro, Dalk. *EH22* 57 BY25
Woodburn Ln, Dalk. *EH22* 57 BY24
Woodburn Medway,
  Dalk. *EH22* 57 BY25
Woodburn Pk, Dalk. *EH22* 57 BY25
Woodburn Pl *EH10* 42 BD16
Woodburn Pl, Dalk. *EH22* 57 BY25
Woodburn Prim Sch *EH22* 57 BY24
Woodburn Rd, Dalk. *EH22* 57 BX24
Woodburn St, Dalk. *EH22* 57 BY24
Woodburn Ter *EH10* 42 BD16
Woodburn Ter, Dalk. *EH22* 57 BZ25
Woodburn Vw, Dalk. *EH22* 57 BZ25
Woodend Pk, Ros. *EH25* 67 BH32
Woodfield Av *EH13* 50 AV21
Woodfield Pk *EH13* 50 AV21
Woodfield Pk (Bils.),
  Ros. *EH25* 61 BF29
WOODHALL 50 AU21
Woodhall Av, Jun. Grn *EH14* 50 AT21
Woodhall Bk *EH13* 50 AV22
Woodhall Dr, Jun. Grn *EH14* 50 AT21
Woodhall Gro *EH13* 50 AV22
Woodhall Millbrae,
  Jun. Grn *EH14* 50 AU21
Woodhall Rd *EH13* 51 AW21
Woodhall Ter,
  Jun. Grn *EH14* 50 AT21
Woodlands Gro *EH15* 29 BN12
Woodrow, Gore. *EH23* 70 BY34
Woods Ct, Bonny. *EH19* **3** 63 BR28
Woodside Dr, Pen. *EH26* 69 BB38
Woodside Gdns,
  Muss. *EH21* 32 CA13
Woodside Ter *EH15* 30 BS12
Woodstock Pl *EH16* 44 BK18
Woodville Ter *EH6* 16 BJ8
Woolmet Cres (Dand.),
  Dalk. *EH22* 45 BR19
Wright's Hos *EH10* 42 BD14
Writers' Museum & Makars'
  Court *EH1* **6** 7 BF11
Wyvern Pk *EH9* 43 BF15
Wyvis Pk, Pen. *EH26* 69 BC36

Y

Yardheads *EH6* 15 BH6
Yarrow Ct, Pen. *EH26* 69 BC36
Yeaman La *EH11* 26 BB13
Yeaman Pl *EH11* 26 BB13
Yewlands Cres *EH16* 44 BK20
Yewlands Gdns *EH16* 44 BK20
York Bldgs *EH2* **7** 7 BF10
York La *EH1* 7 BF10
York Pl *EH1* 7 BF10
York Rd *EH5* 15 BE5
Young Av, Tran. *EH33* 35 CM14
Young St *EH2* 6 BD11
Young St La N *EH2* 6 BD11
Young St La S *EH2* 6 BD11

Z

Zetland Pl *EH5* 14 BD5

In busy areas street names are shown on the map with a number.
Use this list to identify the street names represented by numbers in each grid square.

Page 6
BC10 1 Learmonth Vw EH4
BC11 1 Convening Ct EH4
      2 Dean Path Bldgs EH4
      3 Drumsheugh Pl EH3
      4 Well Ct EH4
      5 Hawthorn Ter EH4
      6 Melville Pl EH3
BC12 1 Douglas Ter EH11
      2 Argyll Ter EH11
      3 Atholl Ter EH11
      4 Grove Ter EH3
      5 Breadalbane Ter EH11
      6 Walker Ter EH11
      7 Cobden Ter EH11
      8 Bright Ter EH11
      9 St. David's Pl EH3
     10 St. David's Ter EH3
     11 McLaren Ter EH11
     12 Lewis Ter EH11
BD10 1 South E Circ Pl EH3
      2 Jamaica St W EH3
BD11 1 Rutland Pl EH1
BD12 1 Festival Sq EH1
      2 Rutland Ct EH3
      3 Cambridge St La EH1
BD13 1 Leven Cl EH3
      2 Chalmers Bldgs EH3
      3 Lochrin Ter EH3
BE10 1 Nelson Pl EH3
      2 Northumberland Pl EH3
      3 Thistle Ct EH2
BE11 1 Playfair Steps EH2
BE12 1 Heriot Cross EH1
      2 Inglis Ct EH1
      3 Spittal St La EH3
      4 Brown's Pl EH1
      5 Portsburgh Sq EH1
      6 Castle Wynd S EH1
      7 Chapel Wynd EH1
      8 Thomson's Ct EH1
      9 Victoria Ter EH1
     10 Websters Land EH1
     11 Castle Wynd N EH1
     12 Dunlop's Ct EH1
     13 Hunter's Cl EH1
     14 Patrick Geddes
         Steps EH1

Page 7
BF10 1 North Clyde St La EH1
      2 Regent Br EH1
      3 St. Ninian's Row EH8
      4 West Register St La EH2
      5 Elder St E EH1
      6 Gabriel's Rd EH2
      7 York Bldgs EH2
BF11 1 Advocates Cl EH1
      2 Bell's Wynd EH1
      3 Borthwick's Cl EH1
      4 James' Ct EH1
      5 Carrubber's Cl EH1
      6 Lady Stair's Cl EH1
      7 Melbourne Pl EH1
      8 Upper Bow EH1
      9 Old Assembly Cl EH1
     10 North Br Arc EH1
     11 Anchor Cl EH1
     12 Tron Sq EH1
     13 Fleshmarket Cl EH1

     14 Barrie's Cl EH1
     15 Warriston's Cl EH1
BF12 1 Charlesfield EH8
      2 College Wynd EH1
      3 India Bldgs EH1
      4 Solicitor's Bldgs EH1
BG10 1 Baxter's Pl EH1
      2 Union Pl EH1
      3 Marshall's Ct EH1
      4 Glenorchy Pl EH1
      5 Greenside Pl EH1
      6 Greenside End EH1
      7 Upper Greenside La EH1
BG11 1 Coinyie Ho Cl EH1
      2 Boyd's Entry EH1
      3 Wilson's Ct EH8
      4 Chalmers Cl EH1
      5 Dickson's Cl EH1
BG12 1 North Richmond St EH8
      2 Marshall St EH8
      3 Niddry St S EH1
      4 Simon Sq EH8
      5 New Arthur St EH8
      6 Grays Ct EH8
      7 Gilmour's Entry EH8
      8 Brown St La EH8
      9 St. John's Hill EH8
BG13 1 Hope Pk Sq EH8
      2 Lamb's Cl EH8
      3 St. Patrick St EH8
      4 Summerhall Cres EH9
      5 Hamilton's Folly Ms EH8
      6 Windmill Pl EH8
BH11 1 Reid's Ct EH8
      2 Robertson's Ct EH8
      3 Cooper's Cl EH8
      4 Crichton's Cl EH8
      5 Bull's Cl EH8
      6 Slater's Steps EH8
      7 Jackson's Entry EH8
      8 Gentle's Entry EH8
      9 Nether Bakehouse EH8
BH13 1 St. Leonard's Crag EH8

Page 8
AB3   1 Echline Steadings,
         S Q'fry EH30
      2 Echline, S Q'fry EH30
AD2   1 Bellstane, S Q'fry EH30
      2 Hill Ct, S Q'fry EH30
      3 West Ter, S Q'fry EH30
      4 Hillwood Pl,
         S Q'fry EH30
      5 Harbour La,
         S Q'fry EH30

Page 9
AE2   1 Hamilton's Cl,
         S Q'fry EH30
      2 Mid Ter, S Q'fry EH30
      3 Vennel, S Q'fry EH30
      4 East Ter, S Q'fry EH30
      5 Smith's Land,
         S Q'fry EH30
AE3   1 Ferryburn, S Q'fry EH30
      2 Scotstoun Gro,
         S Q'fry EH30

Page 11
AR4   1 Riverside EH4

AR5   1 Almond Bk Cotts EH4

Page 12
AU7   1 Southbank EH4
      2 Southbank Ct EH4
      3 Southlawn EH4
      4 Westbank EH4
      5 Easter Pk Ho EH4
      6 Northlawn Ct EH4
      7 Rose Ct EH4

Page 13
AX5   1 Granton Mill W EH4
AY5   1 Granton Mains Bk EH4

Page 15
BE4   1 Lamb's Ct EH6
BE5   1 Auchinleck's Brae EH6
BF4   1 Great Michael Sq EH4
      2 Fishmarket Sq EH6
      3 Wester Cl EH6
      4 Great Michael Cl EH6
BF6   1 Mulberry Pl EH6
BG5   1 Hamburgh Pl EH6
      2 Hawthornbank Ter EH6
      3 Portland Ter EH6
      4 North Leith Mill EH6
BG6   1 Industry Home EH6
BG7   1 Bonnington Gait EH6
BH5   1 West Cromwell St EH6
      2 Citadel St EH6
BH6   1 Ballantyne La EH6
      2 Brewery La EH6
      3 Quayside Mills EH6
      4 Henderson Gdns EH6
      5 St. Anthony Pl EH6
      6 St. Anthony St EH6
      7 Spier's Pl EH6
      8 Bowling La EH6
BH7   1 Cunningham Pl EH6
      2 Newkirkgate EH6
      3 Springfield Bldgs EH6

Page 16
BJ5   1 Commercial Wf EH6
BJ6   1 Bowie's Cl EH6
      2 Chapel La EH6
      3 Links La EH6
      4 New Bells Ct EH6
      5 Seaport St EH6
      6 Water's Cl EH6
      7 Broad Wynd EH6
BJ7   1 Cochrane Pl EH6
BJ9   1 Crawford Br EH7
BK7   1 Rosevale Pl EH6
      2 Elm Pl EH6
      3 Fingzies Pl EH6
BL7   1 Seacot EH6
      2 Boothacre Cotts EH6
BL9   1 Marionville
         Medway EH7

Page 18
CG10 1 Burnside, Pres. EH32
      2 Cookies Wynd,
         Pres. EH32
CH10 1 Salt Preston Pl,
         Pres. EH32
      2 Woodbine Gdns,
         Pres. EH32

	3	Ayres Wynd, Pres. *EH32*
	4	Glebe Gdns, Pres. *EH32*
CH9	1	Sir Walter Scott Pend, Pres. *EH32*
	2	East Sea Side, Pres. *EH32*
	3	Fowlers Ct, Pres. *EH32*
	4	Rosemount Ms, Pres. *EH32*
CJ10	1	South Vw, Pres. *EH32*
	2	Cross Cotts, Pres. *EH32*
	3	Preston Cross Cotts, Pres. *EH32*
CK7	1	Hawthornbank (Cock.), Pres. *EH32*
	2	North Lorimer Pl (Cock.), Pres. *EH32*

Page 19

CL7	1	Winton Ct (Cock.), Pres. *EH32*
	2	Elcho Pl (Port S.), Pres. *EH32*
	3	East Lorimer Pl (Cock.), Pres. *EH32*
CM7	1	Bayview (Port S.), Pres. *EH32*

Page 20

AD10	1	Square, The, K'lis. *EH29*

Page 23

AQ11	1	Affleck Ct *EH12*
	2	Finlaggan Ct *EH12*
AQ12	1	Toward Ct *EH12*
	2	Rowallan Ct *EH12*
	3	Kilchurn Ct *EH12*
	4	Neidpath Ct *EH12*
AQ8	1	Braehead Row *EH4*
AR10	2	North Bughtlin Pl *EH12*
	3	North Bughtlin Neuk *EH12*
AR12	1	Kisimul Ct *EH12*
	2	Dunollie Ct *EH12*
	3	Caerlaverock Ct *EH12*
	4	Barntalloch Ct *EH12*

Page 24

AS13	1	Featherhall Cres *EH12*
AT13	1	Oswald Ter *EH12*
AU12	1	Clermiston Ter *EH12*

Page 25

AX12	1	Western Cor *EH12*
AX9	1	Muirdale Ter *EH4*
AY10	1	Marischal Pl *EH4*
	2	East Ct *EH4*
AY9	1	Craigcrook Pl *EH4*
AZ12	1	Murrayfield Pl *EH12*
	2	Roseburn Gdns *EH12*

Page 26

A12	1	West Stanhope Pl *EH12*
	2	Surrey Pl *EH12*
	3	Eglinton St *EH12*
	4	Hampton Pl *EH12*
11	1	Belford Ter *EH4*
	2	Hawthorn Bldgs *EH4*
	3	Douglas Gdns Ms *EH4*
	4	Ravelston Ter *EH4*
12	1	Easter Dalry Pl *EH11*

BB13	1	Regent's Ct *EH11*
	2	Murieston Cres La *EH11*
	3	Easter Dalry Rigg *EH11*
BC9	1	Mary's Pl *EH4*
	2	Comely Bk Pl Ms *EH4*
BD9	1	Baker's Pl *EH3*
	2	Malta Grn *EH4*
	3	Patriothall *EH3*
	4	Saxe-Coburg Ter *EH3*
	5	Glanville Pl *EH3*
	6	Gabriel's Rd *EH3*
	7	Glenogle Pl *EH3*

Page 27

BE8	1	Munro Pl *EH3*
	2	Canonmills Br *EH3*
	3	Canon Ct *EH3*
BF9	1	East Broughton Pl *EH1*
	2	Old Broughton *EH3*
	3	Barony Pl *EH3*
BG9	1	Antigua St *EH1*
	2	Shaw's Sq *EH1*
BH9	1	Brunswick Ter *EH7*
	2	Brunton Gdns *EH7*

Page 28

BJ10	1	Dalziel Pl *EH7*
	2	Jane Ter *EH7*
	3	Kirkwood Pl *EH7*
	4	Sunnybank Ter *EH7*
BL10	1	Deanery Cl *EH7*
	2	Parsons Grn Ter *EH8*
	3	Piershill La *EH8*
	4	Piershill Pl *EH8*
	5	Wilfrid Ter *EH8*
	6	Wolseley Ter *EH8*
	7	Meadowbank Pl *EH8*
	8	Wolseley Gdns *EH8*
	9	Wolseley Pl *EH8*
	10	Hillend Pl *EH8*
BM11	1	Northfield Hts *EH8*
BM12	1	Abercorn Ct *EH8*
BM15	1	Back Sta Rd *EH16*

Page 29

BQ10	1	Westbank Ln *EH15*
	2	Electra Pl *EH15*
	3	Great Cannon Bk *EH15*
	4	Hillcoat Ln *EH15*
	5	Hillcoat Pl *EH15*
	6	Bridge St La *EH15*
	7	Spa Pl *EH15*
	8	William Jameson Pl *EH15*
	9	Ramsay Pl *EH15*
	10	Law Pl *EH15*
	11	Aitchison's Pl *EH15*
	12	Brickfield *EH15*
	13	Harbour Pl *EH15*
	14	Pottery, The *EH15*
BQ11	1	Williamfield Sq *EH15*
	2	Whins Pl *EH15*
BQ12	1	Southfield Vil *EH15*
BQ14	1	Duddingston Yards *EH15*
BR10	1	New Twr Pl *EH15*
	2	Bath Pl *EH15*
BR11	1	Vernon Cotts *EH15*

Page 30

BS12	1	Brunstane Gdns Ms *EH15*
BS15	1	Niddrie Cotts *EH15*

Page 31

BW14	1	Stoneyhill Gdns, Muss. *EH21*
BX13	1	Bush Ter, Muss. *EH21*
BZ12	1	Paddock, The, Muss. *EH21*
BZ13	1	Dambrae, Muss. *EH21*
BZ14	1	Grannus Ms (Inv.), Muss. *EH21*
	2	Inveresk Gate (Inv.), Muss. *EH21*

Page 32

CA13	1	Linkfield Ct, Muss. *EH21*
CB13	1	Pittencrieff Ct, Muss. *EH21*

Page 33

CD14	1	Forthview Dr (Wall.), Muss. *EH21*
	2	Albert Cl (Wall.), Muss. *EH21*
CD15	1	St. Clements Cres (Wall.), Muss. *EH21*

Page 34

CG11	1	Bellfield Sq, Pres. *EH32*
CH11	1	West Ln Ct, Pres. *EH32*
	2	Robert De Quincy Pl, Pres. *EH32*
CJ11	1	Doo'Cot Pl, Pres. *EH32*

Page 35

CL12	1	Wallace Pl, Tran. *EH33*
	2	Gardeners Pl, Tran. *EH33*
	3	Hope Pl, Tran. *EH33*
CL13	1	Caesar Way, Tran. *EH33*
	2	Elphinstone Ct, Tran. *EH33*
	3	George Way, Tran. *EH33*
	4	Potter's Path, Tran. *EH33*
	5	Viewforth Ter, Tran. *EH33*
	6	Viewforth Gdns, Tran. *EH33*
	7	Coal Neuk Cor, Tran. *EH33*
CL14	1	Dequincey Wk, Tran. *EH33*
	2	Wilson Wk, Tran. *EH33*
	3	Kerr-McNeill Service Rd, Tran. *EH33*
	4	McNeill Wk, Tran. *EH33*
	5	Kerr Way, Tran. *EH33*
	6	Elphinstone Wk *EH33*
	7	Pinkie Wk, Tran. *EH33*
	8	Seton Ct, Tran. *EH33*
CM13	1	Civic Sq, Tran. *EH33*
	2	Plough La, Tran. *EH33*
	3	Cadell Sq, Tran. *EH33*
CM14	1	Fa'side Av, Tran. *EH33*
	2	Fa'side Cres, Tran. *EH33*

Page 39

AP14	1	Gyle Av *EH12*

Page 40

AS19	1	Quarryview *EH14*
	2	Middlepark *EH14*
	3	Middleshot *EH14*
AU18	1	Walkers Ct *EH14*

Page 41
AW17 1 Longstone Cotts *EH14*
AX16 1 Laichpark Ln *EH14*
AX17 1 Graysknowe *EH14*
AY15 1 Chesser Cotts *EH11*
      2 Coxfield La *EH11*
AZ14 1 Wheatfield Ter *EH11*

Page 42
BA14 1 Laurel Ter *EH11*
BA15 1 Lily Ter *EH11*
      2 Sinclair Cl *EH11*
      3 Daisy Ter *EH11*
BA19 1 Morham Lea *EH10*
      2 Syme Pl *EH10*
      3 Morham Gdns *EH10*
      4 Syme Rigg *EH10*
      5 Morham Pk *EH10*
      6 Morham Gait *EH10*
BB14 1 Ardmillan Ter La *EH11*
BB19 1 Ashy Path *EH10*
BD14 1 Alvanley Ter *EH9*
BD16 1 Eden Ter *EH10*

Page 43
BF15 1 Esdaile Pk *EH9*
BF16 1 Glenisla Gdns La *EH9*
BG14 1 Lord Russell Pl *EH9*
      2 Sciennes Pl *EH9*
      3 East Preston St La *EH8*
      4 Summerhall *EH9*
      5 Summerhall Pl *EH9*

Page 44
BJ17 1 Nether Liberton Ct *EH16*
BL17 1 Saddletree Ln *EH16*
BL20 1 Stennis Gdns *EH17*
BL21 1 Carnbee Dell *EH16*
BM16 1 Peffermill Ct *EH16*

Page 45
BP20 1 Ferniehill Gro *EH17*
BQ16 1 Great Carleton Sq *EH16*
      2 Niddrie Ho Gro *EH16*

Page 49
AQ23 1 Pentland Vw Ct, Currie *EH14*

Page 50
AT21 1 Juniper La, Jun. Grn *EH14*
AT22 1 Pentland Vil, Jun. Grn *EH14*
AU20 1 Alcorn Rigg *EH14*

Page 51
AW21 1 Cuddies Ln *EH13*
AW22 1 Bonaly Steading *EH13*
AX20 1 Rustic Cotts *EH13*

Page 52
BA20 1 Stark's Cotts *EH13*
BB21 1 Oxgangs Path E *EH13*

      2 Oxgangs Bdy *EH13*

Page 54
BK22 1 Balmwell Pk *EH16*
BK23 1 Southhouse Sq *EH17*
      2 Burdiehouse Crossway *EH17*
BL26 1 Green, The, Lnhd *EH20*
BL27 1 George Cres, Lnhd *EH20*
BM27 1 Fowler Cres, Lnhd *EH20*
      2 Fowler Sq, Lnhd *EH20*
      3 Linden Pl, Lnhd *EH20*

Page 55
BQ26 1 West Mill Ct, Lass. *EH18*
BQ27 1 Melville Vw, Lass. *EH18*

Page 56
BS27 1 Viewbank Cres, Bonny. *EH19*
BT27 1 Bellfield Vw, Bonny. *EH19*
BU25 1 Weir Ct, Dalk. *EH22*
      2 Eskbank Ct, Dalk. *EH22*
BU26 1 Fairhaven Vil, Dalk. *EH22*
      2 Westfield Ct, Dalk. *EH22*
      3 Westfield Dr, Dalk. *EH22*
BV23 1 Bridgend, Dalk. *EH22*
BV25 1 New Meadowspott, Dalk. *EH22*

Page 57
BW24 1 Maxton Ct, Dalk. *EH22*
      2 Plummer Ct, Dalk. *EH22*
      3 Pettigrew's Cl, Dalk. *EH22*
      4 Eskdaill Ct, Dalk. *EH22*
      5 Jarnac Ct, Dalk. *EH22*
      6 Parkside Ct, Dalk. *EH22*
      7 White Hart St, Dalk. *EH22*
BX24 1 Newmills Ter, Dalk. *EH22*
BY24 1 Place Charente, Dalk. *EH22*
BY25 1 Primrose Ter, Dalk. *EH22*
BY26 1 Easthouses Pl (Easth.), Dalk. *EH22*
BY27 1 Parkhead Pk (Easth.), Dalk. *EH22*
BZ24 1 Robert Burns Ms, Dalk. *EH22*

Page 58
AL26 1 Quarry Howe, Bal. *EH14*

Page 61
BG28 1 Sycamore Path, Lnhd *EH20*
BH28 1 Fir Vw, Lnhd *EH20*
      2 Willow Path, Lnhd *EH20*

Page 62
BL28 1 Mayfield Ct, Lnhd *EH20*

      2 Harnes Ct, Lnhd *EH20*

Page 63
BQ28 1 Polton Ter, Lass. *EH18*
BQ30 1 Cockpen Pl, Bonny. *EH19*
      2 Poltonhall, Bonny. *EH19*
BR28 1 Leyden Pl, Bonny. *EH19*
      2 Arniston Pl, Bonny. *EH19*
      3 Woods Ct, Bonny. *EH19*
      4 Moorfoot Ct, Bonny. *EH19*

Page 64
BS29 1 Dickson Gro, Bonny. *EH19*
BT29 1 Sherwood Wk, Bonny. *EH19*

Page 65
BW30 1 Deanpark Ct (Newt.), Dalk. *EH22*
BX29 1 Lady Rd Pl (Newt.), Dalk. *EH22*
BX31 1 Lingerwood Cotts (Newt.), Dalk. *EH22*
BZ29 1 Blackcot Pl (Mayf.), Dalk. *EH22*
BZ30 1 Dougall Rd (Mayf.), Dalk. *EH22*
      2 Bevan Rd (Mayf.), Dalk. *EH22*

Page 69
BB39 1 Bankmill Vw, Pen. *EH26*

Page 70
BX34 1 Greenhall Cres, Gore. *EH23*
BY34 1 Emily Ct, Gore. *EH23*
      2 Redheugh Ln, Gore. *EH23*
BY37 1 John Bernard Way, Gore. *EH23*
BZ36 1 Harvieston Vil, Gore. *EH23*

Page 71
CA29 1 Laurelbank Pl (Mayf.), Dalk. *EH22*
CA30 1 Ruskin Pl (Mayf.), Dalk. *EH22*
      2 Westhouses St (Mayf.), Dalk. *EH22*
      3 Westhouses Dr (Mayf.), Dalk. *EH22*
      4 Ramsay Wk (Mayf.), Dalk. *EH22*